Rethinking the
Developmental State

Rethinking the Developmental State

India's Industry in Comparative Perspective

VIBHA PINGLÉ

St. Martin's Press

ISBN 0-312-21995-4

Library of Congress Cataloging-in-Publication Data

Pinglé, Vibha, 1966-
    Rethinking the developmental state : India's industry in
comparative perspective / by Vibha Pinglé.
    Includes bibliographical references and index.
    ISBN 0-312-21995-4 (cloth)
    1. Industries—India. 2. India—Economic conditions—1947-
I. Title. II. Title: India in comparative perspective.
HC435.2.P56   1999
338.954—DC21   98-54383
                                                    CIP

Design by Orit Mardkha-Tenzer

First published: September 1999

10 9 8 7 6 5 4 3 2 1

FOR MY PARENTS AND FOR ASHU

Contents

Preface

Conversations with umpteen Indian industrialists and businessmen suggests that the state bureaucracy has been a significant part of India's problem; it has been one of the many institutions that have restricted the pace of India's development. Especially until 1991, India's economy was best described as a "license, quota, and permit raj." Private firms required as many as eighty different licenses before they could begin production, increase production, or change their product mix. And getting any one of these licenses required patience, ingenuity, and in many cases, involved corruption.

But the bureaucracy has not only played a negative role in India's development. Stability is critical for economic growth, and the Indian bureaucracy has been critical in maintaining order. Wars, assassinations, and political crises have caused only temporary disruptions, and while riots have been more frequent than desirable, they have caused mostly localized disruptions to everyday life. For this, the Indian bureaucracy deserves credit.

Moreover, it is difficult to ignore the positive and innovative policy contributions made by some Indian bureaucrats to India's development. How does one explain these success stories? Should we credit them to the unique personalities of a few bureaucrats, or can we offer an institutional explanation for it? The latter will help us understand how the Indian bureaucracy should be reformed.

Consider the steel, automobile and software industries. Regarded as the cornerstone of India's development strategy after independence in 1947, the performance of the steel industry has been dismal. The automobile industry has performed better. The software industry, by contrast, has been a remarkable success; it is *the* most internationally competitive of Indian industries. Interestingly, the very same bureaucracy that may be held responsible for the poor performance of the steel industry deserves credit for handling the software industry very differently.

This book argues that this variation in the performance of the Indian bureaucracy and consequently of Indian industry is best understood in terms of the differences in the pattern of relations between the bureaucracy and industrial actors, and in the structure of the bureaucracy. Evidence from the Indian steel, automobile, and software industries suggests that an institutional arrangement consisting of a cohesive and autonomous bureaucratic structure, political encouragement for innovative policy-making, together with close relations between bureaucrats and industrialists is effective at fostering industrial development.

This book grew out of my dissertation research and is based on field work I conducted in India from 1991 onward. The advice and support of my dissertation committee, Dietrich Rueschemeyer, Morris D. Morris and Paget Henry was invaluable. I am especially grateful to Dietrich Rueschemeyer for his time and encouragement. I would also like to thank Alice Amsden, Bruce Carruthers, Peter Evans, Peter Katzenstein, Richard Swedberg, and Myron Weiner for their advice, comments and support. My thanks also to friends and colleagues at Brown, Harvard and Rutgers, for their support. Finally, this book would not have been possible without the help and cooperation of a large number of Indian bureaucrats, industrialists, trade unionists, and journalists. They gave generously of their time and shared many personal experiences.

Karen Wolny, my editor at St. Martin's Press, and Amy Reading helped make the process of publishing this book considerably easier. During the last stages of editing, I was in Johannesburg studying Black-owned small business in South Africa. Members of the Centre for Policy Studies, where I was based, demonstrated much warmth, patience and kindness.

I am not sure how I can ever thank my family for their support while writing this book. My parents proved to me yet again not just how supportive they are as parents, but also how patient, warm and gracious they are as human beings. They continue to inspire me. Ashu helped make the process of publishing this book substantially easier. Always willing to help, he put aside his own work to read and comment upon my drafts. But most of all I would like to thank him for both flying with me and helping me keep my feet on the ground. This book is for Ashu and for my parents.

List of Tables

List of Abbreviations and Acronyms

ACMA	Automotive Component Manufacturers Association
AIAM	Association of Indian Automobile Manufacturers
AIEI	Association of Indian Engineering Industries
AITUC	All India Trade Union Congress
ALL	Ashok Leyland Limited
API	Automobile Products of India
ASSOCHAM	Associated Chambers of Commerce and Industry
BJP	Bharatiya Janata Party
BMS	Bharatiya Mazdoor Sangh
CACI	Central Advisory Council of Industries
CEI	Confederation of Engineering Industry
CII	Confederation of Indian Industry
CITU	Centre of Indian Trade Unions
CKD	Completely knocked down
CSI	Computer Society of India
CV	Commercial vehicle
DCM	Delhi Cloth Mills
DGTD	Directorate General of Technical Development
ECIL	Electronics Corporation of India Limited
EML	Eicher Motors Limited
FERA	Foreign Exchange Regulations Act
FICCI	Federation of Indian Chamber of Commerce and Industry
HCL	Hindustan Computers Limited
HML	Hindustan Motors Limited
HMS	Hindustan Mazdoor Sangh
HSL	Hindustan Steel Limited
IAS	Indian Administrative Service
ICS	Indian Civil Service
IISCO	Indian Iron and Steel Company
IMSC	Inter-Ministerial Steering Committee
INTUC	Indian Trade Union Congress
LCV	Light commercial vehicle
M&M	Mahindra & Mahindra
MAIT	Manufacturers Association for Information Technology
MHCV	Medium and heavy commercial vehicles
MITI	Ministry of International Trade and Industry

MNAL	Mahindra Nissan Allwyn Limited
MOU	Memoranda of Understanding
MRTP Act	Monopolies and Restrictive Trade Practices Act
MSP	Mini-steel plant
MUL	Maruti Udhyog Limited
NASSCOM	National Association of Software and Service Companies
PAC	Public Accounts Committee
PAL	Premier Automobiles Limited
PCS	Patni Computer Systems
SAIL	Steel Authority of India Limited
SAL	Sipani Motors Limited
SDF	Steel Development Fund
SEEPZ	Santa Cruz Export Processing Zone
SFAI	Steel Furnace Association of India
SML	Swaraj Mazda Limited
SMPIL	Standard Motor Products of India Limited
TCS	Tata Consulting Services
TELCO	Tata Engineering and Locomotive Company
TI	Texas Instruments
TIFR	Tata Institute of Fundamental Research
TISCO	Tata Iron and Steel Company
TUL	Tata Unisys Limited

Rethinking the Developmental State

1.

Introduction

The offices of India's Ministry of Steel and Department of Electronics are similar. Both are overflowing with dusty files, well-worn furniture, and clerks who seem to fill every nook and cranny. The differences between these two offices, however, are more striking. They begin as soon as one enters the buildings. Getting past the receptionist at the Ministry of Steel requires documents, phone calls, and security checks. In contrast, the encounter with the receptionist at the Department of Electronics is a breeze. One only needs to sign the guest book. The contrast gets more conspicuous as one proceeds. Directions to the various offices and officials are clearly marked in the Department of Electronics. The Ministry of Steel is a maze. Meetings with senior officials at the ministry are hard to come by; it's quite the opposite at the Department of Electronics. The manner in which industrialists from the steel and software sectors interact with the two agencies is also remarkably different. Owners of steel plants rarely visit the Ministry of Steel. Their liaison officers do. Software manufacturers frequently interact directly with Department of Electronics officials. And the discussion is informal and goes beyond issues concerning business.[1] While relations between software entrepreneurs and Department of Electronics bureaucrats are marked by shared understandings, those between steel manufacturers and the Ministry of Steel are not.

The relations between the state and industrialists in these two industries, thus, greatly differ. By examining the steel, software, and the automobile industries in India, this book argues that this difference and the variations in the internal structure of the concerned agencies have been key factors in the making of entrepreneurial bureaucrats and in shaping the performance of

Indian industries. Consequently, variations in the performance of these industries cannot be understood by the currently dominant analytical approaches (neoclassical, positive political economy, cultural, or sectoral arguments).

No scholar would argue that India's industrial performance since the country's independence in 1947 has been spectacular. Many would insist that what the rest of the world ought to learn from the Indian experience is how *not* to promote industrial development. Yet close study of Indian industry reveals that poor performance was not universal; certain industries performed remarkably well (e.g., computer software), while others were successful at certain times and not others (e.g., automobile and steel). The puzzle, then, is to understand why all Indian industries were not unsuccessful all of the time. Solving this empirical puzzle would help develop theoretical propositions about the process of industrialization, the state's role in it, and the specific conditions under which the state can promote development. In other words, it will help us specify the institutional basis of policies that promote entrepreneurial perspectives among industrial actors.

Evidence offered by this book indicates that "pockets" of shared understandings are important for rapid industrial transformation. Shared understandings between bureaucrats allow the state to not fall prey to societal and political interests and to function smoothly. Shared understandings among industrialists increase their ability to get the infrastructure and collective goods necessary for further growth. And shared understandings between industrialists and the bureaucracy facilitate the transfer of information between them, the formulation of appropriate policy, and, thus, industrial development. Shared understanding between industrialists and bureaucrats also helps motivate bureaucrats to act. The presence of such a pattern of relations between the state and industry actors facilitates the continual responsiveness of policy to industry needs. And as the discussion of the development of the steel, automobile, and software industries shows, successful industrial performance is dependent upon the continual resynchronizing of policy to the needs of the industry. In other words, when policy was responsive to the needs of the industry, the industry performed well. Software policy has been responsive, while steel policy has not, and automobile policy has been responsive to the needs of some firms and not others.

To explicate how and why the pattern of relations between the state and industry actors influences industrial performance, I use the concept of the developmental ensemble and argue that it is essential for rapid industrial transformation. The developmental ensemble has four dimensions: a cohesive state structure, bureaucratic autonomy from societal interests, encouragement from political superiors, and informal channels of communication between bureaucrats and industrial actors. Once in place, such institutions can help develop policies that, as a consequence of their better "fit" with the social structure, are likely to promote industrial entrepreneurship faster. In other words, this book suggests that the presence of a developmental ensemble makes it likely that appropriate growth-promoting policies will emerge.[2] Rather than merely search for policies, states should focus on constructing the developmental ensemble.

The challenge, therefore, is to reform state structures in the developing world. Instead of focusing merely on importing industrial policies from more successful economies, decision makers should seek to establish state institutions that are autonomous, embedded, coherent, and flexible, i.e., whose bureaucrats are institutionally enabled to act as policy entrepreneurs. Policy entrepreneurs are not born; they are created by their institutions. This book discusses how a few policy entrepreneurs have been created in India in an otherwise vast sea of bureaucratic ineptitude. In doing so, it attempts to learn how this process might be replicated elsewhere in the developing world.

THE INDIAN STEEL, AUTOMOBILE, AND COMPUTER SOFTWARE INDUSTRIES

The steel, automobile, and computer software industries developed within India's overall regulatory and restrictive policy regime, which was changed only in 1991. All three have been administered by the same state apparatus, staffed by members of India's bureaucratic service, the Indian Administrative Service (IAS). Further, workers in all three industries have been governed by identical labor laws and organized by common trade union federations.

There are, however, fundamental differences in the industries. First, the performance and trajectory of the three industries have varied considerably. They have experienced substantial differences in growth rates, exports, and production efficiencies. Of these three industries, the computer software industry has performed the best. It continues to grow at a rapid pace (an average annual growth rate of around 50 percent between 1989 to 1990 and 1998 to 1999), is internationally competitive, is highly entrepreneurial, and is beginning to move up the technological ladder (from body-shopping to developing software).[3] The automobile industry has performed only moderately well. During the 40 years after independence; the Indian automobile industry (with a few exceptions) produced substandard vehicles, was inefficient, and showed little evidence of entrepreneurship. The industry began turning around during the mid- to late 1980s. The quality of Indian vehicles and components is improving, and especially components exports are looking up.[4] Automobile production grew at an average annual rate of 11.10 percent between 1989-90 and 1995-96, with all segments of the industry contributing to this growth.[5] The steel industry has performed the worst. After an initial period of rapid growth of 10.66 percent until 1964-65, steel production grew at the rate of 3.76 percent between 1965-66 and 1984-85. In addition to the decline in growth rates, capacity utilization remained poor, as did the quality of steel produced. One might expect that faced with a slowly growing steel industry, the state would have responded by modifying its policies. This, however, was not the case.[6] Despite the industry's overall poor performance; the state more or less retained its initial policy framework until 1991. Steel production has improved since then, growing by an annual average rate of 8.87 percent between 1989-90 and 1995-96, although it remains a weak performer in terms of capacity utilization, product quality, and when seen in international perspective.[7]

Second, similar kinds of policy instruments had remarkably different outcomes in these three industries. State-owned enterprises (SOEs) were established in all three industries. A key aim of the SOEs was to lead the way for private entrepreneurs, inject dynamism, and improve the technological base in each industry. The results, however, were uneven. While the automobile SOE succeeded in leading the private manufacturers forward and injecting entrepreneurship, the same cannot be said for the other two. The steel SOE has performed substantially better than the computer software SOE, where the contribution has been dismal.

Third, while the initial policy toward all three industries was more or less similar, over time these policies diverged considerably. The state initially invested in the steel sector, established state-owned steel plants, and placed restrictions on private production. The state's policy response to the computer software sector was almost identical. However, in the case of automobiles, the state imposed restrictions on private enterprises and made no initial state investment.

Subsequently, state investment in steel and computers declined. At the same time, while restrictions on private steel production remained, restrictions increased for some segments of the automobile industry and declined for others. For the computer sector, restrictions on private enterprise were somewhat eased.

Over time, the growth of steel production declined, inefficiencies in production increased, and the state-owned enterprises in particular performed poorly. The performance of automobile firms varied considerably. While some segments grew, others either stagnated or experienced declining production levels. The performance of the private computer software firms (in terms of production and exports) remained good.

With regard to the automobile industry, the state continued its particularistic policy regime as well. The only policy modification was the establishment of a state-owned automobile firm. While steel policy continued unchanged, computer policy was frequently fine-tuned much before 1991 in response to the needs of the sector. In addition, while steel and automobile policy sought to restrict the growth of private entrepreneurs, computer software policy aimed at nurturing private firms.

The contrast between steel and automobile policy on one hand and computer software policy on the other is striking at this point. If computer software policy was initially similar to steel policy, the difference between them by the late 1980s was substantial. Unlike the steel and automobile policy, computer policy had changed from being merely regulatory to fostering long-term entrepreneurial perspectives among the industrial actors. Not unexpectedly, while the steel industry continued to stagnate, the computer software industry grew remarkably well.

Three basic questions therefore arise: (1) Why did the state not change its policy response to the steel sector given its poor performance? (2) Why did the state-owned automobile firm perform well while the state-owned steel plants (and the computer software SOE) did not? (3) Why, beginning in the 1980s, did the state adopt a developmentalist approach with regard to computer software and not for the steel and automobile industries? These questions form the key empirical puzzle of this book.

THE DEVELOPMENTAL ENSEMBLE

To explain this puzzle we need a theoretical framework that will help in understanding the role of the state in economic development and the factors underlying developmental state activity.[8] The comparative institutional or social-structural perspective offers useful building blocks for constructing such a model. Rooted in arguments offered by Max Weber, this perspective has been elaborated by scholars seeking to explain variations in economic performance in terms of institutions and social structure.[9] The explanatory variables, in other words, are the structures of the state and of society. The intervening variable is policy. To understand variations in economic performance, therefore, the perspective considers the institutional and social basis of policy and how policies in different institutional contexts influence economic performance.

The state in this perspective is defined in Weberian terms, as an institution "invested with the authority to make binding decisions for people and organizations juridically located in a particular territory and to implement these decisions using, if necessary, force."[10] Such an understanding of the state has two advantages. First, this definition does not assume that all members of the state necessarily have similar self-interested interests and goals. It does allow for the possibility of tensions and contradictory interests within the state apparatus. Second, it also allows for the possibility that the state under certain circumstances can and does act as a corporate actor. According to Weber, the state's ability to act in this manner is a function of the structure of its bureaucracy. The bureaucracy is characterized by strict rules of recruitment, meritocracy, long careers, and a clear hierarchy of authority. For Weber, the state was concerned primarily with maintaining order in society—order that allowed markets to function smoothly.[11] And the modern state, Weber noted, was "structurally enabled" to do so. But what enables the state to be successful at fostering entrepreneurship and, more generally, promoting development?

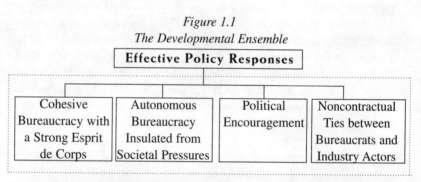

Figure 1.1
The Developmental Ensemble

As depicted in figure 1.1, this book argues that four factors are essential. These are: a cohesive bureaucratic structure with a strong esprit de corps, an autonomous bureaucracy insulated from societal pressures, political encouragement for bureaucratic innovation, and noncontractual ties between bureaucrats and industry actors that allow for the transfer of information but do not lead to the capture of the latter by the former. I call such an institutional arrangement, "the developmental ensemble." Effective policy responses and improved industrial performance are likely in the presence of the developmental ensemble.

A Cohesive Bureaucratic Structure
A cohesive bureaucracy is essential for unified and focused state action. As Weber noted, without coherent bureaucratic structures, states would find it

difficult to maintain order in society. A strong esprit de corps (defined as shared understandings, norms, and values) helps the state apparatus cohere and work toward unified goals. This becomes an especially critical issue as the state actively intervenes in the economy and seeks to promote entrepreneurship. Intervention exposes the state to the perils of contestation and to attempts by private actors to capture state agencies, which may be aggravated by decentralization. "Deeply penetrating state actions make necessary a decentralization," which can undermine state cohesion and thus the ability of the state to be a corporate actor.[12] A strong esprit de corps enables the state to function effectively despite decentralization. Intra-bureaucratic interaction is smoother with greater cohesiveness.

An Autonomous Bureaucracy

Developmental state activity also requires autonomous bureaucrats, who are more likely to adopt policies beneficial to the industry as a whole than are bureaucrats captured by one or another societal interest. State autonomy may be defined as the ability of the state to "formulate and pursue goals that are not simply reflective of the demands or interests of social groups, classes, or society."[13] If industrial policy is to promote overall industrialization, not merely enable a select group of firms or a class of people to prosper, state autonomy would appear to be essential. It would enable bureaucrats to consider all the relevant policy options and not develop biased policies as a result of societal pressure.

Theoretically, autonomy results when: the dominant group in society has serious divisions and consequently no group can control the state; or pressure from subordinate groups forces the dominant group to grant the state greater autonomy; or the subordinate groups acquire the power necessary to "undo monolithic political control by the dominant classes."[14] Thus, at a minimum, the extent of a state's autonomy is a consequence of the relationship between the state, and the dominant and the subordinate groups.[15]

With regard to industrial policy, state autonomy is an outcome of the relationship among bureaucrats, industrialists, and trade unions. The degree of bureaucratic autonomy is determined by the extent to which industrialists and labor leaders are able to influence the policymaking process and the extent to which politicians representing popular demands shape industrial policy. Industrialists' ability to capture the state is dependent on their financial clout and their connections to the political elite, while that of labor leaders is dependent on the strength of labor and the extent to which labor laws permit trade union mobilization.

However, autonomy also depends on the state's internal structure, which may be understood in terms of two dimensions: the bureaucrats' length of tenure in any department or agency and the extent of bureaucratic cohesion. State agencies whose incumbents are frequently transferred and thus have shorter periods of contact are less likely to have the same rate of capture by industrialists than incumbents with longer tenures. Second, the stronger the bureaucratic cohesion, the greater the resources bureaucrats have to withstand societal pressure. A unified bureaucracy is harder to penetrate. This, of course, was the colonial government's raison d'être for setting up the cohesive Indian Civil Service as a bureaucracy, which was relatively autonomous from the "natives."

Bureaucratic agencies subject to a substantial degree of political interference are likely to face constraints on their autonomy. Especially in democracies, politicians act as conduits for societal interests. If political influence in policymaking is greater than bureaucratic input, the policies formulated might reflect specific societal interests rather than those of an autonomous state. The extent to which political influence hampers policymaking depends on the degree of bureaucratic cohesion. Bureaucracies with strong intrabureaucratic ties are likely to better withstand the pressure of politicians than bureaucracies without such ties. A bureaucrat's institutional control increases with the strength of these ties. Strong ties, not surprisingly, are likely to strengthen her ability to stave off political pressure effectively.

Political Encouragement

The role of politicians in promoting developmental state action is, however, not merely negative. By encouraging bureaucrats to undertake developmental action, politicians can facilitate industrial growth. The case of politicians and bureaucrats in Japan is instructive here. Chalmers Johnson observes that successful developmental states separate the tasks of reigning and ruling. While politicians reign, the bureaucrats rule. Johnson concludes: "Bureaucrats cannot rule effectively if the reigning politicians fail to perform their positive tasks, above all, to create space for bureaucratic initiative unconstrained by political power."[16]

Political encouragement of bureaucratic innovation is essential especially in bureaucracies that do not provide organizational incentives (in terms of merit-based promotions and salary raises) for developing and implementing a responsive policy regime. Bureaucrats need to be willing to take policy risks to institute effective policy responses. Bureaucratic organizations, on the other hand, tend to promote risk-aversion among the bureaucrats, emphasizing predictability over entrepreneurialism. Organizational incentives linking salaries or promotions to performance can overcome this tendency toward risk-aversion or even toward maintaining the status quo. Yet organizational incentives are not always advisable, since they tend to undermine the bureaucratic esprit de corps and cohesiveness. In the absence of such incentives, political encouragement can act as a substitute.

Noncontractual Bureaucrat-Industrialist Ties

Finally, for developmental state action not only do bureaucrats have to be autonomous and cohesive, receive political or organizational encouragement, but they also have to be embedded in society. The downside of autonomy is isolation. While insulation grants bureaucrats autonomy and aids the process of policymaking, it tends to promote their isolation. Isolated bureaucrats are less likely to develop effective industrial policies than those who are keenly aware of the issues facing industries. The challenge for states therefore is to develop bureaucracies that are not only autonomous but also have some hands-on knowledge of the industries concerned. Such knowledge can be acquired in two ways: via formal institutional links and through informal noncontractual relations. Formal links include institutional arenas that bring bureaucrats and industrialists together, such as industry-state boards and national industry associations. Informal noncontractual relations refers to informal social networks between bureaucrats and industrial entrepreneurs. Industries whose entrepreneurs have such ties with bureaucrats are in a better position to inform autonomous (and insulated and isolated) bureaucrats of the needs and concerns facing the industry. This information is critical if the bureaucrat is to be able to fine-tune policy and develop effective policies.

Bureaucrat-industry ties are, however, likely to be affected by the presence of close ties between politicians and industrialists. Industrialists who have the financial clout to establish contact with leading politicians are unlikely to have informal contacts with the mostly middle-class and upper-middle-class bureaucrats. Bigger industrialists are more likely to deal directly with senior politicians than are smaller industrialists. At the same time, bureaucrats aware of close ties between specific industrialists and politicians are likely to steer clear of them as, in the absence of clear rewards, stepping on political toes is not likely to be an attractive proposition. By conceptually distinguishing between politicians and bureaucrats and by explicating how politician - industrialist relations influence the emergence of relations between industrialists and bureaucrats, we can further specify the conditions under which informal relations between bureaucrats and industry actors are likely to emerge.

Fine-tuning of policy is, however, possible only if the overall policy framework is relatively flexible. In other words, state agencies with the listed characteristics are likely to be more effective at promoting growth and development so long as the policy framework allows them relative industry-specific flexibility. States with rigid policy frameworks (whether ISI or liberal) set by the political regime, in which senior and middle bureaucrats have little input, are unlikely to foster entrepreneurship. Inflexible policy frameworks are less likely to allow bureaucrats to develop responsive policies.

The developmental ensemble, then, is a specific arrangement of institutions that has the four key dimensions of: state cohesion, state autonomy, political encouragement, and the presence of non-contractual relations between the state and industry. It is such an arrangement of institutions that makes for entrepreneurial bureaucrats, allows them to develop responsive policies, and fosters entrepreneurial perspectives among the industrial actors.

Figure 1. 2
The Developmental Ensemble and Policy Frameworks

Faster Industrial Growth	Slower Industrial Growth
A the developmental ensemble *plus* market oriented policy framework (example: Indian software industry, post-1991)	**B** market-oriented policy framework *without* the developmental ensemble (example: Indian steel industry, post-1991)
C the developmental ensemble *plus* ISI policies (example: Indian software industry, pre-1991)	**D** ISI policies *without* the developmental ensemble (example: Indian steel industry, pre-1991)

Figure 1.2 suggests that industrial growth is faster under A than B and under C as compared to D. This is not to argue that policies are irrelevant; it is indeed likely that growth under A is higher than that under C and faster under B compared to D. The major point, however, is that without the developmental ensemble, policies alone will not be enough for rapid industrial transformation. In other words, if my argument is correct, growth under A is likely to be faster than growth under both B and C.

The World Bank has recently noted: "Good policies by themselves can improve results. But the benefits are magnified where institutional capability is also higher. . . . Good policies such as those being pursued . . . by many countries in Latin America and Africa would increase growth in income per capita by around 1.4 percent a year. . . . But it would be even higher with good policies *and* strong institutions."[17] I present evidence supporting this argument, and suggest that good institutions and high institutional capability are best understood via the conceptual category of the developmental ensemble. India's post-1991 industrial performance indicates that industrial growth following the adoption of a structural adjustment policy package is likely to be stronger when these policies are supported by appropriate institutions.

The experience of a number of African economies negatively bear out this conclusion. The weaknesses of state institutions are widely regarded as the reason why structural adjustment polices in Africa have rarely been successful.[18] However, even countries with seemingly strong and capable state structures appear to have problems with industrial performance following liberalization. The experiences of Chile and Venezuela, two well-established Latin American states, support the argument made in this book. The developmental ensemble helped sustain Chile's post-1973 industrial performance, while Venezuela's weaker performance since 1989, it has been argued, was partly a consequence of the absence of such institutional arrangements.[19] Thus, having stable state structures alone does not ensure post-liberalization economic success. Appropriate institutions are also important.

China's economic performance since the 1980s offers additional evidence in favor of my argument. What has contributed most to China's remarkable industrial achievement since 1980 is not the performance of the state-owned enterprises but that of the township and village enterprises (TVEs), which are collaborations between private and local governments. These enterprises have succeeded in an environment where property rights are unclear at best. Evidence suggests that an important factor contributing to this success is the presence of institutions approaching the ideal type of the developmental ensemble at the local level.[20]

The theoretical framework and the concept of the developmental ensemble presented in this book draws to a considerable extent on the theoretical arguments offered by Peter B. Evans.[21] Like Evans's concept of embedded autonomy, the concept of developmental ensemble considers the structure of the state and the state's relationship to societal institutions as explanatory variables. The argument presented here, however, differs from the Evans's in three ways. First, by studying variations in industrial performance within one country, this book controls for historical contingency and variations. Evans focuses on one industry in three countries; this book deals with three industries in one country. Second, it examines the micro-foundations of policymaking and in doing so identifies the incentives and constraints influencing state action. This allows an understanding of the institutional mechanisms that promote developmental state action and of not only why bureaucrats act entrepreneurially but also of what makes them willing to do so. Evans primarily deals with what enabled the state to act developmentally; this book also considers why state and bureaucrats would be willing to act thus. Enabling conditions do not necessarily offer incentives for action. Third, Evans tends to ignore the role of politicians in the process of industrial transformation. This book argues that to understand state action, one must distinguish between bureaucrats and politicians. Statist perspectives tend to conflate these two sets of actors.

Conflating bureaucrats and politicians is especially problematic in democratic countries. Politicians and bureaucrats frequently have differing interests. A politician's actions are influenced by the nature of the political system, while a bureaucrat's actions are shaped by the incentives and constraints generated by the structure of state apparatus. The interests of both politicians and bureaucrats influence their specific relations with industrial actors. More important, the interests of the politician indirectly influence the relationship that the bureaucrat has with entrepreneurs or labor and vice versa. For example, if the politician enjoys a close relationship with an industry actor, bureaucrats are likely to steer clear of such an industrialist for fear of treading on the politician's toes. At the same time, industrialists would have little incentive to develop close relations with bureaucrats. Not only does the presence of politician-industrialist ties not create incentives for the development of such ties between bureaucrats and industrialists, it might also create disincentives. To understand state-industry relations and specifically why some industry actors have close informal relations with bureaucrats, we must conceptually distinguish between politicians and bureaucrats.

ALTERNATE PERSPECTIVES

The Neoclassical Argument

Neoclassical economists have long argued that state intervention in the process of industrial development undermines industrial performance. Only a state concerned with providing adequate infrastructural facilities and maintaining macroeconomic stability is likely to aid industrialization. State "intervention" via industrial policies, incentives, and guidelines is likely to lead to "rent-seeking" and distortions in market signals and therefore hurt industrial growth. Krueger, for instance, has argued that state intervention in the market leads to inefficiencies and losses and that efforts by the state to promote growth are inherently contradictory and unsuccessful.[22] Summarizing this argument, Colander notes that "rent-seeking occurs primarily through the political process and . . . that the best way to limit rent-seeking is to limit government."[23]

By now it is clear that the performance of the East Asian economies between the mid-1960s and mid-1990s offer evidence to the contrary.[24] Not only did industrial policy in Japan, South Korea, and also Taiwan *not* undermine development, it was "developmental"—facilitating the region's massive industrial transformation.[25] On the other hand, it is also clear that state intervention in Latin America, Africa, and South Asia led to slow industrialization. The difference appears to be the *kind* of state intervention, not state intervention per se.

Problems also arise when one examines the performance of different industries in the same country, that is, when one moves from an intercountry to an intracountry industry comparison. As I will show, the reasons why software in India did so well has less to do with the absence of state intervention and more to do with the emergence of policies that actively promoted entrepreneurialism. Such promotion was absent in steel and only partly present in automobiles. Why was this the case? The neoclassical economic perspective is theoretically unable to explain this empirical puzzle.

The Positive Political Economy Arguments

By employing concepts such as transaction costs, the positive political economy perspective, unlike the neoclassical economic perspective, provides a way of understanding inter-industrial variations. The costs of market transactions alter the theoretically expected neoclassical results. Transaction costs include the costs of deciding, planning, arranging, and negotiating the actions to be taken and the terms of exchange when two or more parties do business; the costs of changing plans, renegotiating terms, and resolving disputes as changing circumstances require; the costs of ensuring that parties perform as agreed. Transaction costs also include any losses resulting from inefficient group decisions, plans, arrangements or agreements; inefficient responses to changing circumstances; and imperfect enforcement of agreements. In short, transaction costs include anything that affects the relative performance of different ways of organizing resources and production activities.[26] This argument has been applied to the study of costs incurred in market interactions and also in intra-firm interactions. The organization of the market and of the firm, it is argued, influences the efficiency of market interactions and intra-firm activities respectively. Variations in the costs of transaction explain why some business interactions even in a market economy lead to suboptimal results. Neoclassical economics does not consider the costs of transactions.

The transaction cost argument may be used to explain variations in state performance in the following manner: State agencies that face lower transaction costs are likely to be more effective at their tasks, and agencies with higher transaction costs are likely to be weaker performers. In other words, the policy responsiveness of agencies or departments is explained in terms of the costs of the transactions involved in policy formulation. As Kreps notes, the "study of markets and organizations that transactions take place in becomes a study of the relative transaction costs within the organization."[27] The inability of the Indian Ministry of Steel to respond to the needs of the industry, as opposed to ability of the Department of Electronics to do so, might therefore be explained in terms of variations in transaction costs.

The concept of transaction costs is, however, less than helpful for explaining the performance of *public* organizations such as the state and state-owned enterprises. The transaction cost perspective assumes, for example, that managerial action seeks to lower transaction costs as a consequence of its interest in maximizing profits. In the case of public agencies, it is impossible to adopt such an assumption. At the very least, the goals of state agencies include fostering growth, stabilizing the economy, satisfying societal and political demands, and providing employment.[28] Moreover, while one might reasonably assume that political leaders "care enormously about retaining their posts," it is not possible to make such an assumption with regard to the bureaucrats.[29] Job security, by definition, is more or less guaranteed in a bureaucracy.[30] Not only are the interests of bureaucrats less clear (when compared to those of private entrepreneurs, managers, and even political entrepreneurs), they are also often internally contradictory.

Consider a bureaucrat in India's Ministry of Steel.[31] He or she is likely to be interested in: formulating long-term policy; responding to the interests of steel manufacturers (large, medium, and small); responding to the demands of the steel trade unions; satisfying his or her political superiors, dealing satisfactorily with the elected members of Parliament; being an effective boss to the managers of the state-owned steel enterprise; managing the day-to-day business of the ministry; supporting the interests of the Ministry of Steel vis-à-vis other ministries; finding a suitable position once his or her tenure at the ministry has been completed; and the like. This list is not comprehensive; nor are the bureaucrat's interests necessarily ranked in this order. Only by understanding the specific constraints and incentives applicable to the concerned agencies can bureaucratic interests be identified. The transaction cost argument of positive political economy is useful for explaining variations in bureaucratic behavior only once one assumes that bureaucrats actors have clear and noncontradictory goals. Making such an assumption is problematic. How the unclear and often contradictory interests of a bureaucrat are eventually balanced cannot be determined deductively. More empirical research is necessary.

Douglass North's arguments about institutional change also fall within the purview of the positive political economy perspective. For North, the crucial variable that explains variations in economic performance is the nature of institutions (i.e., the rules of the game). The actions and interests of organizations can lead to changes in institutional structure. This institutional change is slow and incremental, though over time it might lead to a qualitative transformation in the economic regime (say from feudalism to capitalism). Thus, North argues that institutions "are the underlying determinant of the long-run performance of economies."[32]

North's theoretical argument is not useful for explaining the empirical puzzle noted earlier for two reasons. First, while his framework offers insights regarding the process of long-term economic change (e.g., feudalism to capitalism, mercantile capitalism to manufacturing capitalism), it is less helpful for examining short-term changes or variations in industrial performance, which is the main concern of this book.

Second, North's assumption of maximizing actors is problematic. His framework is better suited for explaining how private firms and entrepreneurs might bring about change, than for understanding how the state agencies might do so. For North, as for the other proponents of the positive political economy perspective, the interests of the state are identical with the interests of its rulers, and these interests are comparable to the interests of private economic actors.[33] As I shall show, bureaucrats have to be distinguished from both economic actors and politicians. While the assumption of self-interest may be applicable to politicians (not the subject of this book), its application to bureaucrats is highly problematic. Bureaucratic interests, as already stated, are not clear and often are internally contradictory.

The Cultural Perspective

If the rapid industrial growth of East Asia has provided evidence for critiques of neoclassical economic arguments, it has also strengthened the hand of cultural arguments. The essential tenet of this perspective is that East Asian culture has been critical in helping them succeed economically. One of the leading proponents of this view, Ezra Vogel, has argued that the key factor underlying East Asia's performance is "the institutional practices and underlying attitudes, what Robert Bellah and others call the 'habits of the heart,' that [the present generation has] absorbed in growing up in their culture."[34] These habits "gave the present generation the ability to achieve the needed complex levels of organization."[35]

Another proponent of the cultural approach, Peter Berger, suggests that social and cultural factors such as "a very strong, achievement-oriented work ethic; a highly developed sense of collective solidarity, both within the family and in artificial groupings beyond the family; the enormous prestige of education, with the concomitant motivation to provide the best education for one's children; and severe . . . meritocratic norms and institutions" have all played a critical role in promoting development.[36]

Such cultural arguments might well explain, for example, why the Japanese steel industry has performed better than the Indian steel industry, or why the South Korean automobile industry has been more successful than the Indian automobile industry. They cannot effectively explain why the Indian automobile industry has performed better than the Indian steel industry or why the computer software industry has performed substantially better than the Indian steel industry. Clearly greater disaggregation is needed.

The Sectoral Analysis

One also could argue that certain sectors as opposed to others are more likely to perform better as a result of their inherent attributes. Shafer, for example, contends that: "sectors have an optimal economic organization [that] poses distinctive economic challenges to all producers and states" and "states with similar sectoral bases face similar political constraints when they address these challenges, do so from similar institutional positions, and arrive at similar policy outcomes."[37] Using this analytical framework, Shafer argues that sectors marked by high capital intensity, high economies of scale, high production inflexibility, and high asset/factor inflexibility are likely to pose greater challenges to state autonomy and capacity and consequently to the ability of the state to restructure the sector than those marked by the opposite. "High/high sectors" create vicious cycles, while "low/low sectors" create virtuous cycles for themselves.

There are three reasons why this sectoral analysis is unable to explain our empirical puzzle. First, according to the sectoral analysis, high/high sectors are likely to face continual problems with regard to restructuring. Drawing on the experiences of Zambia, Sri Lanka, South Korea, and Costa Rica, Shafer observes that the former two countries have been unable to effectively restructure and improve the performance of their leading industries (mining and tea respectively). This inability, he argues, is a function of the high/high nature of their leading industries. South Korea and Costa Rica, on the other hand, did not face this problem since their leading sectors (light manufacturing and coffee respectively) were low/low. The experience of India's automobile industry, however, raises problems for the sectoral analytical framework, which is unable to explain how and why the automobile (a high/high) industry turned around in India or why the computer software industry (low/low) performed poorly until the 1980s. This perspective cannot adequately handle such intertemporal variation.

Second, India's multisectoral economy may well be the reason why the experience of the country's automobile industry does not support the sectoral analysis. As Shafer himself notes, while his sectoral perspective is useful for understanding the performance of sectors in economies dominated by single sectors, its validity for a multisectoral economy is unclear, because in such economies, actors not connected to a leading sector but powerful nevertheless might influence the development of that sector. In Zambia or Sri Lanka, the most powerful actors are all involved with the dominant sector. In multisectoral economies like India, dominant actors such as large conglomerates are interested in more than one sector. For this reason, while insights gained by the sectoral analysis may be used to explain parts of our empirical puzzle, it needs to be substantially reworked.

Third, Shafer's model assumes that politicians and bureaucrats are *willing* to introduce change but are *unable* to do so only as a result of the sector's political-economic dynamics. Rather than merely assuming that bureaucrats and politicians are willing to act in a developmental manner, one needs to explain what leads them to be willing. A bureaucrat with a secure job, with promotions not linked to performance, may have little incentive to take risks, innovate, and act in a developmental manner.

Thus in order to determine why some industries grew and others did not, we need to investigate why bureaucrats were willing and able to act in a developmental manner at certain times and not others, and in some industries, not others. The formulation of any new policy or significant changes in existing policies depends on state managers having the will and the ability to do so.[38] This is better explained by the social-structural perspective and the concept of the developmental ensemble.

The concept of the developmental ensemble constructed from within the social-structural perspective has clear advantages over these three alternate explanations. In contrast to neoclassical economic arguments, the concept of the developmental ensemble can explain how and why the state can promote industrial development. Vis-à-vis the positive political economy perspective, the argument about the developmental ensemble can more effectively explain change in industrial performance over the short run and also explain the behavior of public organizations. While the sectoral argument is insightful when it comes to understanding single-sector economies, it is less capable of explaining industrial performance in multisectoral economies. The cultural perspective, in contrast to the concept of the developmental ensemble, cannot explain intra-bureaucratic behavior.

RESEARCH METHODOLOGY

Given the small number of industrial sectors, in this study I use a comparative-historical methodology, which involves the study of "how different conditions or causes fit together in one setting [in] contrast [to] how they fit together in another setting."[39] Thus, I examine the conditions plausibly associated with shifts in industrial policy for one industrial sector at any one point in time; compare it with a similar examination of the other industrial sectors at a comparable point in time; and also relate it to a comparable analysis of the same sector at other times. Through the logical juxtaposition of the characteristics of the three industrial sectors, I identify valid causes and associated factors.

Since the book focuses on *Indian* industrial policy, the danger of presenting an analysis that confuses its unique characteristic with its more generalizable ones always exists. In an effort to overcome such a problem, I relate the cases under focus to comparable earlier studies. By using such associated analyses as checks, I strengthen my argument beyond the cases under study and arrive at theoretical propositions with considerable support.

ORGANIZATION OF THE BOOK

The book is organized as follows: Chapter 2 reviews India's overall economic/industrial strategy, the structure of its state apparatus, its trade union structure, and industry associations. The chapter examines industrial policies adopted since independence in 1947 that apply to the three sectors under review. It also considers the organizational structure of the Indian Administrative Service whose members are in charge of administering the industrial policies. Finally, it reviews the history of the union movement and the labor laws and discusses the implications of this trade union structure for the role trade unions play in the policymaking process.

The Indian steel, automobile, and computer software sectors are examined in chapters 3, 4, and 5, which focus on the growth of each sector and the changes in policy for each one. These three chapters also discuss the factors underlying the shifts or lack of shifts in policy for each sector. Finally, chapter 6 discusses the empirical and theoretical conclusions, examines the implications of the analysis, and places it within an international comparative context.

2.

The Indian Context

Before examining the development of the steel, automobile, and computer software industries in India, we need to review the country's economic, bureaucratic, labor, and industry structure. This review will give us an understanding of the institutional context in which these three industries have developed. Such an understanding is a building block in the construction of a social institutional argument. It is essential for understanding the similarities and differences among these industries.

THE ECONOMIC CONTEXT

India's Initial Economic Strategy

In line with the dominant perspectives in development economics prevalent during the late 1940s and in the 1950s, the Indian government adopted a course of planned development. [1] The goal of the development program was to create "an economic structure which will yield maximum production without the concentration of private monopolies and the concentration of wealth and which will create the proper balance between urban and rural economies."[2] With this in mind, the state passed an Industrial Policy Resolution in 1948 (hereafter called Industrial Policy Resolution-48). The resolution argued that the emphasis of the development programs should be on increasing agricultural and industrial production with the state playing a progressively active role in industrial development.

The Industrial Policy Resolution-48 stated that the central government would have exclusive monopoly over the manufacture of armaments, atomic energy production, and management of the railway network. The establishment of any new units/plants in the following industries was to be the sole responsibility of the state: coal, iron and steel, aircraft and shipbuilding, mineral oils and manufacture of communication facilities such as telephones, telegraph and wireless apparatus. The state also was given the right to acquire any private enterprise in these industries whenever warranted by public interest. Eighteen industries were to be open to private entrepreneurs.[3] The state was to regulate the growth and production of these industries. The state retained the right to participate in these sectors as well as to intervene in specific private units when deemed necessary.

In 1951 the state passed the Industries (Development and Regulation) Act, which provided the licensing system covering the industries falling under the purview of the Industrial Policy Resolution-48. According to the act, a license was required for establishing a new industrial unit, manufacture of a new product by an existing unit, increasing production capacity, and changing the location of any existing unit. Small-scale industries (those having assets below a certain amount) as well as cottage industries were exempted from these licensing requirements. Together, the Industrial Policy Resolution-48 and the Industrial (Development and Regulation) Act created an elaborate licensing system.

Meanwhile, in 1950 the Planning Commission was set up to oversee the implementation of India's Five Year Plans. Members of this commission included economists, politicians, and even the odd industrialist. Situated directly under the Prime Minister (who is also its chair), the commission performs an advisory role. Its recommendations and policy advice are submitted to the Ministerial Cabinet for approval and consideration. In practice, however, the relationship between the cabinet and the Planning Commission has been less than clear. Under Jawaharlal Nehru, the Planning Commission became the Prime Minister's organizational tool with regard to economic policy, and it had a good deal of authority vis-à-vis other ministries.

The status of the Planning Commission has, however, declined in the years since Nehru's death in 1964. Political exigencies have led subsequent Prime Ministers to reduce the commission's authority while increasing that of the Prime Minister's Office and the cabinet. In recent years, the Commission's ability to shape the planning process has been determined more by political interests and conflicts and less by its members' expertise and skill.[4] Bureaucrats in the Prime Minister's Office and administrative ministries now have greater autonomy from the Planning Commission with regard to economic policy decisions.

The Planning Commission presented its First Five Year Plan covering the years 1951 to 1956 in 1951. The plan focused on agricultural development, irrigation, and associated infrastructure. It addressed the industrial sector to the extent that it was essential for the growth of agricultural production. Only 7. 6 percent of the total plan outlay was allocated for industrial development. Agriculture, irrigation and community development, on the other hand, were to receive 32 percent of the total outlay.

During the mid-1950s, the state changed its approach to planned development. Its new approach emphasized the role of industrial development for overall economic development and the responsibility of state-owned enterprises in the development of core industries. Heralding this new economic strategy was the Industrial Policy Resolution of 1956 (hereafter cited as Industrial Policy Resolution-56).

This resolution classified industries into three categories. While the Industrial Policy Resolution-48 had presented the general guidelines for private enterprise and state intervention in the economy, the Industrial Policy Resolution-56 *specified* the extent of the state's role. The state was given the sole right to establish industries listed in the first categories. Existing private companies in these sectors were permitted to operate and their expansion was not proscribed. Industries in this category included: iron and steel, atomic energy, arms and ammunition, heavy plant and machinery manufacture, coal, mineral oils, mining, aircraft, shipbuilding, railway transport, telephone and telephone cables and heavy electrical plants.

The second category comprised industries "which will be progressively State-owned and in which the State will, . . . generally take the initiative in establishing new undertakings, but in which private enterprise will also be expected to supplement the effort of the State."[5] These industries included: machine tools, drugs, plastics, fertilizers, ferro alloys, and road transport. Thus, while the first resolution had proposed that the state would regulate, and if necessary, intervene in the noncore sectors, the second resolution went substantially further.

The third category consisted of all other industries. Private enterprises were viewed as central for the development of these remaining industries. The Industrial Policy Resolution-56 also stressed the role of cottage and small-scale industries. Support for these industries was to be provided via differential taxation, subsidies, and by restricting the production of the non-small-scale and cottage sector. This was Nehru's concession to the Gandhian legacy of the Indian national movement.

The development focus of the Industrial Policy Resolution-56 was reiterated and concretized by the Second Five Year Plan, which covered the years 1956 to 1961. Placing industrialization at the center of economic development, the Plan argued that "the country must aim at developing basic industries and industries which make machines to make machines needed for further development."[6] Such a focus, the plan noted, implied an expansion of India's iron and steel, coal, cement, nonferrous metals, and other "basic" industries.

Related to the focus on basic industries was the emphasis (in line with the perspective of the Industrial Policy Resolution-56) on public sector development. The plan argued that the main responsibility for developing the core industries lay with the central government, since the implementation of the specific projects required considerable financial investment as well as organizational and administrative capabilities. The programs "of industrial development during the Second Plan place on the Government responsibility, among other things, for new steel plants, coal mines, heavy machine building factories, fertilizer factories, manufacture of heavy electrical equipment and oil exploration and development."[7]

The Third Five Year Plan, covering 1961 to 1966, retained the prior plan's emphasis on the development of basic industries and the responsibilities of the public sector. The critical difference between the plans was the focus on self-reliance. With the Third Plan, an additional goal of self-reliant development was added. The goal of self-reliance "was interpreted to mean import-substitution and/or self-sufficiency because of the crucial premise of export pessimism on the part of the planners."[8]

National income grew by 3.6 percent during the First Plan period, and by 4.0 percent and 2.2 percent during the next two plan periods, respectively. Industrial production grew by 7.3 percent, 6.6 percent, and 9.0 percent during the first three plan periods, respectively. The Indian economy, however, ran into problems toward the end of the Third Plan period. The agricultural sector did not perform as expected during the plan period's first three years and frequent droughts in subsequent years hampered progress, resulting in food crises. The war with Pakistan in 1965-66 and a decline in foreign aid also hurt the economy and especially industrial production. As a result of these disruptions, public investment declined and hindered the growth of industrial production. The reduction in industrial production was particularly apparent in the basic and capital goods industries.

Severe financial constraints during the mid-1960s made the formulation and implementation of the Fourth Plan difficult. The financial situation improved to a limited extent after the state received a loan from the International Monetary Fund in 1966. Despite this, however, poor agricultural performance created additional economic problems. The Fourth Plan was therefore postponed.

A "plan holiday" was declared for the years 1966 to 1969 and three annual plans were drawn up. During this period, the state emphasized investment in the agricultural sector, particularly in irrigation infrastructure. The direction adopted during the Second and Third Plans was somewhat reversed. As during the First Plan, the emphasis was now on the agricultural sector rather than on heavy industry. During these three years national income declined by 6 percent, and industrial production increased marginally by 2.0 percent.

The Fourth Five Year Plan, covering 1969 to 1974, was introduced in 1969. In comparison to the previous plans, this plan was accompanied by a shift in plan outlays from heavy industry toward agricultural infrastructure. This shift was a consequence of the populist stance adopted by Prime Minister Indira Gandhi.

Heavy industry in particular and large industry in general faced with increased regulatory controls. At the same time, there were only modest increases in plan outlays for the development of industry. The new regulatory policies were in the form of the Monopolies and Restrictive Trade Practices (MRTP) Act in 1969 and the Foreign Exchange Regulation Act (FERA), which was introduced in 1973. MRTP companies (firms falling under the purview of the MRTP Act, in other words, firms with assets exceeding Rupees 2 million) were permitted to enter only the core and heavy industries not previously reserved for the public sector. FERA introduced similar regulatory measures for foreign companies in India. Credit and finance facilities available to the large industries were also controlled and regulated following the nationalization of the banking industry in 1969.

Besides directly increasing regulatory control over large industry, the Fourth Plan also sought to contain its development by further emphasizing the role of small-scale industries in the process of industrialization. The strategy with regard to these industries was transformed from one of promotion to protection.

The 1973 oil crisis constrained economic planning and development during the early part of the decade. The almost fourfold increase in the price of crude oil was accompanied by an increase in the prices of cereals, fertilizers, machinery and equipment, non-ferrous metals. The balance-of-payment situation was adversely affected, and crisis necessitated a loan from the International Monetary Fund for Rs. 4,850 million in 1974 to 1975. [9]

Given the shift in political agendas and policy emphasis as well as the financial crunch, the rate of public investment (as a percentage of gross domestic product) during the Fourth Plan period remained low. Planners (and most economists) acknowledged this as one of the principal factors leading to a decline in the rate of economic growth. Low public investment also adversely affected industrial production and productivity levels. Public investment in infrastructure declined. This, together with the poor management of the infrastructure, undermined the economy. National income grew by only 3.3 percent and industrial production by 3.0 percent.

As a result of India's fiscal situation during the mid-1970s, the Fifth Plan did not include dramatic increases in state investment. Plan outlays were kept at modest levels. No new projects in the industrial sector were planned. The national income grew at an annual average rate of 5.0 percent and the GDP by 5.2 percent during the Fifth Plan period. The rate of both industrial and agricultural production grew at a better (average annual) rate than during the previous plan period—4.3 percent versus 2.9 percent for agriculture and 5.9 percent as opposed to 3.0 percent for industry. The improvements in these indices were partly a reflection of the improvements in the agricultural sector, especially irrigation facilities, and of the relative stabilization of the balance-of-payments position toward the end of the decade. While the oil price hike in 1973 had created balance-of-payments problems, by the late 1970s remittances of India's migrants in the Middle East had begun to stabilize the situation.

The Sixth Five Year Plan, from 1980 to 1985, was implemented following Mrs. Gandhi's reappointment as prime minister. The plan's stated objectives were very similar to those of the earlier plans. However, a few significant changes were made in the economic and industrial policies adopted during this period.[10] One significant shift was the focus on exports.

India's export performance between 1951 and 1980 had been mediocre. It's share of world exports had fallen from 2.42 percent in 1948 to 0.41 percent by the end of the 1970s.[11] The volume of India's exports had grown slower than the exports of developing countries.[12] The relative lack of focus on exports was reversed starting with the Sixth Plan. Liberalization of policy regarding the import of up-to-date technology, especially for export-oriented industries, supported the emphasis on exports. The shift toward a more liberal economic/industrial policy was probably influenced by Indira Gandhi's political calculations as well as by a loan from the International Monetary Fund granted in 1981.

The Industrial Policy Statement (1980) specified the contours of this policy shift. It presented new policy initiatives with regard to the licensing requirements for private industrial production, small-scale industries, state-owned enterprises, and export-oriented industrial units. The licensing requirement for industries in the core sectors was liberalized. Industrial units in the core sector or those directly linked to the core sectors were permitted to increase their production capacity. The new policy initiatives also sought to reduce the industrial regulations applicable to smaller-sized firms by redefining the category of small-scale industries, such as, raising their upper limit on assets. This enabled a larger number of industrial units to receive benefits available to small-scale industries (i. e., comparatively lower taxes, fewer licensing requirements, and easier credit facilities).

The policy statement of 1980 also presented new initiatives aimed at improving the productivity of state-owned enterprises. The focus was on improving the managerial capacity of these enterprises. Drawing on the relationship between state-owned enterprises and the state in France, the 1980 Industrial Policy Statement proposed the establishment of the practice of "memoranda of understanding" (MOU) to be signed jointly by the state and the state-owned enterprises covering a period of one to three years. These MOUs were expected to act as production targets and thus govern production patterns and strategies at the state-owned enterprises. The MOUs were regarded a mechanism to help reduce interference by the various ministries in the day-to-day activities of the SOEs.

By the end of the Sixth Plan period the target of 5.2 percent aggregate growth rate had been achieved. Two factors contributed to this achievement: good agricultural production and the rapid growth of the service sector. Mining and manufacturing, however, continued to perform well below expectations. Especially inadequate was the performance of basic industries such as steel, fertilizer, textiles, and cement. Productivity and capacity utilization in these sectors remained low.

Following Mrs. Gandhi's assassination in October 1984, Rajiv Gandhi was elected leader of the Congress party, and in December 1984 he led his party to a landslide electoral victory. During the election campaign Rajiv Gandhi presented himself as a new kind of politician and as a leader capable of "leading India into the twenty-first century."

The Seventh Five Year Plan, for the period 1985 to 1990, reflected this shift in economic ideology and political perspectives. It extended the Sixth Plan's focus on exports and liberalization with regard to industrial production. While the Sixth Plan had sought to shift the focus on export into the existing economic framework, the Seventh Plan recognized the need to modify industrial and monetary policy in order to support the changes in trade policy.

The modifications in industrial policy, however, remained incomplete. While export-oriented industries were encouraged and industrial regulations were modified, the overall economic and industrial policy framework remained. Key industrial acts, such as the MRTP Act and FERA, as well as protection for small-scale industries, continued with only minor alterations. The changes were introduced largely at the sectoral level.

The pseudo-liberalization measures soon ran into political problems. Opposition from within his party (i. e., the Congress party) compelled Rajiv Gandhi to rescind some of the newly introduced modifications. If the word 'socialism' had not been mentioned in the first budget speech presented by Rajiv Gandhi's finance minister (V. P. Singh), the socialist rhetoric used by Nehru and Indira Gandhi had been reintroduced by the end of the 1980s. During the Seventh Plan period, national income grew by 5.5 percent and industrial production by 8.5 percent. The Seventh Plan period also saw a sharp increase in the budget deficit. And this was a critical factor in the economic crisis of 1990-91.

The 1990-91 Economic Crisis and Its Aftermath
The next major shift in India's economic policy framework followed the crisis of 1990-91 that developed partly as a consequence of the rising budget deficits of the 1980s. The budget deficit grew from 6.4 to 9 percent of the GDP through the 1980s, partly as a result of increased defense spending, governmental wages and salaries, and subsidies. The major contributing factor, however, was the continual failure of state-owned enterprises to generate profits and increase government savings.

Economic conditions reached their nadir during 1990-91. The precipitating factor was the Iraqi invasion of Kuwait in August 1990. Remittances from Indian workers in the Gulf (which formed a significant portion of India's foreign currency earnings) fell drastically. The invasion of Kuwait led to a sharp increase in the price of crude oil. Along with the fall in remittances, the rise in the price of crude oil exacerbated the pressure on India's foreign currency reserves.

By the end of 1990 there was a serious possibility of default. In January 1991 the government accepted a loan from the Compensatory and Contingency Financing Facility of International Monetary Fund for $1.8 billion. Toward the middle of 1991 the new government, headed by Prime Minister Narasimha Rao, turned to the IMF for another loan, which was accompanied by conditionalities regarding the control and reduction of the budget deficit as well as the implementation of structural reforms.

The Industrial Policy Statement (1991)
In July 1991 the state presented a new Industrial Policy Statement, which brought about a radical change in the overall economic/industrial policy framework. If the earlier attempts at liberalization had altered only certain aspects of the policy regime, the 1991 statement fundamentally changed the overall framework. The industrial licensing system was abolished, foreign

investment rules were liberalized, technological collaborations were regarded as essential for improving growth rates, state-owned enterprises were de-emphasized in the development approach, and restrictions on large private companies (the MRTP companies) were removed.

Along with eliminating most licensing requirements, the Indian government also revised its views regarding foreign investment. For the first time in over 40 years, the Indian state emphasized the advantages of foreign investment such as "technology transfer, marketing expertise, introduction of modern managerial techniques and new possibilities for promotion of exports" and welcomed it.[13]

The MRTP Act, which had proven to be the bête noire for private entrepreneurialism, was finally modified. Large private companies no longer had to receive prior clearance from the MRTP Commission for investment decisions.

In 1991 the Indian government also altered its perception of the role of state-owned enterprises in the development strategy. The new approach did argue for increased support for state-owned enterprises in strategic sectors (i.e., infrastructure, oil exploration, defense products), but it also called for a review of existing state-owned enterprises engaged in sectors where "the private sector has developed sufficient expertise and resources."[14] The state-owned enterprises were now to be considered essential only in sectors where private investment was inadequate or undesirable for reasons of national security (i. e, defense equipment).

The reform retained some links with the earlier policy regime, however. The labor laws and industrial relations laws were left untouched, and more specifically, the reform package did not include an exit policy (i. e., firm closure policy).[15] The financial sector reforms (recommended by the international financial institutions) also have not been fully implemented. While private banks and mutual funds are now permitted, nationalized banks continue to dominate the banking sector. And while privatization of state-owned enterprises has begun, it is still relatively rare. There has been limited sale of equity of state-owned enterprises.

The Indian economy has, nevertheless, clearly stabilized and gone through a structural adjustment since 1991. The balance-of-payments position has improved. From a situation where India's foreign currency reserves covered only two weeks of imports (in 1991), the reserves as of May 1999, were $31.3 billion. Inflation, which had reached record levels of 16 percent in 1991, was at 7.7 percent in May 1999.[16] Exports have grown at an average annual rate of around 13 percent since 1992 to 1993. The economic growth rate since then has been around 6 percent a year, and the industrial growth rate has been around 7 percent a year.[17]

In the years since independence, the gains in the overall economy have been primarily in terms of: considerable success in agricultural production, the elimination of famines, and the creation of an industrial base.[18] India's rate of economic growth, while it may have been faster than its population growth, has not been spectacular when compared to that of other industrializing countries. Between the years 1965 and 1973, the Indian economy grew at an average annual rate of 3.7 percent. Between 1970 and 1980 the average annual growth rate remained more or less the same (at 3.4 percent). During the years 1980-1988, this figure increased to 5.6 percent. Following a significant decline during the balance-of-payments crisis of 1991, the rate of growth bounced up to 6.0-7.0 percent and even over 7.0 percent during the mid-1990s. India's GDP declined to 5.0 percent in 1997-98 from 7.8 percent in 1996-97 partly as a result of the fallout of the East Asian crisis. By 1998-99 the economy recovered somewhat and grew by 5.8 percent.[19]

In comparison, South Korea's economy grew by 10.1 percent during the years 1970 to 1980, and between 1980 and 1993, it grew at the rate of 9.1 percent. The Malaysian economy during the periods 1970 to 1980 and 1980 to 1993 grew by 7.9 percent and 6.2 percent respectively. Indonesia grew at the rate of 7.2 percent and 5.8 percent during the same two periods.[20]

Thus, compared to the economic performance of South Korea and other East Asian and South east Asian countries, India's economic growth appears dismal. However, when compared to other developing countries (i. e., some in sub-Saharan Africa), India's overall performance is, if not spectacular, not entirely disastrous. For the period 1965 to 1980, while India was not one of the 20 fastest-growing economies (a list that included Taiwan, South Korea, Brazil, and Indonesia), it also was not among the 20 slowest-growing economies (included here were Chile, Ghana, and Jamaica). For the period 1980 to 1991, India was the eighteenth fastest-growing economy, ahead of Turkey, Egypt, Kenya, Israel, and Zimbabwe but following South Korea, China, Taiwan, Indonesia and Malaysia.[21]

India's industrial performance has almost consistently been short of the targets set in the various plans. Following the initial spurt in industrial growth (7.9 percent average annual rate), Indian industry grew at an average annual rate of 4.2 percent during the period 1951 to 1980. Between 1980 and 1995 a period of relatively rapid industrial growth ensued, but it is nowhere comparable to the East Asian performance. Consider the comparison with South Korea. Industrial production in South Korea has grown at a rate of 16.0 percent. And in the 1980s South Korean industry grew at 12.6 percent. Casting a wider net, for the period 1980 to 1990 India's industrial growth rate was the fourteenth fastest rate, ahead of Turkey, Indonesia, Singapore, and Uganda but following South Korea, China, Thailand, and Malaysia.

Apart from a relatively slow growth rate, the list of failures of India's industry includes the disappointing performance of state-owned enterprises.[22] Capacity utilization by these firms remains low. The state-owned firms that dominate the basic and infrastructure industries have, in particular, performed poorly. India's export performance has also been poor. Its share in world exports declined from 2.42 percent in 1950 to 1.1 percent in 1960, 0.65 percent in 1970, and 0.41 percent in 1980. Finally, productivity levels in the manufacturing sector have not gone up significantly.

India's one major industrial achievement has been the substantial extent to which industry has diversified over the past 40 years. "At Independence, India inherited an industrial structure which was dominated by textiles and sugar industries."[23] Today, however, India's industrial structure is markedly different. Years of a self-reliant approach have led to industries that manufacture an entire range of products (capital goods, consumer goods) and that offer a variety of services and consequently have reduced imports. Policies aimed at ensuring the regional diversification of industries also have been successful.

THE STRUCTURE OF THE INDIAN BUREAUCRACY

The Indian Administrative Service

The complex licensing framework and regulatory economic policies described in the previous section have since independence been administered by a gargantuan bureaucratic apparatus. The Indian Administrative Service (IAS) is the dominant and elite segment of the state bureaucracy. Created at the time of independence in 1947 to replace the colonial Indian Civil Service (ICS), the 3,000-odd members of the IAS are assigned to key positions in the central ministries (i.e., Finance, Commerce, Steel, and Industry) and also in the various state governments. The Cabinet Secretary is the senior-most bureaucrat in the country and is always a member of the IAS. Secretaries, the bureaucratic heads of the various ministries, are also mostly IAS members. Consequently, senior policymakers in the bureaucracy are inevitably IAS officers. To understand how and why bureaucrats are willing and able to promote industrial development, therefore, it is important to understand the structure of the Indian Administrative Service.

Training

As with the ICS, entry into the IAS is on the basis of a competitive nationwide examination. Examinees are tested in two areas of their choice. Following this examination selected candidates are interviewed. Once accepted into the service, trainees undergo two years of training. Since the beginning the entire recruitment process has been biased toward selecting candidates with a liberal, generalist education. While technical specialists (such as engineers and doctors) have been selected, the civil service cadre has tended to be dominated by humanities and social science majors.

Upon selection, the IAS officials are trained at the National Academy of Administration in Mussoorie for a year. Training there consists of a foundation course on India's constitutional, economic and social framework.[24] In addition, trainees are taught the principles of public administration and the ethics of the civil service. After the foundation course, they are taken on a cultural-study tour of India. Upon their return trainees spend time at a military base, at a police training college, and at the Parliament. Apart from the foundation courses and the field trips, trainees are instructed in the areas of law, emergency work, developmental programs, use of weapons, and horseback riding.

Not only is the program at Mussoorie similar in terms of formal content to the ICS training regime, but further, it attempts to instill in the IAS probationers an appreciation for an upper-class English lifestyle. The informal training at the academy includes instruction on the "appropriate" attire for formal and casual occasions (formal for men means suits, and for women, Indian clothes), English table manners ("remember to use the correct silverware"), gender relations, and the "proper" way of addressing senior IAS officials (always as "sir").

The informal instruction has been clearly aimed at altering the trainees' lifestyle and norms of social interaction. According to Potter, "gentlemanly norms relating to social calls, formal invitations, table manners, dress, civic manners, and ceremonial functions were actually printed privately for probationers in a 'Handbook on Etiquette and Manners.'"[25] And he further notes that these "manners" were "precisely the form insisted upon by senior ICS Europeans when shaping ICS Indians in the 1920s and 1930s. The manners and etiquette are not just 'western,' they come straight out of behavior patterns common amongst ICS gentlemen in the days of the raj."[26]

In a survey of IAS officers, Potter notes that most respondents identified the inculcation of ICS social norms and values as playing a central role in homogenizing the IAS probationers who came from various regions within India.[27] It also had the effect of generating among IAS members an esprit de corps. The esprit de corps is of course strengthened by the small size of the IAS cadre (around 75 to 80 chosen annually in recent years). In addition, during the generalist training, the various IAS cohorts are not divided. In other words, the training and organizational structure of the IAS and the resultant esprit de corps help link mutual attachment, loyalty, pride in membership on one hand with shared outlook, values, assumptions, and policy orientations on the other.

At the end of a year-long training period, the IAS probationers (as the trainees are called) are assigned to a state cadre and sent to that state for a year of district training.

In the course of their careers IAS officers are posted at various levels in their cadre state, and at senior positions in the central ministries (such as the Ministry of Industry, Steel, Finance, Commerce, etc.). Changing one's cadre state is possible only under the most extraordinary circumstances. This training occurs at various levels within the district and focuses on the areas of revenue collection, judicial work, and grass-roots development work. Following their training the IAS officers are assigned their first posts in their state cadre.

Lifestyle

The life of a colonial bureaucrat resembled the status driven life of a feudal lord or of a rich landlord (the Indian equivalent). Life revolved around the civil service. In towns and larger districts, the local officers' club was the center of social activity. Colleagues were neighbors, and neighbors dominated one's circle of friends. Noncontractual ties with non-ICS members were if not discouraged, clearly inhibited. And both their personal and professional life were supported by a multitude of junior officers, clerks, peons, and servants.

This lifestyle more or less continued after 1947. The IAS bureaucrats are, in fact, given the same offices used by the ICS members. Up until the 1960s, a majority of the junior officials and street-level bureaucrats in these offices had received their training under the supervision of senior ICS members. Apart from being placed in the very same office buildings and assigned the same subordinate officers, IAS officials live in the same houses, maintained by a retinue of servants. They are members of the same clubs, which are now open to Indians. Their lifestyle further strengthens their esprit de corps.

Overall, the training and lifestyle of the IAS probationers has the following consequences: (1) it tends to create a strong esprit de corps and strengthens intra-IAS ties; (2) it bolsters the IAS's elite and exclusive status, professionally as well as socially, and distances members from the society they are to administer (uncannily like the way in which the ICS was separated from the "natives"); (3) it retains the law-and-order focus of the ICS; (4) it places more emphasis on regulatory than on developmental tasks; and finally, (5) it does not equip the bureaucrats with an in-depth knowledge of specific industries they would be expected to promote later in their careers.

The IAS Career

Despite the bias in the training program and in their initial work experience toward local administration and law and order, IAS officials in the course of their careers are placed in middle and senior positions within most state-level and central departments and ministries. More specifically, they are assigned the task of promoting economic and industrial growth, areas in which they have neither received formal instruction nor work experience. [28] Qualified specialists, technocrats, and political appointees are assigned to these positions only under the rarest of circumstances. This is true not only of ministries and departments concerned with general administration but also of those involved with technological, scientific, and industrial development. In the Ministry of Steel, for example, all positions from the rank of joint secretary and above are reserved for members of the IAS. The situation is identical in most of the other ministries concerned with formulating and implementing economic and industrial policies, including the Ministries of Industry, Finance, Labor and Commerce. The argument offered by current officials regarding why this is not a problem is similar to the perspective of the erstwhile ICS officials: that administration is administration; being a member of the IAS enables one to undertake any of the tasks required of a state bureaucrat.

Rules and regulations regarding transfers stipulate that the tenure of under secretaries at the various central ministries is three years; deputy secretaries, four years; and joint secretaries, five years. In reality, the pattern of IAS transfers is very different. Data suggest that "a staggering 80 percent or more of the entire IAS in the early 1980s [for example], actually held their posts for less than two years before moving on."[29] IAS officers are on a never ending merry-go-round of transfers.

In interviews, IAS bureaucrats remarked that the frequent transfers often did not permit them to understand the dynamics of the various issues and concerns they are required to administer.[30] More important, even when they are able to grasp the finer points and subtleties of their duties, they were never in the position long enough to effectively formulate and implement a policy response. Thus, frequent transfers, which were essential for insulating members of ICS from the "hostile masses," do not appear to be suitable for performing non-routine duties. The generalist character of the IAS that is fostered during the training period is, therefore, reinforced by the frequent transfers of the IAS bureaucrats.[31]

Apart from being transferred every few years, IAS bureaucrats are also transferred to positions that tend to be dissimilar in content and tasks. As a result, the IAS bureaucrats tend to have or acquire a nonspecialist career path. The pattern of transfers along with the frequency of transfers thus reinforces the generalist training they receive as probationers. It also strengthens intra-IAS ties. Posted to a new position and often to a new town every few years, IAS bureaucrats tend to depend on contacts with colleagues from within the IAS to establish themselves both professionally and socially. At the same time, these moves reduce the possibility of developing ties between industrial actors and IAS bureaucrats; in other words, they further reduce the possibilities of non-contractual ties emerging between industrial actors and the IAS.

The frequent and "random" transfers also have the effect of discouraging bureaucrats from performing innovative tasks (in contrast to routine ones). The average tenure at any post, as noted above, is barely adequate to understand the tasks at hand, let alone devise and implement effective and innovative policies and programs. Frequent turnover tends to ensure that routine tasks are completed, but tasks requiring a greater gestation period are forsaken or at least put on hold.

Thus the pattern of transfers, and more specifically the period of postings and the career paths of the bureaucrats, has the following consequences: it reinforces the generalist training of the IAS bureaucrats; it strengthens intra-IAS ties; it reduces the possibility of developing ties with industrial actors; and finally, it increases incentives for performing routine rather than innovative tasks.

One factor that might undermine the intra-IAS cohesiveness and esprit de corps is competition among its various members over the course of their careers, If promotions, for example, are based on performance or periodic evaluations, then it is likely that the resulting competition would reduce the cohesiveness of the civil service cadre. Promotions for IAS officials are, however, not based on performance but are automatic. Every five to seven years IAS bureaucrats are promoted and their salaries raised. While evidence of corruption or other criminal behavior interrupts the automatic promotions, average performance or even mildly inadequate performance leads to little censure; IAS officials need to display only reasonable competence and reliability.[32]

Despite these drawbacks, the IAS does have a number of positive characteristics. First, the IAS cadre has functioned as India's "steel frame." Especially during times of political and/or social crises, the IAS is widely regarded as the most reliable component of the Indian state apparatus. During the period of the Emergency (1975-1977), it was to the IAS cadres that Prime Minister Gandhi turned to for support. The IAS's experience and ability to perform routine administrative tasks and maintain law and order made it the preeminent choice. The very characteristics that have made it impossible for IAS members to act as agents of development and entrepreneurship have made it possible for the IAS to be regarded as the nation's steel frame. Second, the autonomy and insulation resulting from the IAS's cohesive structure and frequent transfers has ensured that while the IAS is not free of corruption, it is certainly not as corruption-ridden as the lower ranks of the Indian bureaucracy.[33]

Thus, the organizational factors that curtail IAS bureaucrats' ability to act in a developmental manner include: (a) the generalist training and career focus; (b) the frequent transfers; and (c) their control over personnel policy which has effectively prevented reform of the IAS structure.[34] The generalist training combined with frequent transfers (which tend to follow a generalist pattern as well) restricts their understanding of the various industrial issues and problems they are assigned to tackle. Changes in the organizational structure of the IAS to encourage specialization and reduce the frequency of transfers would eliminate this problem. However, the IAS members' control over personnel policy and the lack of interest on the part of the political leadership to push for change have ensured that the IAS structure has remained more or less the same almost 50 years after Independence. Despite early declarations to the contrary over the years, the political leaders have tended to promote rather than undermine the power of the IAS.[35]

With no monetary incentives to act in a developmental manner, and in the absence of information from industrialists, IAS bureaucrats are *unwilling* to improve their performance and, more important, do not always know how to improve it. IAS bureaucrats lack the knowledge of "how and what to do," and the incentives to promote developmental statism. Therefore, if the IAS bureaucrats could be guided with regard to "how and what to do," and were given the incentives to do so, they could conceivably promote and nurture industrial growth. Thus, one might expect that in government agencies and departments where conducive conditions exist, IAS bureaucrats would in fact be acting in a developmental manner.

Such conducive conditions would include: longer tenures for IAS bureaucrats in specific posts, so as to encourage IAS officials to undertake projects with long gestation periods; greater informal and formal interaction with industrial interests, such that IAS officials would overcome the generalist mold and know what specific actions would promote industrial development and foster long-term entrepreneurial perspectives among the industrial elite.

A bureaucrat's ability and willingness to promote development, however, is a function not only of the organizational structure but also of the structure and interests of the other concerned actors and institutions. Chapters 3, 4, and 5, examine how specific interests (of politicians, trade union leaders, industrialists) and institutions (trade unions, industry associations, and the structure of concerned state agencies) in the steel, automobile, and computer software industries influence the bureaucrats' and the state's willingness and ability to act in a developmental manner.

Figure 2.1

Organizational Structure of the IAS

IAS Structure	Incentives and/or Constraints Created	Implications for IAS Bureaucrats' Ability to Act in a Developmental Manner
Generalist training	Officials lack knowledge of the needs of specific industries.	Does not make bureaucrats able to promote industrial growth.
ICS traditions maintained	Creates a relatively strong esprit de corps; reinforces the IAS' elite and exclusive status; strengthens intra-IAS ties; inhibits the formation of ties between IAS officials and industrial actors.	Restricts the ability of the IAS bureaucrat to formulate industrial growth promoting policies.
Law and order focus in training	Emphasis is on regulatory rather than developmental tasks.	Encourages a regulatory approach towards industry; reduces IAS officials' willingness and ability to promote industrial growth.
Frequent transfers	Reduces ties with industrial actors; strengthens intra-IAS ties; reinforces the generalist training; increases incentives for performing routine tasks; reduces incentives for non-routine tasks and major policy changes.	Does not enable the IAS officials to gather adequate knowledge about specific industries and their growth.
Cohesiveness	Reinforces IAS elite and exclusive status; strengthens intra-IAS ties; inhibits the formation of ties between IAS officials and industrial actors.	Restricts the ability of the IAS bureaucrat to formulate industrial growth promoting policies.
Promotions not contingent on performance	Incentives for improving performance are lacking.	Incentives to counter the constraints created by the IAS's other features lacking.
IAS lobby powerful	Given the IAS officials' control over personnel policy changes in the organization of the IAS have been forestalled.	The character of the IAS remains unchanged; attempts to alter the bureaucrats approach to industrial growth have been blocked.

THE LABOR STRUCTURE

Indian politicians of all persuasions have historically turned to trade unions while mobilizing electoral support. Political parties helped establish firm-level trade unions and national trade union federations in an attempt to mobilize grass-roots support for the independence movement, and this close association between political parties and trade unions has continued ever since. Divisions within India's political parties and alliances between parties have been replicated by trade unions. Firm-level trade unions are aligned with national-level trade unions federations. And these federations, in turn, are affiliated with different political parties. This trade union structure has been shaped during the post-independence years by India's labor laws. Given India's emphasis on socialism, especially until 1991, and the fact that nearly every large political party claims to represent the interests of the working class and has a trade union wing, one might expect labor to play an especially central role in India. This, however, is not the case. This section examines the Indian labor structure, and considers the role of labor in the process of economic and industrial policymaking.

Labor Laws

Two labor laws have played a key role in shaping Indian labor: the Trade Unions Act (1926) and the Industrial Disputes Act (1947).[36] The Trade Unions Act was adopted by the colonial government in 1926. With only a few relatively minor modifications, however, it remains the cornerstone of India's labor policy regime. The act established procedures and regulations regarding the formation and registration of unions. It stipulated that any "seven or more members of a Trade Union may, by subscribing their names to the rules of Trade Union and by otherwise complying with the provisions of this Act with respect to registration, apply for registration of the Trade Union under this Act."[37]

While the Trade Unions Act defines the features of trade unions, the Industrial Disputes Act specifies the extent and nature of state involvement in management-worker disputes. It grants the state the authority to refer any industrial dispute on its own initiative to adjudication by industrial tribunals. Interested parties in a dispute, such as political parties, trade union federations, management, and firm-level unions, also are permitted to refer the matter to the tribunals. While arbitration proceedings are in progress, the workers are prohibited from striking. The decisions rendered by the tribunals or courts are binding.

The Industrial Disputes Act also regulates worker layoffs and retrenchment and the exit (closure) of firms. Layoffs, retrenchment of workers, and the exit of firms have been deemed illegal unless permitted by the state. All firms are required to notify the state prior to taking any such action. A permit is granted by the state following an inquiry, and the decision is binding on all parties.

Implications of the Labor Laws for Trade Unions

These labor laws have had profound implications for the structure of Indian trade unions, their relations with political parties, and their ability to achieve their stated goals. First, while enabling the formation of trade unions, Indian labor laws have had the unintended effect of encouraging the splintering of trade unions by permitting any seven workers to form a union. This in turn has influenced the unions' financial status. Fearful of divisions and competition at the plant level, unions more often than not do not force members to pay union dues regularly. As Myers and Kannappan note, "Such practices are encouraged due to the climate of competitive unionism, and attempts to impress the members, especially on the occasion of a publicly aired labour dispute."[38] In addition, small unions usually have trouble supporting their staff and operational overhead even if dues were paid regularly. The unions' financial situation, therefore, tends to be rather dismal.

Due to their poor financial status, unions are susceptible to co-optation by both management and local political interests, which further encourages the splintering of trade unions. Consider the case of Premier Automobiles Limited. When the management of this automobile company entered into an agreement with one trade union, union members displeased with it formed their own trade union. Charges of being co-opted by management were leveled by the breakaway union members, who for their part turned to local political parties for financial resources.

As this example illustrates, the inability to depend on membership dues for financial support forces trade unions to turn to either management or political parties for financial resources. The dependence of any one trade union on management support tends to encourage the further fragmentation of the unions at the firm. The fragmentation is also facilitated when one union aligns itself with a political party. Breakaway members or opposing trade unions are likely to seek affiliation with the opposing political party. Thus, the fragmentation and the weak financial status of trade unions in India make the resolution of industrial disputes via collective bargaining that much more difficult.

Second, the financial weakness of the trade unions and their lack of a solid membership leads to their dependence on outside leaders to guide them.[39] In the absence of a secure, relatively permanent income and membership, unions are unable to support the necessary staff. As a result, trade unions at the firm level tend to be dependent on the national trade union federations for financial resources and leadership. The national trade union federations are in turn dependent on the resources of national and local-level political parties. Indian labor laws allow half of any trade union's leaders/staff/officers to be outsiders.

Another factor that draws in outside leadership is the issue of recognition. The legal registration of a union does not ensure that employers would "recognize" the union for purposes of negotiation. That remains a political issue. In a discussion about union recognition, Tulpule notes that "without recognition, the process of collective bargaining cannot even begin, and unions would also be handicapped in the task of securing for the workers the protection and the benefits provided by labour legislation."[40] The threat of fragmentation and the presence of rival trade unions lead unions to seek recognition as the sole representative of the workers. In their pursuit of recognition unions draw on outside leaders and political parties in their attempt to persuade (or compel) management to recognize them. According to Karnik, a union without recognition "has nothing else to do but to exist as a centre for agitation and propaganda. The agitation and propaganda tend to become more and more political when it is denied the opportunity to work for solving immediate economic problems through representations and negotiations."[41]

Political opportunists and sundry leaders, as a result, tend to dominate the leadership of trade unions. These outside leaders guide unions, lead strikes, and participate in employer-worker negotiations. Outside leaders (prominent and not-so-prominent political leaders) with few direct ties to firms or industries flit around different firms, stirring up tensions, if not creating conflicts. Labor disputes are quickly transformed into political battles with the union rank-and-file having little say in the process of negotiation or the demands made.

At Premier Automobiles, rivalry between union leaders and political parties accounted for two-thirds of strikes, work stoppages, and industrial relations problems between the years 1978 and 1990. Out of a total of 63 disruptions, 42 were largely the consequence of nonfirm factors. And prominent among these factors were interunion rivalry, political party conflicts, and conflicts stirred up by outside leaders for grievances not related to the firm.[42]

In 1973 IISCO, a private steel company, was nationalized in response to serious labor-management tensions, interunion rivalry, and the subsequent decline in steel production. After years of discussion, the Ministry of Steel, which was now in charge of IISCO, succeeded in getting the various IISCO trade unions to sign a Memorandum of Understanding regarding the modernization and operations of the plant. What is interesting about the memorandum is the number of signatories. Eleven management representatives signed and on the side of labor, 5 trade unions were involved. Each trade union was represented by anywhere from 5 to 12 leaders, many of whom were outsiders.

Thus, apart from drawing trade unions closer to the political parties, the Trade Unions Act has led to the emergence of a peculiar labor aristocracy. The labor aristocracy in India consists of the upperstratum of the trade union leadership. In other words, of the total Indian workforce, the labor aristocracy comprises the leaders of the unions in the organized sector. These trade union leaders, more often than not, are not employees at the firm and are instead career politicians. The labor aristocracy tends to use the problems and conflicts associated with fragmentation and recognition for its own ends, ignoring the interests of the workers, with regard to representation, benefits, work conditions and so on. Thus, giving priority to its own political interests. In addition, the labor laws have encouraged the emergence of a hierarchy within the organized sector. According to Lloyd and Susanne Rudolph, "trade union activity [has] benefited middle-class and lower-middle-class employees whose condition was already good in comparison with that of the vast majority of the nation's wage earners."[43] Distinct "'islands of privilege' have emerged, especially among public employees but also in the private sector."[44]

Third, union interests tend to be marginalized within almost all political parties. As noted earlier, all parties profess to represent the interests of the workers (i. e., organized workers) with equal vigor.[45] However, they are all also supported by other groups: industrialists; businesspeople; and ethnic, caste, and language groups. Thus, trade union interests reflect only a portion of any party's resource base and, hence, agenda. In the absence of a party representing only trade unions, the existing political parties (Congress, Janata Dal, Bharatiya Janata Party, etc.) have no incentives, and face little pressure, to offer more than lip service to trade union demands. The absence of a trade union party allows the various political parties room to maneuver and even adopt policies contrary to the interests of their affiliated union. The interests of the rank-and-file workers are, therefore, marginalized within the trade unions and also within the various political parties. Moreover, even the labor aristocracy is unable to prevent its own marginalization within the political parties.

As a result, Indian unions have been almost universally unable to influence wider issues of economic development. As the Lloyd and Susanne Rudolph note, the "ideological, partisan, and territorial fragmentation of unions and the much more rapid proliferation of unions than of unionized workers weaken the capacity of organized labor to affect economic bargaining, political competition, and policy formulation. Proliferating unions have tended to struggle among themselves over the control of a relatively fixed sum of organized workers rather than expand the sum of organized workers."[46]

Reviewing the Indian trade unions' ability to shape issues such as education, health, housing, and development strategies, Karnik argues that "unions have not yet started speaking in a loud enough voice and in a determined manner. In . . . public life as a whole their voice is yet feeble, though strikes and demonstrations attract a good deal of attention and give a different impression. In the legislatures they have few representatives—though a few union leaders get elected as representatives of various parties. . . . Immediate problems of existence . . . absorb most of the attention of unions."[47]

Fourth, trade unions do, however, retain power over issues concerning exit and privatization. The previous point argues that political parties have some autonomy from unions; however, this autonomy has clear limits. One indication of these limits, and of the power of the unions, is the inability of the Congress government, despite its intentions to adopt a new exit policy (i. e., a policy identifying the rules and procedures regarding closure of firms and dismissal of workers) following the 1991 economic liberalization. In 1993 the Ministry of Labor proposed revisions in labor laws that would have restricted the number of trade unions the workers of any one firm could form. In addition the ministry suggested the adoption of an exit policy that while it would "not cater to the industry's demand for a 'hire-and-fire policy,' it would nevertheless give employers the prerogative to check inefficient and errant workers."[48] Further, the proposed exit policy was intended to ensure "that the employer-employee relationship was not regulated by law and recourse to law would be taken only in extreme cases and under difficult circumstances."[49]

The proposed amendments were, however, not even presented in Parliament. Nationwide strikes by employees of both state-owned enterprises and private firms ensured this. Trade unions affiliated to all the opposition parties participated in the strike. Initially, even the Indian National Trade Union Congress (or INTUC), the union affiliated with the then-ruling Congress party, had agreed to join the strikers. However, subsequent pressure from the Congress leadership ensured that INTUC, while it did not oppose the strike, did not participate in it. INTUC's nonparticipation notwithstanding, the furor created by the other trade unions and supported by the opposition parties persuaded the Congress government to back down.

The privatization of state-owned enterprises has run into similar opposition. The larger and relatively more powerful trade unions at large private firms and at the SOEs have, over the years, been effective in preventing privatization. Strikes have been the primary tool used to assert their demands. Faced with competitors supporting nonprivatization (i. e., the status quo), unions (even those affiliated with the ruling party) have been compelled to unite against the interests of the political leadership in order to retain their members' support.

Consider the case of IISCO. Following its nationalization, the Ministry of Steel embarked on a program to restructure the steel company with the aim of making it profitable again. Facing financial constraints, the ministry began, in the 1990s, considering the possibility of reprivatizing IISCO. Offers had been received from private industrialists. However, opposition from the various trade unions at IISCO left the ministry unable to proceed. Faced with unions stridently opposed to privatization plans, and the threat of losing worker support, even INTUC, the union affiliated with the ruling party, was unable to side with the privatization plans.[50] Thus, the dynamics of competition, the threat of fragmentation, the marginalization of unions' voice within political parties, the logic of political patronage, and, most important, the overall dependence on political parties have together ensured that unions are more effective at retaining the existing labor policies and supporting entrenched interests than at adopting policies favoring the interests of labor.[51]

The Trade Unions and the Bureaucracy

The presence of strong formal-institutional and informal relations between the trade unions and the politicians has preempted the development of noncontractual relations between the bureaucrats in the central ministries (i.e., Steel, Industry, Finance, and Labor) and the trade union leadership. In interviews, prominent trade union leaders frequently stated that for assistance regarding arbitration or adjudication proceedings they turned to their well-established ties with the politicians rather than to the bureaucrats.[52] Thus, political alignments established prior to independence along with the trade union labor laws have led to the close association between trade unions and the political parties, and the presence of these ties has not encouraged the trade union leadership to seek the support of bureaucrats.

The structure of the IAS also has prevented the establishment of ties (involving capture or noncapture) between bureaucrats in the central ministries, and union leaders. The elite character of the IAS, its small size, and its dominance within the state apparatus, as noted earlier, has lent it a significant degree of cohesion. Frequent transfers, the cohesive structure, and its esprit de corps have discouraged the establishment of informal ties and channels of communication between the bureaucrats and trade union representatives.[53] In other words, the IAS bureaucrats are more likely than their political superiors to be relatively autonomous from and to lack informal relations with trade unions.

Three conclusions may be drawn about the role labor is likely to play in the process of industrial policy formation. First, the marginality and multiplicity of unions enables trade union action to be effective only with regard to issues such as privatization and exit policy, not with regard to other aspects of industrial policy. Second, presence of close ties between unions and politicians and the absence of close ties between unions and bureaucrats induces trade unions to frustrate the process of policy changes (even those not relating to privatization or exit policy) by drawing wider political conflicts and interested actors into firm and industry-level debates. Third, this suggests that policymaking for industries lacking organized labor (i. e., small firms or firms in the unorganized industries) is likely to proceed more smoothly than for others.

However, these conclusions will be tempered as our analysis proceeds insofar as trade unions operate, not independently but in conjunction with industrialists, bureaucrats, and politicians in industrial policymaking. It is likely that characteristics of the industry, firm, bureaucrats, or politicians have enabled specific firms or even industries to overcome the ability of the union leadership to frustrate policy changes.

INDUSTRY ASSOCIATIONS

At the national level, India's diversified industrial structure has been represented by three industry associations. These are: the Federation of Indian Chambers of Commerce and Industry (FICCI), the Associated Chambers of Commerce and Industry (ASSOCHAM), and a relatively recent entrant, the Confederation of Indian Industry (CII).

FICCI and ASSOCHAM

FICCI was the leading body representing Indian industry from the 1920s to the 1980s. It was established in 1927 by a prominent industrialist, G. D. Birla, to counter the power of British industry in India. Its members included, apart from the Birlas, the Modi, and the Sri Ram groups. Most of the industrialists affiliated to FICCI were closely involved in India's independence movement. As Kochanek observes, "the federation saw itself as the economic arm of the freedom movement led by the Indian National Congress."[54] ASSOCHAM was set up in 1920 and represented British capital prior to independence. After independence in 1947, it also came to represent Indian industrialists, and particularly, professionally managed manufacturing and trading companies and large multinational corporations. FICCI, on the other hand, tended to represent traditional businesspeople.

FICCI's close relations with the independence movement enabled it to be the dominant industry association in the early decades following independence. Birla had especially close relations with Gandhi and other prominent members of the Congress party. Yet this close association with India's prominent politicians did not ensure FICCI's success as an industry association. Internal conflicts led to the resignation of two of its larger members, Tatas and

Mafatlal, which subsequently joined ASSOCHAM. Internal conflicts continued within FICCI, leading to a split in 1986. Besides the problems resulting from internal divisions, changes in the political climate further undermined FICCI's strength. Indira Gandhi's turn toward populism in the 1970s had weakened the close ties between her party (Congress) and FICCI's members. The MRTP and FERA laws affected its larger and more powerful members.

The breakaway group joined ASSOCHAM. As a result, ASSOCHAM appeared poised to emerge as the more powerful of the two national industry associations; its membership increased from 220 to 388 individual member companies. However, increased membership did not automatically translate into an equivalent increase in ASSOCHAM's status. Its ability to play a more prominent role in the process of industrial policymaking was restricted by its relative lack of contact with politicians and bureaucrats in New Delhi. It was also curtailed by the growing power of CII, which was formally formed in 1992.

CII

The FICCI split also strengthened a third, much less prominent association, the Association of Indian Engineering Industry (AIEI). AIEI was formed by the merger of two industry associations in 1972, the Indian Engineering Association, established by British entrepreneurs in 1895, and the Engineering Association of India, set up by Indian businessmen in 1942. In 1986 AIEI changed its name to Confederation of Engineering Industry (CEI), and in 1992 it changed its name again, to the Confederation of Indian Industry (CII), and began representing not just engineering industries but all of industry. Today CII has become India's most influential industry association.

Four factors enabled CII to rise to this position. First, CII does not depend on member contributions but raises funds via promotional activities. Second, CII has a greater export focus than either FICCI or ASSOCHAM. By focusing on the international market, rather than on capturing each others' domestic share, CII has helped promote collective action among its members. Third, especially during the early 1990s, CII's membership list was dominated by India's rapidly growing medium- and small-size manufacturing and high-tech firms (electronics, software and computer firms). Finally, unlike FICCI and ASSOCHAM, CII adopted a proactive approach and thus played a role in establishing India's policy agenda.

CII's rapid rise to prominence soon made it more attractive than either FICCI or ASSOCHAM to India's large business houses. However, some of these large business houses are key members of the Bombay Club, an informal association of India's traditional business houses with the stated agenda of restricting foreign competition. The group was formed following the adoption of structural adjustment policies in 1991.

The interests of the Bombay Club clearly clash with the stated goals of India's medium and small companies who constitute the bulk of CII's members. Yet members of this group continue to be active participants in the federation. What explains this? There are two possibilities: either members of the Bombay Club are only halfhearted in their desire to restrict foreign competition, or CII is not fully committed to policies increasing competition. Meetings with CII members, other concerned industrial actors, and bureaucrats familiar with both CII and the Bombay Club, suggest that both answers are partly valid. Bombay Club members are genuinely concerned about foreign competition; however, in the absence of strong political opposition to it, they are unable to control CII's policy agenda. CII, for its part, has always supported foreign competition. Its action cannot be fairly perceived as halfhearted. However, it is hamstrung by its broad and rather unwieldy constituency. To not support its prominent, albeit nonsupportive members would mean having a lower profile. The large firms lend it cachet, prominence, and strength in the public arena. Moreover, retaining its larger members also helps retain the smaller ones; the latter gain individual/selective benefits as a result (via personal contacts with the larger members).

It remains unclear what the precise implications of Bombay Club members playing a prominent role within CII are for CII's goals and its future status. Interviews with bureaucrats and industrialists suggest that CII's position and ability to represent Indian industry has been somewhat undermined in recent years.

The State and Industry Associations

Reviewing the role of these three industry associations in the 50 years since independence suggests that especially FICCI and ASSOCHAM have, by and large, been ineffective at influencing policy changes. While individual industrialists have been able to influence politicians to secure special benefits and privileges, industrialists collectively have been more or less ineffectual at the national level. In an early study of industry associations, Kochanek has observed that although specific industrialists were "successful in gaining specific, individual, distributive benefits . . . business collectively has not been able to influence the broad outline and direction of public policy in India."[55] Compared to FICCI and ASSOCHAM, CII has had a somewhat better track record. It played a relatively influential role in the policy process during the early 1990s. So what explains the overall ineffectiveness of industry associations? And why has CII been more successful?

Three factors have contributed to the ineffectiveness of national level associations (especially FICCI and ASSOCHAM): close relations between prominent industrialists and politician that obviate and undermine collective industry representation, the absence of informal ties between the industry associations and bureaucrats, and the lack of useful formal arenas of interaction between industry associations and IAS bureaucrats.

As noted earlier, prominent members of the two older associations, FICCI and ASSOCHAM, have had links with India's political leadership since the pre-independence era. These links emerged out of the shared political and economic interests of its leading members, J. R. D. Tata, G. D. Birla, Shri Ram, Kasturbhai Lalbhai, and the leaders of the national movement. Both the Indian industrialists and the leaders of the national movement were critical of British capital, and the colonial government. As India's leading industrialists saw it, the colonial government favored British at their expense. For the nationalist leaders, it was more a question of political self-determination, but they too were acutely concerned about the restrictions imposed on Indian business and the colonial government's protection of British capital. This shared interest was formalized in 1943 with the formulation of the Bombay Plan.

The Bombay Plan was a strategy for economic growth developed by leading economists and industrialists (nearly all of whom were actively involved with the Congress party) including J. R. D. Tata, G. D. Birla, Sir Ardeshir Dalal, Sir Shri Ram, Dr. John Mathai, and Kasturbhai Lalbhai. The plan articulated a development strategy that emphasized the central role of the state. The authors of the Bombay Plan "argued for the development of basic and heavy industries, particularly power; active government intervention and a predominant role for the public sector; and State control over the private sector."[56] The plan demarcated the sphere of activity of the private sector and recommended that the profits of private entrepreneurs and industrialists be restricted via mechanisms such as price controls, restrictions on dividends, and higher taxes.

The plan, its tone, and argument thus brought India's industrialists and politicians together. Industrialists could better develop their critique of the colonial government with the political and ideological help of nationalist leaders. Nationalist leaders, on the other hand, found ties with industrialists particularly useful insofar as they provided essential financial resources. Shared interests gave rise to a mutually dependent relationship.

Following independence, this close relationship between the leading industrial actors and the political leadership was maintained to a significant extent. This relationship did not, however, lead to a close ties between FICCI or ASSOCHAM and the state, it primarily involved specific industrialists and politicians. Kochanek notes, that the "political leadership has been more inclined to establish close relations with individual business leaders than with the business community as a whole."[57] It nevertheless offered a channel of communication between the "reigning" political leaders and industry. The particularistic nature of these relations, however, made them somewhat tenuous. Changing political inclinations undermined their stability and strength. Indira Gandhi's populist/leftist turn in late 1960s, for instance, and the subsequent policy changes (MRTP Act and FERA) of the 1970s weakened some of these ties.

More important, the ability of prominent industrialists to influence, even moderately, politicians for particularistic reasons undermined collective industry action. As the leading industrialists saw it, collective action was a waste of resources when personal ties work. While industrialists supported the formal agendas of the associations, in private interactions with politicians they voiced contrary opinions. A senior administrator at one association lamented that its formal petitions and discussions with the government were pointless since his prominent members pressured politicians to do the opposite.[58]

Given the pivotal position of the bureaucracy in the policymaking process, industry associations and individual industrialists have continually sought to develop channels of communication with them. However, success has not been easy to come by. As discussed earlier, the structure of the IAS forestalls the formation of close ties between senior and middle-level bureaucrats and industrialists. "Indian business did not enjoy the rapport with the colonial bureaucracy that English business easily maintained. Thus, there were no long-term personal contacts, no long-established strategies of access to fall back on when the bureaucracy became, after independence, a center of power in its own right, by virtue of its pivotal position in the planned and controlled economy."[59]

Industrialist-bureaucrat interactions have tended to consist primarily of liaison officers and public relations personnel contacting IAS officials for various clearances and licenses. There was limited direct interaction between IAS officials and industrialists. As noted, industrialists have tended to prefer to interact with the political leadership, with whom they had a better history of interaction, than with IAS officials. In other words, if industrialists want to influence the policy process, they tend to pressure politicians. When they need to get around red tape, they send their liaison officers to the IAS officials.

There are formal arenas (committees, councils, etc.) that bring industrial associations and senior bureaucrats together. However, these arenas tend to be rather ineffective. Consider the Central Advisory Council of Industries (CACI). It meets once a year for a day, which is spent making ceremonial speeches. In other words, the CACl does not facilitate the informal exchange of information between industrial associations and the state. While IAS bureaucrats note in public that such councils are useful, in private they remain critical, viewing them as window-dressing. And industrialists concur.[60]

In recent years, not only has CII emerged as the dominant of the three national associations, it also has been more successful at influencing the policy process. One might argue that CII's success is consequence of the reforms of 1991: with fewer regulations and lesser protection, collective action improves. But this does not explain why CII has been more successful than FICCI or AS-SOCHAM. This is better explained by CII's greater emphasis on export promotion and its development of ties with those who "rule," the IAS officials.

As Kochanek notes, CII was very similar to FICCI and ASSOCHAM until the late 1980s. Like them CII was largely ineffectual, acting "as a supplicant its dealings with government."[61] The change occurred in 1990-91 when CII began emphasizing exports to a greater extent. This offered a good rallying point for its members. Given India's poor industrial export performance, none of the large industrial houses were in direct competition with each other regarding the export market. CII's new emphasis therefore strengthened the association.

It also had the effect of improving relations with the state, for the emphasis on exports resonated well with the liberalization of 1991. At the same time, CII began to actively develop strong informal relations with senior IAS bureaucrats. In interviews, CII members remarked that this has been critical for their association's recently acquired dominant position among industry associations.[62] Kochanek notes that "CII leaders and staff select key bureaucrats in critical economic ministries and attempt to build a trusting relationship with them."[63]

However, while CII might be more effective at influencing the overall direction of industrial policy, it is less likely to be effective at shaping industry-specific policy. This is because CII is a national-level association. While its members might agree on certain *general* issues (say, export promotion), they are unlikely to agree on specific policies. Automobile manufacturers might be at odds with automobile component manufacturers on the *extent* to which the state should promote the export of components. If component manufacturers found the export market more attractive, Indian automobile manufacturers might face an increase in costs. In other words, despite CII's greater abilities today, it is unclear whether it can effectively act as an advocate for all its members. And this has become an especially critical issue, with the formation of the Bombay Club and the active participation of its members within CII. Industry-specific associations, such as the Association of Indian

Automobile Manufacturers (AIAM) and National Association of Computer Software and Service Companies (NASSCOM), might be able to play a more effective role in promoting entrepreneurship. Their role is discussed in chapters 3, 4, and 5.

This chapter has examined four key features that are shared by the Indian steel, automobile, and computer software industries. They all share a common labor policy regime. Governed by identical labor laws, industrial relations in the three industries are therefore likely to be similar. The industries are all administered by a state apparatus whose upper ranks are filled by IAS bureaucrats from a common pool. IAS officials are key actors in the process of policy formulation for all three industries. Third, all three industries have developed within the same economic policy regime, and all have experienced economic/financial crises, foreign exchange shortages, and swings in political ideologies. Finally, all three industries were represented at the macro level by industry associations discussed above.

In the next three chapters I examine the specific development path of the steel, automobile, and computer software sectors. My aim is to identify why, despite these similarities, industries have had fundamentally different growth trajectories and policy responses. The trajectories and policies, however, have not been uniformly dissimilar. At various times they have been almost alike, while diverging significantly at other times. What explains these patterns? Why, despite being shaped by identical labor and economic policies and administered by the same state apparatus, have the policies diverged, but only at certain times?

3.

The Steel Industry

I ndian steel policy has been highly regulatory—controlling steel production (entry, exit, and production capacity of firms), distribution, and prices.
The state initially adopted a similar approach with regard to automobiles and
computer software. However, while computer-software policy changed over
time and adapted itself to the changing economic and industry requirements,
overall steel policy continued unchanged until 1991, even when its effective-
ness was clearly in doubt. Reviewing Indian steel policy, Etienne notes that
while "teething troubles and lack of experience could be understood in the
early phase, the repetition of these shortcomings lacks rationale."[1]

The history of the Indian steel industry may be divided into three phases.[2]
The first phase (late 1940s to late 1960s) was marked by the establishment of
state-owned steel plants and the rapid growth of steel production. During the
second phase (1970s to mid-1980s) the state-owned steel plants experienced serious problems and their performance began to decline. Mini-steel plants mushroomed during these years, although their performance on average was poor.
The third phase began with steel (price and distribution) decontrol in 1991. In a
reversal of policy, private entrepreneurs were permitted (even encouraged) to
establish steel plants, and licensing regulations were eased considerably.

Thus the state promoted steel production in the 1950s and 1960s. In the
1970s and 1980s the state responded to the needs of the sector in a manner
that was ineffective at best, and harmful at worst. The 1990s saw the transformation of steel policy and the emergence of a developmentalist stance on
the part of the state.

Currently the Indian steel sector is dominated by state-owned plants (Bhilai, Bokaro, Durgapur, Rourkela, IISCO, and Vizag). There is one private

integrated steel plant—TISCO. Of the steel produced by the integrated steel plants, the state-owned plants currently produce 80 percent with TISCO contributing the remaining 20 percent. Besides these seven steel plants, the steel sector in India also consists of rerolling units, sponge-iron plants, and mini-steel plants (electric arc furnace units). Nearly all the rerolling units and the mini-steel plants are privately owned.

The steel sector in India has not fared well over the years in terms of export earnings, meeting the domestic demands, quality of the products manufactured, and the growth rate of the sector as a whole. The current condition of the Indian steel sector is placed in perspective when one considers the analyses of the sector made during the 1950s and the 1960s. In a 1966 study, Johnson argued that "India's achievement of virtual self-sufficiency in steel and her production at relatively low costs is very good evidence that India possesses a comparative advantage in the production of steel."[3] Today, however, the utilization of this comparative advantage is much in doubt.

Industrialists, World Bank officials, industry analysts, and even bureaucrats attribute the condition of the Indian steel industry between 1947 and 1991 to the nature of state intervention in the sector.[4] In the 1989 annual report, the chairman of the Steel Authority of India (SAIL, the state-owned steel company) observed that the steel policy, instituted in the 1950s, is not helping the industry adapt to the changing needs of the market and that the time has come to review its usefulness.

Steel policy between 1947 to 1991 aimed at discouraging private sector expansion. Entry of new firms was not even considered. The price and the distribution of steel was controlled. Between 1947 and 1970, investment in steel was accorded priority over investment in most other industries. This priority declined thereafter. Throughout the years 1947 to 1991 the steel industry remained a highly regulated industry "partly because of the belief that steel is especially important to India's economic growth" and partly due to institutional constraints and political interests to be discussed.[5]

The structure of Indian steel policy was changed finally in 1991 in the midst of a severe balance-of-payments crisis and the introduction of a structural adjustment program. Distribution and price controls were abolished, and the integrated steel plant sector was opened to both Indian and foreign private entrepreneurs.

The central question of this chapter is: Why, despite indications that the steel industry was performing poorly, were bureaucrats in charge of steel policy neither willing nor able to modify policy so as to promote its growth and development prior to 1991?

In order to answer this question I explicate the process of steel policy formulation and relate it to the relationship among bureaucrats, industrial actors, labor leaders and politicians in the sector. The chapter first traces the origins of the steel industry in India, then reviews the various policies adopted and their implications. Finally, I discuss the manner in which the pattern of relations between key players (bureaucrats, industrialists, labor leaders and political actors) has influenced steel policy.

THE ORIGINS OF THE STEEL INDUSTRY IN INDIA

The history of the (modern) iron and steel industry in India can be traced to the end of the eighteenth century. The availability of iron ore and charcoal led colonial entrepreneurs to attempt to produce pig iron. Integrated steel plants were established in the first quarter of the twentieth century. The Indian Iron and Steel Company Limited (IISCO) was established by Burn & Co. in 1918 at Hirapur. In the early years, IISCO was an iron producer—making pig iron for manufacturers of castings or steel. By 1924, however, IISCO had started steel production.

Indian entrepreneurs also entered the fray in the early 1900s. In 1904 Jamshedji Tata established India's first integrated steel plant—the Tata Iron and Steel Company (TISCO). The company had an initial capacity of 100,000 tonnes of ingot steel and 72,000 tonnes of finished products. A third steel plant was built by the government of the princely state of Mysore. The plant (later to be named Mysore Iron and Steel Works) started producing pig iron in 1923.

In terms of financial stability, plant capacity, and plant modernization, TISCO was the most successful. By the 1950s it had increased its plant capacity to 1 million tonnes per year (tpy), and by the end of the 1950s plant capacity touched 2. 0 million tpy. Reviewing the firm's development, N. R. Srinivasan notes that much of TISCO's relative success could be attributed to its ability to innovate and successfully experiment with the available resources.[6]

Several mini-steel plants using the electric arc furnace technology were set up during the first half of the century. The colonial government set up the first one at Cossipore in 1902. Nearly all the plants were linked to steel foundries and produced relatively unsophisticated products mainly for the railway companies and for local requirements, using locally generated scrap for their raw material.

As part of the war effort, the colonial government controlled most aspects of the steel industry (including steel distribution and pricing) during the first half of the twentieth century. The Defense of India Rules (81 and 84) "made a blanket provision for 'regulating or prohibiting the production, treatment, keeping, storage, movement, transport, distribution, disposal, acquisition, use or consumption of articles or things of any description whatsoever.' It also provided 'for controlling the prices (or rates) at which articles or things of any description whatsoever may be sold.'"[7] Thus these rules granted the imperial government the legal authority to intervene in nearly all aspects of the economy. The India (Central Government and Legislature) Act of 1946 ensured the continuation of these controls after World War II. And, following independence, the Indian state incorporated the regulatory and control measures into its political philosophy and planning framework. Rakesh Mohan and Vandana Aggarwal note that "[even] the language used in much of decision making today continues to be that which was appropriate to a war economy."[8]

In 1941 the state imposed statutory control over steel prices (as well as over distribution) via the promulgation of the Iron and Steel (Control of Production and Distribution) Order. Under this order, the Iron and Steel Controller was given the authority to fix the maximum prices for the various steel products sold by producers or other persons.[9] Two years later scrap was also brought under the purview of this order.

Steel price controls emerged in India during World War I when TISCO offered to sell its products to the state at a fixed price, less than the price of imported steel products and less than the then current market price. These practices of informal price control and informal production and distribution control (since the primary buyer of steel was the state, TISCO considered the state's requirements before making production decisions) continued into the 1930s and 1940s, when, during World War II, the colonial state and TISCO negotiated the price of steel for military use. There thus emerged during the war years a close relationship between TISCO and the colonial government a relationship which sustained TISCO through the depression.

The Tata Group also maintained close relations with the leaders of the India's independence movement. J. R. D. Tata, the chairman of TISCO, was particularly close to Nehru. This relationship was not, however, one based on political patronage. Rather, common interests and goals brought Tata and Indian politicians together. For Nehru, the support of Indian businessmen was both useful and essential. For Tata, supporting the independence movement was one way of promoting a state that was likely to favor to Indian businessmen over European businessmen.

The relationship between J. R. D. Tata and Nehru (as well as other politicians) continued after independence and served TISCO well. When cries for nationalization of private industry surfaced immediately following independence and again in the early 1970s, TISCO remained untouched. The company's superior performance along with its ties with India's leading politicians clearly enabled it to escape nationalization.

PHASE I: THE ORIGINS OF INDIA'S STEEL STRATEGY

The ideological basis of steel policy during the early years of independence was Fabian-Socialism, which emerged as the dominant ideology within the Congress party especially after the mid-1950s. As presented by its leading Indian advocate, Jawaharlal Nehru, Fabian-Socialism viewed public sector dominance and the strict regulation of private enterprise as critical for economic development. The presence of state-owned enterprises at the "commanding heights" of the economy (i. e., the steel sector) was regarded as essential for the growth of downstream industries and more crucially for ensuring the reduction of economic and social inequities in society. And the adoption of the Fabian-Socialist approach is clearly indicated in the Industrial Policy Resolution-48 and even more so in the Industrial Policy Resolution-56.

Two sets of policies shaped the development of the Indian steel industry: the industrial licensing system, which restricted the entry, production, and growth of private steel firms and state investment policies that determined the growth and production of the state-owned integrated steel plants; and price control policies and steel distribution policies.

First, consider the licensing and investment policies with regard to steel. Recognizing that a major steel production program would be necessary to provide the basic infrastructure for accelerated industrialization, Industrial Policy Resolution-48 emphasized the role of the steel sector. According to the resolution, the state was to be solely responsible for the establishment of new iron and steel units. However, if required, the state would consider the further involvement of private entrepreneurs/enterprises in the development of iron and steel units.

The resolution granted the state the inherent right to acquire existing steel plants as and when required in the interests of the nation, and proposed that existing private units be given a ten-year test period, during which they would be allowed "all facilities for efficient working and reasonable expansion."[10] The state, however, retained its right to acquire any unit following a ten-year performance review.[11]

The resolution also stated that while foreign technology and investment is invaluable for industrialization, every individual case of involvement of foreign capital will require the approval of the state. Further, the resolution stated that "as a rule, the major interest in ownership, and effective control, should always be in Indian hands. . . . In all cases, however, the training of suitable Indian personnel for the purpose of eventually replacing foreign experts will be insisted upon."[12]

While this resolution stated the state's overall intentions regarding the fundamental aspects of industrial policy and steel policy in particular, the

Industries (Development and Regulation) Act of 1951 created a licensing system drawing on prior policy and planning intentions. The act required all industrial units in the steel sector (rerollers, ancillary units, and firms employing more than 50 workers) to obtain a license for: establishing a new industrial undertaking; manufacturing a "new article"; substantially expanding the capacity of an existing unit; and changing a unit's location. The act permitted a few exemptions, largely at the discretion of the civil servants in the concerned ministry, that is, the Ministry of Steel.

The licensing regime restricted and regulated the entry, production, and growth of the private steel plants, and the various Five Year Plans shaped the development of the sector insofar as they specified the extent and form of state investment. Given that new production capacity was largely restricted to state-owned steel units, state investment played an important role in growth and decline of the Indian steel industry.

During the 1950s and 1960s, steel production by the private steel plants, TISCO and IISCO, was supplemented with production by state-owned steel plants. The First Five Year Plan (1951 to 1956) allocated Rs. 800 million to set up one state-owned steel plants with a production capacity of 350,000 tonnes of pig iron per year. However, soon after entering the plan period it became apparent that more than one additional steel plant would be required to fulfill the rising demand for steel.

At the recommendation of the World Bank, the Indian government set up a Technical Commission to examine the country's current and future demand for steel. As the demand was expected to only increase, the government was forced to decide to set up three new integrated steel plants even before the Commission's report was completed.

Before deciding on establishing state-owned steel plants, the then minister of industries, T. T. Krishnamachari (a successful industrialist, and a confidant of Prime Minister Nehru, and later the Minister of Steel invited Indian industrialists to set up steel plants. However, none of the industrialists agreed to satisfy the conditions (i. e. the strict emphasis on self-reliance and the foreign exchange regulations) set by policymakers. As a result, Krishnamachari became convinced that the development of the steel industry (as well as other heavy industries) would not be possible without active state participation.

The establishment of three state-owned integrated steel plants was proposed—a 1.0 million tonnes per year plant at Rourkela, another at Bhilai, and a third at Durgapur. All three plants were constructed with the help of foreign collaboration and aid (Soviet, German, and British). These plants were placed under the newly created Hindustan Steel Limited (HSL). Staffed by technical and administrative personnel who were hired directly,

HSL was assigned the task of managing the day-to-day operations at the various plants.

The Second Plan (1956 to 1961), focused much more than the first plan on heavy industries. Its explicit aim was to utilize surplus labor, and its intent was to promote India's economic self-reliance. The plan was based on the argument that India

> shall be able to use her own iron ore and with her own hands produce steel; and then use the steel to produce more machinery to produce more steel and tools; and also to produce machinery to make more consumer goods. India will then not have to worry about foreign exchange every time [India] wishes to start a new factory as . . . now. [India's] dependence on foreign supplies will be greatly reduced. The main obstacle to rapid industrialization being thus removed, India shall be able to increase production and employment quickly and raise the level of living.[13]

In addition to allocating resources for the completion of the three state-owned integrated steel plants, the plan also proposed that the private integrated steel plants be allowed to increase their capacity. Part of the financing for the capacity expansion at TISCO and IISCO came from the state in the form of loans. The rest was financed by World Bank loans, with the state acting as the guarantor.

The total capacity of steel production all plants was about 6.0 million tonnes per year by the end of the 1950s. TISCO had a capacity of 2.0 million tpy, and the other plants each had a capacity of 1.0 million tpy.

The three state-owned steel plants were expanded under the Third Five Year Plan (covering 1961-62 to 1965-66). The capacity of the Bhilai Steel Plant was to be increased to 2.5 mtpy, of the Rourkela plant to 1.8 mtpy, and of Durgapur to 1.6 mtpy. In addition, the establishment of a fourth plant was proposed at Bokaro in Bihar. Planning for the Bokaro plant began in the late 1950s.

The project was to be supported by American technical and financial assistance. However, the United States withdrew its support because of differences over the project within the U. S. Congress. As a result India turned to the Soviet Union for assistance. In her study of the history of the Bokaro plant, Desai suggests that the one factor which had a determining effect on the plant's planning, construction, and management of the plant was the overriding interest of the Indian state in self-reliance.[14]

The problems with technical and financial assistance were compounded by, the Indian government's insistence that Indian materials be used to the maximum extent in its construction and by the demand of the Bihar government that only residents of Bihar be employed unless absolutely essential. As a result, the Bokaro integrated steel plant was unable to begin steel production on schedule. Plant construction began in 1967 and the first phase (with a capacity of 1.7 mtpy) of the Bokaro Steel Plant was commissioned in 1976.

Second, consider the price and distribution policies. If the regulatory and investment policies directly and indirectly controlled entry, production capacity, and production strategy of both state-owned and private steel plants, the price and distribution policies controlled the output of the steel plants. The statutory price controls established in 1941 were retained following independence. Under this system, steel was purchased from the manufacturers at a state-established "retention" price. The price paid by consumers (the selling price) was higher than this retention price. The state used the difference to equalize the consumer price of steel across the country. Thus, for the consumer, the price of steel was the same irrespective of different freight charges.

The office of the Iron and Steel Controller, a department within the Ministry of Steel, determined the statutory price during the 1950s and early 1960s. The retention price was increased periodically. Between 1956 and 1964 the retention price was raised 30 percent to cover increases in costs of production. For most years the retention price was uniform for all the steel companies, private and public. By offering the same price for different qualities of steel, the statutory price system tended to encourage manufacturers to produce more steel rather than better steel.

The Office of the Iron and Steel Controller was also in charge of steel distribution. Steel consumers were required to place an "indent" with the Iron and Steel Controller, which accepted indents for a minimum of one railway wagon load. To purchase lesser amounts, buyers had to contact middlemen known as stockists who in turn placed indents with the Iron and Steel Controller. Upon reviewing the indents, the Controller placed orders with the various steel plants. All requests for importing steel were also routed through the Controller's office.

The Iron and Steel Controller received over 50,000 indents every year. Not unexpectedly, the review of the various indents received was not foolproof, and at least a few were rejected or accepted arbitrarily. Unsure of being granted the total amount of steel requested, buyers inflated their indents to protect against possible cuts. Faced with excessive demand, the Iron and Steel Controller began prioritizing buyers. This, along with the Iron and Steel Controller's inability to prevent resale of steel, led to a black market.

Given the high state and private demand for steel, the statutory selling price of steel could not be maintained without distribution controls. And failures to control distribution led to failures in regulating prices. Problems with the statutory controls became increasingly obvious by the early 1960s. In an attempt to rectify the situation, the Minister of Steel set up the Joint Plant Committee, which included representatives of the main steel producers (TISCO and HSL), and the railways (the transporters and one of the largest consumers). The Iron and Steel Controller (a civil servant) was to be appointed as chair of the committee. He was also an ex-officio Joint Secretary in the Department of Steel.

The Joint Plant Committee was to fix the prices of all steel products in consultation with the main producers and the railways, although all prices required the prior approval of the state. Thus after nearly two decades, statutory price control was abolished, and the Joint Plant Committee was made the arbiter of steel prices, although State approval was required. The Joint Plant Committee was also assigned the task of steel distribution. This structure of price and distribution controls and the office of the Joint Plant Committee were retained for the next two decades. Steel price and distribution policies were liberalized further only in the 1980s, when Joint Plant Committee price modifications were exempted from prior approval from the Ministry of Steel.

Performance of HSL, TISCO, and IISCO (1950s and 1960s)

Following its establishment in 1954, HSL managed the three state-owned steel plants at Rourkela, Bhilai, and Durgapur. It continued to perform this task until 1973, when it was replaced by the Steel Authority of India Limited. While production grew at HSL, profits and capacity utilization gradually declined during the 19 years of its existence.

After an initially rapid average annual growth rate of 144.2 percent during the first four years after its establishment, HSL's production of ingot steel slowed down to an average annual growth rate of 2.59 percent between 1965-66 and 1972-73. Productivity during this period remained below par. According to a study of the Indian iron and steel industry, while "steel production had increased several fold . . . [productivity in] the industry did not come up to planned expectations."[15] HSL's capacity utilization followed a similar trajectory. After achieving a high of 101 percent by 1964 to 1965, HSL's capacity utilization fell to 68 percent by 1972-73.

If HSL's production levels grew slowly and even declined for a few years, and capacity utilization declined after increasing during the initial few years, its performance in terms of profits remained uniformly poor. In fact, HSL never succeeded in making a profit, suffering losses every year until 1973 when the Steel Authority of India Limited took over its functions. HSL's cumulative losses during its 19 years of operations reached Rs. 2.5 billion.

Thus, in terms of production, capacity utilization, productivity, and profitability, HSL's performance was less than adequate and even poor. Comparison with private Indian steel plants, especially TISCO, further highlights HSL's inability to rise to expected levels. The government replaced HSL with a new state-owned managing company, SAIL, in an attempt to address this problem.

Of the two private steel plants, TISCO was more successful during the 1950s and 1960s. The increased demand for steel during World War I had proven beneficial to it, when it had become a critical source of steel for British government operations in Asia. Production and profit levels again increased during the Second World War II. However, the increased production strained the plant machinery considerably.

As a result, and following approval by of the Planning Commission, TISCO began a modernization and expansion program in the 1950s. Part of the modernization program undertaken with technical help from Kaiser (USA) was financially supported by loans from the World Bank and the Indian government. Both programs were completed by 1958.

TISCO had a production capacity of 2.00 million tonnes during the 1950s and 1960s. Government restrictions on capacity expansion limited the company's growth rate. Where TISCO did succeed was in having a higher capacity utilization and superior product quality. It approached the state in 1961 and again in 1965 with proposals for further expansion. While the first proposal was turned down by the government, the second project was deferred by TISCO due to internal factors (labor problems, fall in profitability). The first proposal was rejected since the government expectated that the production targets set by the Planning Commission could be met by the expansion of the three-state-owned plants and a new one at Bokaro. Later, however, the state asked TISCO to consider possible expansion during the Fourth Plan period. And as Johnson notes "only when it became evident that third Plan and proposed fourth Plan targets could not be achieved without private sector participation, did the government give tentative approval to the expansion of" TISCO.[16]

The other private steel plant, IISCO, performed moderately well during the 1950s and early 1960s, but overall it was not as successful as TISCO. In 1947 IISCO had a plant capacity of about 0.3 million tonnes. By the end of the 1950s the plant capacity had been increased to 1.0 million tonnes, making it the second largest private steel plant in India. During the first half of the 1960s, IISCO's capacity utilization exceeded 100 percent (i. e., total production was greater than the plant's production capacity) and was even better than TISCO's.

Meanwhile, IISCO approached the state with a proposal to increase its production capacity via improved technology and using better quality coal. IISCO turned to the World Bank for financial assistance, and in 1966 the bank approved a $30 million loan. However, the project was canceled due to IISCO's internal management problems. There was a decrease in steel production toward the late 1960s, "owing to the lack of adequate maintenance and timely replacement, and labor problems."[17] And in 1972, during the Fourth Five Year Plan, with management and technological problems at IISCO increasing, the state nationalized the company.

Administrative Machinery in the Steel Sector

To administer this rapidly growing sector, the cabinet created a Ministry of Steel and Mines. The ministry was concerned with the implementation of steel policy and the management of the state-owned steel enterprises. Until 1950 steel policy was formulated directly by the political leadership. After 1950, the Planning Commission became the nodal agency for steel policy formulation. The Ministry of Steel interacted with the Planning Commission regarding the formulation of steel policy. However, the role of the Ministry of Steel in steel policy formulation during this period (1950s and early 1960s) was limited to making policy recommendations and managing the state-owned steel plants. The policies and five year plans formulated by the Planning Commission were guided by Nehru's ideological framework. Insofar as it followed the approach of the Bombay Plan, these policies and plans also reflected the interests of a few leading industrialists, such as J. R. D. Tata and G. D. Birla.

The Ministry of Steel was headed by a Minister (a political appointee). The chief bureaucrat was the Secretary in the Department of Steel. Below the Secretary came the Additional Secretary, the Joint Secretaries, the Deputy Secretaries, and the Under Secretaries. Nearly all these bureaucrats belonged to the IAS/ICS cadres.[18] The Department of Steel also included a technical division, which was placed below the Joint Secretaries in the ministry and has been more or less marginalized. The Technical Division is headed by a technical officer (not a member of the civil service). Its main task is to compile data and technical reports regarding the state-owned steel plants and the sector as a whole.

The price and distribution of steel was the concern of the office of the Iron and Steel Controller, which was also a part of the Ministry of Steel. This office had been established by the colonial Government in the early 1940s and was retained after independence to "control distribution and also production of steel and scrap."[19] The responsibility of the Iron and Steel Controller during the initial years of Indian Independence was more or less a continuation of his role from the years of British rule, although its power grew gradually during the 1960s, the 1970s, and the 1980s. The Iron and Steel Controller was assigned the task of periodically revising the retention price of the various steel products.

With the creation of the Joint Plant Committee in 1964, the bureaucracy gained an increased role in the development of the steel industry. Bureaucrats in the Ministry of Steel were now given the authority to negotiate pricing and distribution issues with the management of the state-owned steel plants and of TISCO. Representatives of the state-owned Indian Railways were included in the Joint Plant Committee, as the railways were both the primary mode of transporting steel and one of its largest consumers.

The shift from statutory price and distribution controls (in which the Planning Commission played a critical role) to the establishment of the Joint Plant Committee (of which the Joint Secretary, Ministry of Steel, was the chair) reduced the authority of the Planning Commission while increasing that of the bureaucrats. The overall decrease in the status of the Planning Commission beginning in the 1960s contributed to the autonomy of the Ministry of Steel in the political arena.[20] This autonomy was, however, limited by the overall role of the Ministry of Finance, which, along with the cabinet, had to formally approve all decisions taken by the Joint Plant Committee and the Ministry of Steel.

The greater authority of the Finance Ministry with regard to fiscal policy and financial outlays clearly curtailed the decision-making powers of the Ministry of Steel. The structural hierarchy and distance between the two ministries was, however, undermined by the strong informal and personal ties between the bureaucrats in the two ministries, who belonged to the IAS. Given the generalist nature of the IAS, it was often the case that bureaucrats posted in one ministry had worked in the other at some time in their careers. Also, bureaucrats belonging to the same state cadre (i. e., the state to which they were assigned at the beginning of their career) or the same batch (i. e, the year of entry into the IAS) were often posted in the different ministries. As a result, the organizational limitation on the power and authority of the Ministry of Steel was somewhat overcome by the informal links between the Ministry of Steel and the Finance Ministry.[21]

Besides reducing the role of the Planning Commission in the development of the steel industry, the creation of the Joint Plant Committee had another effect. Earlier the relationship between the managers of the state-owned steel plants and the bureaucrats in the Ministry of Steel had been unequal: the bureaucrats regulated and monitored the managers at the steel plants and had the authority to interfere in their day-to-day operations. By reducing the role of the Planning Commission this relationship became even more unequal, since the Ministry of Steel was now primarily in charge of both policymaking and implementation. At the same time, there were few, if any, informal links between the plant managers at HSL (who were technical or administrative personnel recruited directly) and the IAS bureaucrats in the ministry. As a result, the organizational limitations on the power and authority of HSL managers were not countered by informal ties between the two.

Ties between the trade unions and politicians remained strong, however. All of the large trade unions at HSL were affiliated with the various national trade union federations. The recognized unions at Bhilai, Durgapur, and Rourkela were affiliated with the various national-level trade union federations (i. e., INTUC, HMS, and CITU). As a result of the political support, trade unions have been able to play a substantial role in the Ministry of Steel's management of HSL. Given both historical conditions and the labor policy regime, local and national level politicians were drawn into various issues at the plant. Thus, while labor interests at the steel plants were easily communicated to the state, management interests were not. This situation became particularly problematic as the authority of the Ministry of Steel increased.

While the Joint Plant Committee had the potential of fostering communication between industry and the state, the greater authority of the IAS bureaucrats in the Ministry of Steel counteracted this possibility. This increased authority exacerbated the problem of bureaucratic interference in the day-to-day management of the state-owned steel plants.

In the next phase of the development of Indian steel industry, the problem of bureaucratic interference in the operations of the state-owned steel plants only increased as a consequence of the creation of the Steel Authority of India Limited, which was the Ministry of Steel's response to the declining performance of HSL.

PHASE II: MANAGERS AND BUREAUCRATS TO THE FORE

The declining performance of HSL during the 1960s elicited a response only in the 1970s, when the Ministry of Steel reorganized the state-owned steel sector in its attempt to improve its performance. This action, however, had little impact. In addition, the Ministry of Steel promoted the mini-steel plant segments in an effort to increase overall production. The effort led to more problems than it solved. Yet little was done to improve the productivity of the steel industry until 1991, when the steel industry was decontrolled and delicensed.

SAIL

Between the years 1964-65 and 1971-72 steel production by the state-owned integrated steel plants barely increased, primarily because of the state's lack of investment in technological upgrading and plant maintenance and poor plant management. The Ministry of Steel had two options: increase investment and/or reorganize the management structure. By the early 1970s, the effect of the Bangladesh War (1970), a severe drought (1972-73), and the oil crisis of 1973 led to rising inflation and the worsening of the balance-of-payments situation. In addition, the government began to emphasize poverty removal programs. The new policy emphasis on anti-poverty programs and the changing economic circumstances forced the state to reduce investment in the state-owned enterprises.

The political basis for the decline in investment is clear when one considers that despite the apparent shift in the political ideology and the financial crunch, Prime Minister Indira Gandhi felt it politically prudent to propose the establishment of three new integrated steel plants in the southern states of Karnataka (at Vijayanagar), Andhra Pradesh (at Vizag), and Tamil Nadu (at Salem). This decision was her attempt to win political support and electoral votes from these states.

Unable to invest the necessary capital in technological upgrades, or in infrastructure development (such as power generation or transportation), the Ministry of Steel was compelled to focus on reorganizing the management structure of HSL. The push for this reorganization came primarily from the Minister of Steel, M. Kumaramangalam.

In a lecture in 1972, Kumaramangalam argued that one way to ensure the successful performance of HSL was to adopt a management approach resembling the practices followed by private enterprises. The second, was to have the head of the company (a technocrat) report directly to the Minister.[22] Thus the Minister's proposals aimed at reducing the role of the bureaucrats in HSL operations and giving specialists (technocrats) greater say in the policy-making process.

Kumaramangalam's proposals were adopted, and as mentioned, in 1973 a single holding company for all the state-owned integrated steel plants—the Steel Authority of India Limited (SAIL)—was created. The existing state-owned integrated steel plants—Hindustan Steel Limited, Bokaro Steel, and (the recently established) Salem Steel—became its subsidiaries.[23] SAIL, staffed by technocrats rather than Ministry of Steel bureaucrats, was now responsible for the state-owned steel plants.

SAIL was assigned three tasks: planning, promoting, and organizing "an integrated and efficient development of the iron and steel and associated industries, such as iron ore, coking coal, manganese, limestone, refractories, etc., in accordance with the national economic policy and objectives laid down by Government from time to time"; coordinating "the activities of the subsidiaries, to determine their economic and financial objectives/targets and to review, control, guide and direct their performance with a view to securing optimal utilization of all resources placed at their disposal"; and acting "as an entrepreneur on behalf of the State," identifying "new areas of economic investments and [formulating and recommending] to Government a national policy for the development of iron and steel and related input industries and [advising] it on all policy and technical matters."[24]

SAIL was organized similar to a private corporation—with a chair and board of directors (including five representatives of the state and the managing directors of the various state-owned steel plants).[25] Given the stated intention of having a technocrat head the company, the first chair of SAIL, M. A. Wadud Khan, was a technocrat and was also concurrently the Secretary of Steel.[26]

However one central problem remained. All SAIL decisions regarding capital expenditures beyond Rs. 100 million (later changed to Rs. 200 million), agreements regarding foreign collaborations, annual development plans, and some personnel appointments required the approval of the Ministry of Steel. Thus, despite stated intentions to the contrary, the Ministry remained profoundly involved in the administration of SAIL.

Reviewing the relations between the Ministry and SAIL, the World Bank noted that "the investment review limit . . . is too low even for individual steel plants, let alone for SAIL as a Company."[27] A little further the World Bank report observed that "SAIL's management claims that because of the present low review limit, much needed capital expenditures, including many in the nature of routine (but major) maintenance have suffered inordinate delays, and affected performance." Discussions with officials at SAIL suggests that delays, caused by the need to get the approval of the Ministry of Steel, in plant maintenance and development and in the hiring of personnel have been a problem since the very beginning.

The relations between the Ministry of Steel and SAIL led not only to delays and maintenance problems but also to serious problems in SAIL's production strategy and manufacturing process. Its production strategy was developed by the Ministry officials. According to them, production objectives were the availability of domestic steel at the lowest price possible and the production of steel products required by other state agencies, such as the railways, defense, and so on. Given the lack of coordination between the Ministry of Steel and SAIL, these objectives led to the greater production of low-quality (cheaper) steel rather than the production of more profitable specialized and higher grades of steel (which during the 1970s and 1980s had to be imported). The emphasis on the production of basic steel products discouraged technological innovation at SAIL. In addition, the lack of coordination between the Ministry of Steel and SAIL led to the overproduction of specific steel products at certain times and their shortages at other times. The

SAIL managers' lack of autonomy with regard to product mix and production schedules further discouraged managerial innovation.

The lack of autonomy of SAIL managers with regard to production and management affected industrial relations at the plants also. If it discouraged managerial innovation with regard to production strategies, it did so in the case of labor management as well. Managers, unsure of support from the Ministry of Steel and constrained by bureaucratic regulations, were both unwilling and unable to go out on a limb when settling labor disputes. SAIL managers tended to respond to industrial disputes with a policy of appeasement. Their primary aim was to stave off embarrassing questions in Parliament and resume minimum levels of production.[28]

At the same time, the unions' awareness of these constraints on management reinforced the trade union-political party ties. If the management lacked the ability to satisfy labor's demands, then trade unions would inevitably turn to political leadership for patronage, further undermining SAIL managers' ability and willingness to improve their performance.[29]

The management structure of state-owned steel plants was again reorganized in 1978. The restructuring program changed the relation between SAIL (the holding company) and its subsidiaries. The subsidiaries were now placed directly under the control of SAIL. This was expected to increase the congruence between steel policy and production policies of the individual plants.

As a result, decision making was further centralized, and the Ministry of Steel was, in effect, given a greater (and more direct) involvement in the day-to-day management of the various steel plants, not just of SAIL. The Ministry had administrative control over SAIL's financial decisions, had five representatives on SAIL's corporate board, and also acted as the liaison between SAIL and other relevant ministries, such as Finance and Commerce. This involvement, according to senior officials at SAIL as well as the ministry, has only deepened in recent years. On being questioned about the relations between SAIL and the Ministry, senior managers and members of its board contend that the Ministry was in effect acting like the "corporate office," leaving little or no space for decision making by SAIL management. One senior manager went so far as to suggest that SAIL management had been rendered redundant by the civil servants in the Ministry of Steel, with regard to both corporate strategy and labor management.[30]

At the same time, the Ministry of Steel and SAIL continued to lack channels of communication that might have encouraged the transfer of information between the generalist IAS officials and the technical managers at SAIL. The bureaucrats lacked the specific knowledge to improve SAIL's performance, and SAIL managers who had such knowledge had insufficient capacity to do so. The pattern of relations established impaired performance in two ways: it led to the adoption of inefficient corporate strategies; and it led to an appeasement-oriented labor policy resulting in labor indiscipline, low productivity, and politicized trade unions.

Thus, while the political leadership was successful in establishing of state-owned steel plants, the organizational structure of the trade unions, the Ministry of Steel, and SAIL undermined their subsequent performance. The various attempts at reorganizing the state-owned steel plants only exacerbated the restrictions on their autonomy. The original intention behind the creation of SAIL voiced by Kumaramangalam had been effectively nullified by the structure of the Ministry of Steel and its IAS bureaucrats.

Mini-Steel Plants

While integrated steel plants produce saleable steel from iron ore using blast furnace technology, mini-steel plants (MSPs) use the electric arc furnace method and scrap metal as raw material to produce steel. World steel production via the electric arc furnace process received a major boost with the introduction of the ultra-high-power furnace and oxygen steel making during the 1960s. Further technological developments included large-capacity furnaces and more efficient production mechanisms. The 1970s saw an increase in the output of Indian MSPs as a percentage of total steel production in India from 14 percent in 1970 to 20 percent in 1980. The rise of the MSPs segment in India duplicated the international trend. The steel crisis of the 1970s had led to growth of mini- and midi-steel plants in the major steel manufacturing countries. However, in contrast to the successful growth of mini-steel plants internationally, in India the segment faced serious problems (including shortages of raw material, power, outdated technology, and noneconomies of scale) beginning in the mid-1970s.

The history of electric arc furnaces in India can be traced back to 1902, when an ordnance factory was established at Cossipore. It was followed by the (private) Hukum Chand Electric Steel Company in 1922 in Bengal. The demands of World War I encouraged the growth of the MSP sector. In the years immediately following independence, the growth of the private MSP sector was restricted by the Industrial Policy Resolution (1956), which permitted only the state to set up new steel production facilities.

However, with the increasing demand for steel and the long gestation period of the integrated steel plants established by the state, steel policy was revised in 1959 to permit the entry of private entrepreneurs in the production of steel using the electric arc furnace route. With the expansion of steel production in India during the 1950s and 1960s, the quantity of scrap generated increased. Unable to process all the scrap it generated, India began exporting scrap while at the same time importing finished steel. In an effort to counter this anomalous situation, the state, beginning in the Fourth Plan period, sought to encourage the growth of MSPs by adopting a liberal licensing policy. It initially proposed the establishment of 15 mini-steel plants by private entrepreneurs.[31] The existing industrial licensing policy was to regulate the production and capacity of the MSPs.

The development of the MSPs during the 1970s was also supported by the prevailing ideological framework which favored smaller units over larger industrial plants. MSPs could also be located throughout the country, since they depended upon scrap metal generated locally. This was in accordance with the state's locational policy that sought to disperse industrial development. Political pressure from the various state governments was one critical reason for the rapid growth of the sector. Patronage politics and the desire of the various state governments to produce steel locally led to a spurt and the wide dispersal of MSPs. As a result of the rapid growth, MSPs contributed around 20 percent of the total steel produced in India by the end of the 1970s.

While steel policy facilitated the growth of the MSPs (by permitting and encouraging the entry of private capital), the overall scarcity of steel in India also was a contributing factor. The scarcity of steel was primarily due to the inability of the integrated steel plants to satisfy domestic demand and due to the restrictions on steel import as a result of the balance-of-payments problems during the late 1960s and the early 1970s. Between 1967 and 1974, the capacity of the MSPs increased from 0.5 million tonnes to 3.0 million tonnes per year. The rate of growth of production during this period was slow, and most MSPs operated at low levels of capacity utilization.

During the 1970s MSPs began facing "difficulties in maintaining production and in marketing [their] products at an economic price."[32] The difficulties were largely three. First, the licensing policy encouraged the growth of a large number of small-capacity plants, with most units having a capacity of under 40,000 tonnes per year, while the general capacity of an economically viable plant is over 200,000 tonnes per year.[33] Absence of economies of scale hurt investment in the modernization and technological upgrading of the existing MSPs. Second, with declining state investment in the power sector (during the 1970s following the oil shock and also during the 1980s) and a concomitant fall in the quality of infrastructural facilities, the power-intensive MSPs faced acute power shortages. (The integrated steel plants were comparatively less affected since they depended on captive power generation.[34]) Consequently, production levels at the MSPs were negatively affected. Third, with the rapid growth in the number of MSPs and the slow rate of growth of steel production by the integrated steel plants, scrap metal became scarce. As a result of the three factors just outlined, utilization of existing steelmaking capacity of the electric arc furnace units remained around (or even under) 50 percent.

To ensure adequate supplies of raw material, that is, scrap metal, the state permitted the MSPs to import scrap. Thus India moved from being an exporter of steel and scrap in the late 1960s to being an importer of both in the 1980s.

In an attempt to promote the production capabilities of the MSPs a few "liberal" policy measures were introduced, including the elimination of excise duties on the production of MSPs plants and of customs duty on imported scrap. In addition, "selected mini steel plants were allowed to diversify into production of certain grades of high alloy steel."[35]

The Ministry of Steel has in recent years also encouraged the establishment of sponge iron plants. Sponge iron can be used as a supplement to scrap metal. Most MSPs are technologically capable of using sponge iron to the extent of about 15 to 20 percent as its raw material. New furnaces, and even some existing electric arc furnaces with some technological modifications, can accept raw material containing nearly 70 percent of sponge iron.

Despite the adoption of these relatively more liberal policies toward the MSPs during the 1970s and 1980s, the basic problems faced by these units—the shortage of power, and raw materials as well as the restrictive licensing framework—were not addressed. MSPs also faced the additional problem of inadequate and erratic water supply. As a World Bank report notes, "the situation is frustrating for owners as the demand for steel is rising, and the mini-steel plants have unused capacity which they cannot use because of the shortages of scrap and power which are beyond their control, and because the plants need to be brought up-to-date technically, which will require costly investments."[36] The Ministry of Steel formulated no long-term strategy or plan for the MSP segment. "Most of the studies and presentations prepared by industry associations and leaders have been concerned with reviews of past performance, examinations of technologies and developments in other parts of the world, and pleading for relief or incentives to overcome current plan and there are concerns that the mini-steel industry cannot be relied on to be a long term major contributor to steel production."[37]

The problems plaguing the MSPs remain largely unresolved. MSP owners receive limited encouragement from the government to upgrade their technology and improve their product quality. While the Ministry of Steel has introduced changes in duties and taxes on inputs, little has been done to provide infrastructural facilities required by MSPs, such as electricity and water. In contrast, the Department of Electronics, as discussed in chapter 5, actively sought ways of reducing infrastructural problems faced by software manufacturers.

Other Policy Changes

Apart from reorganizing the management structure of the state-owned steel plants and encouraging MSPs in an attempt to increase production, a few other measures were also introduced. First, to meet the expected demand of 10 million tonnes per year by the end of the Fourth Five Year Plan (1974), the plan proposed the expansion of the Bhilai plant from 2.5 million tonnes to 4.2 million tonnes. And as discussed earlier, the expansion of IISCO's capacity following its nationalization was also proposed. Additionally, the construction of the fourth plant at Bokaro with a capacity of 1.7 million tonnes was envisaged during the first half of the 1970s. The plan proposed expanding this capacity to 4 million tpy. In the 1980s, while no new state-owned steel plants were constructed or proposed, two of the existing plants were expanded and the fifth plant at Vizag was expected to be operational by the late 1980s.

Second, in an effort to generate finances for the modernization of the private and state-owned plants, the Ministry of Steel created the Steel Development Fund (SDF) in 1978. The fund was to be financed by charging a surcharge of Rs. 100 per tonne on steel products. Thus, the selling price now included the retention price and the surcharge besides sundry taxes. The SDF was administered by a committee consisting of representatives of the Planning Commission, Finance Ministry, and the Joint Plant Committee; the head of the Committee was the Secretary of Steel.

Third, given that the low-capacity utilization of the integrated steel plants was partly a function of the nonavailability of inputs such as power and coal, the Ministry of Steel proposed the creation of captive power units at Bokaro, Durgapur, and Rourkela. (TISCO already had a captive power plant.) In addition, the ministry of steel stated that up to 2 million tonnes of coking coal would be imported annually to prevent production stoppages due to shortages.

Fourth, the steel price control policy was liberalized to a limited extent. The Joint Plant Committees' decisions regarding retention prices were now exempted from prior approval of the Ministry of Steel, in attempt to grant greater autonomy to the integrated steel plants vis-à-vis the Ministry. However, institutional and informal ties between the Joint Plant Committee and the ministry undermined this attempt. As the World Banks's report notes, "being headed by a civil servant suggests that the Joint Plant Committee is likely to be more responsive to official attitudes, however indirectly."[38]

Fifth, after Rajiv Gandhi came to power in 1984, there was an attempt to introduce further liberalization measures and reform the state-owned enterprises. This was in sharp contrast to the policies of Indira Gandhi, who throughout the 1970s and 1980s did not question the basic premise that SOEs ought to occupy the "commanding heights" of the economy. In a clear departure from the traditional "self-reliance and state-monopoly perspective," the Minister of Steel under Rajiv Gandhi presented a report of the steel industry that called for a change in the relationship between the Ministry of Steel and SAIL and an internationally comparative focus in the development of the sector.

Bureaucratic inertia, however, ensured that none of the proposals was adopted, and little changed in the Ministry of Steel's strategy. A little later the Minister who presented the "radical" report resigned for sundry political reasons. And although he continued to encourage a change in steel policy to improve efficiency in the state-owned enterprises, Rajiv Gandhi's goals remained unaccomplished.

Thus changes introduced during the 1970s and 1980s left the overall steel policy framework more or less untouched. The establishment of SAIL, which was intended to alter the face of the Indian steel industry, did not quite do so. The liberal entry policies that encouraged the growth of MSPs did little to solve the problems plaguing the sector, and in fact exacerbated them. The problems faced by the Indian steel industry during the 1960s continued more or less intact throughout the 1970s and 1980s.

SAIL's Performance

SAIL's production levels grew slowly. In 1973-74 SAIL had an installed production capacity (for ingot steel) of 5.3 million tonnes per year. However, its production level in 1973-74 had yet to reach even 4.5 million tpy. Ten years after its establishment, SAIL had increased its production capacity to 7.6 million tpy. Production, however, had grown to only 6.64 million tpy growing at an average annual rate of 4.75 percent (1974-75 to 1983-84).

From 1984-85 to 1990-91 SAIL's production grew at an average annual rate of 4.32 percent. Its capacity utilization during this period was considerably better than that during the previous decade, although it succeeded in achieving close to full capacity utilization only at the very end of the 1980s. As Nayar notes, the cuts in investment, delays in planning, and inefficiencies in management that continued through the 1980s and early 1990s have ensured that the state-owned steel plants have not achieved the dominance or success originally intended by planners and political leaders, and steel production has remained below targets.[39] Despite inefficiencies in production and low capacity utilization, SAIL's increased capacity ensured that its state-owned steel plants together with IISCO (following its nationalization) were India's primary and dominant producers of basic steel.

IISCO's Performance

Production at IISCO declined beginning in the mid-1960s. Steel production (of ingot steel) at IISCO had reached a high of 1.0 million tonnes a year in 1962-1963. However, by 1972 to 1973, IISCO was producing only 0.43 million tpy. As mentioned, due to labor and financial problems, the expansion program proposed during the Fourth Plan was canceled. And by the early 1970s the state decided to respond to the crisis by nationalizing the company.

IISCO's problems during the 1960s may be attributed to three factors. First, the recession during the mid-1960s reduced the demand for steel. Second, local politicians in conjunction with trade union politics fostered labor-management tension. The local communist leaders, in particular, wreaked "havoc on the management of [the] firm in an effort to wrest control over workers from rival unions."[40] In its 1969 annual report, IISCO management stated that the problematic labor relations were primarily the result of rivalry between unions affiliated with opposing political parties. Third, and perhaps most important, the Joint Plant Committee had not increased the price of steel for several years. When combined with rising costs and concessions to labor, this had affected the country's profitability and viability. And in its 1970 annual report IISCO declared that as a result of continuing labor problems, the plant had been closed down.

Following nationalization, the Ministry of Steel drew up plans to modernize the IISCO plant during the 1980s. If nationalization was intended to improve IISCO's production, however, it clearly failed. Production fell to levels lower than those prior to nationalization in 1972. Plans have been afoot in recent years to privatize IISCO, but these plans, have been effectively scuttled by IISCO's trade unions in conjunction with members of various political parties. In 1995-1996 production at IISCO was 0.32 million tonnes of ingot steel and 0.30 million tonnes of saleable steel. During the late 1990s, the plant has been functioning at a capacity utilization of between 33 and 40 percent.

TISCO's Performance

Throughout the 1970s TISCO periodically upgraded its technology and improved its productivity. It was only toward the end of the 1970s, however, that TISCO embarked on an expansion and modernization project.[41] The first phase (1980-83) of the modernization project cost Rs. 2.25 billion and was completed ahead of schedule in 1983, quite unlike expansion programs undertaken by SAIL, which nearly always faced the problem of cost and time overruns.

The second phase of the modernization program (at the cost of Rs. 8.47 billion) was completed successfully by 1989. While both phases of the modernization program resulted only in a marginal increase in production capacity, they nevertheless helped TISCO improve its overall performance and efficiency, upgrade its plant facilities, and improve the quality of steel it produced.

In 1989 TISCO (with encouragement from the state) decided to embark on another expansion and modernization program. The project (costing Rs. 10 billion) was to be financed by a loan from the Steel Development Fund, internally generated resources, and commercial capital. The completion of the project has, however, been delayed as a result of the foreign exchange crunch and import restrictions of 1991 and 1992. The accompanying devaluation of the rupee also slowed the program by increasing costs.

TISCO's production of ingot steel has increased from 1.72 million tonnes per year in 1974-75 to almost 2.29 million tpy by 1990-91. Production of saleable steel increased from 1.46 million tpy in 1974-75 to 1.94 million tpy by 1990-91. Throughout this period TISCO's average capacity utilization was around 96 to 97 percent for ingot steel and 100 percent for saleable steel. During these years TISCO's performance in terms of productivity, capacity utilization and profits, as compared to SAIL's, was also substantially superior. Between 1973-74 and 1985-86 TISCO made a cumulative profit of Rs. 5.85 billion, while SAIL suffered a cumulative loss of Rs. 1.62 billion during the same period. Why has TISCO performed better than the public sector plant, SAIL?

The answer has seven parts. First, TISCO compared to SAIL had lower production costs. Steel prices on products produced by TISCO and SAIL were set by the Joint Plant Committee throughout the 1970s and the 1980s. The prices were periodically revised to cover increases in the cost of inputs and transportation. Given the concern on the part of the Joint Plant Committee, the Ministry of Steel, and the political leadership to demonstrate the profitability of the state-owned steel plants (especially to parliamentary committees), the price revisions always took into account SAIL's lower productivity. As a result TISCO nearly always profited more than SAIL under the price control regime. As noted by CRISIL: "Due to SAIL's relatively lower cost efficiency, [the] price increases [or revisions] generally tend to benefit TISCO more."[42]

Second, TISCO has been able to alter its product mix and thus dodge the constraints imposed by the price control regime. The prices set by the Joint Plant Committee affected only certain steel products (albeit a large category). By changing its product mix, TISCO has been successful in reducing the effect of price controls. Over the years TISCO has increased its production of finished steel, which is of higher value. "Since [Joint Plant Committee] pricing does not affect higher value finished steel, TISCO is able to price such products independently and obtain higher profits."[43] SAIL unfortunately, has not been able to do the same. Tight controls and monitoring by the Ministry of Steel and the resultant lack of corporate autonomy have reduced its capacity to change its product mix. Third, the steel products controlled by the Joint Plant Committee are meant largely for state consumption (railways, defense, power, etc.). National interest, as a consequence, has also played a critical role in diminishing SAIL's profitability.

A fourth factor that ensured TISCO's profitability is the presence of captive power generating plants and iron ore and coal mines, which reduced its dependence on state-run electric companies (widely regarded as the most inefficient state-run industry in India). It enabled TISCO, as compared to SAIL, to better manage its production process and avoid production stoppages due to input shortages. Fifth, having downstream industrial units as subsidiaries also helped TISCO, enabling it to alter its product mix in accordance with the demands of its subsidiaries and thus improve its profitability and that of the Tata group overall. SAIL's product mix was determined largely by the Ministry of Steel based on the requirements of the defense industry and the railways. Lack of coordination between the state agencies ensured that SAIL, more often than not, did not make production decisions based on economic rationale and economies of scale.

TISCO's ability to play the game of regulatory controls has been helped by the nature of relations between its corporate leaders and the political leadership. TISCO's relations with the government have been cordial, not hostile. And the cordiality has not been ensured by relations of patronage. Since the very beginning (particularly under the leadership of J. R. D. Tata), the Tata group has emphasized the value of maintaining an equidistant position from the various political actors and parties.

Finally, "continuity of management," a conducive work ethic, and "cordial labor relations" also enabled TISCO to perform better than SAIL.[44] Unlike the periodic labor disruptions encountered at the various SAIL plants, TISCO's plants faced few problems.

The negative consequences of the licensing and policy regime were, therefore, countered by TISCO's monopoly hold over a specific niche market, the peculiarities of the pricing system, superior management, and a long-term business strategy (e. g., the establishment of downstream industries and captive power plants). While enabling TISCO to grow, steel policy during this period hindered the growth of the state-owned steel plants as well as the overall development of the Indian steel sector. Throughout the 1970s and 1980s the price of TISCO's shares on the stock market kept rising, making it one the most valuable stocks at the time.

Why No Other Response?

To summarize the argument above, three points can be made: First, bureaucrats in the Ministry of Steel were not captured by TISCO; TISCO's chief executive officer supported all political parties; and TISCO continued to perform well. Second, the mini-steel plant segment was perennially plagued by input shortages and was by all accounts inefficient. Third, the state-owned steel plants kept fumbling; their growth remained slow, and profits reflected the bureaucrats' ability to cook the books rather than improve the actual performance. Yet India's steel bureaucrats did little. While a few cosmetic policy and organizational changes were introduced, little was done to move the Indian steel industry, and especially the state-owned steel plants, toward a trajectory of rapid growth.

What precluded a change in policy? The answer has two parts: factors within the state apparatus and the planning process, and the role and influence of nonstate actors in the steel sector, such as TISCO, mini-steel plants, and labor.

By granting the steel industry a central role in India's industrialization, Nehru (and to a lesser extent Indira Gandhi) created considerable barriers for change. Former bureaucrats in the Ministry of Steel, including the steel secretary, argue that the commanding status of the steel industry, ironically, reduced the number of policy options available to them. Changing steel policy meant altering several other sectoral policies, including automobile, defense, railway, machine tool, and small-scale industry. Steel price and distribution controls were a form of subsidy, especially to the railway and defense industries. Backward and forward linkages united these industries with the steel sector, forming part of an overall planning and industrial vision with steel at its heart. The only remaining alternative available to the bureaucrats was to disregard the implications for other sectors and formulate steel policy unilaterally. This, however, would undermine the dominant ideology: Fabian-Socialism emphasized state control of the "commanding heights" of the economy. Thus, in addition to the economywide implications of changes in steel policy, the Fabian-Socialist ideology deeply entrenched within the political leadership placed additional constraints upon the bureaucrats.

However, these constraints were somewhat softened during certain periods. M. Kumaramangalam, Vasant Sathe, and Rajiv Gandhi pushed for the adoption of innovative policies to spur the growth of the state-owned steel plants. Yet either the modified policy was watered down at the time of implementation by IAS bureaucrats or entrenched interests, such as labor, succeeded in countering the policy changes. Hence, apart from the constraints introduced by the Fabian socialist ideology and economy wide linkages, bureaucratic structures and key actors within the sector appear to have blocked changes in policy.

The non-technical background of the IAS bureaucrats in the Ministry of Steel is particularly noteworthy. The ministry is staffed by members of the IAS cadre. Given their generalist experience and training, these bureaucrats are not entirely familiar with the industrial dynamics of the steel industry. The IAS officials are posted in the Ministry of Steel for 3 to 5 years. Senior and middle-level bureaucrats consistently have noted that it takes them about a year to understand the industrial dynamics and the basic technical issues of the sector. The five-year limit on appointments encourages neither the formation of policy initiatives with long gestation periods nor their follow-through.[45]

In other words, those who had the power and authority to introduce innovative policy did not have the knowledge or the motivation to do so. The bureaucrats' lack of industry experience was compounded by the absence of channels of communication with the managers of the state-owned and/or private plants. Differences in professional (and even social) background were not conducive to the development of informal channels of communication. Finally, as discussed in chapter 2, the Indian Administrative Service offered few incentives to entrepreneurial and innovative bureaucrats in terms of promotions, postings, or salary levels.

Three nonstate actors in the steel sector could have influenced policy and introduced change: TISCO, mini-steel plants, and labor. Why did they not do so?

As the dominant private actor, TISCO clearly had both the institutional and political ability to modify policy. Senior managers at TISCO did present the Ministry of Steel with policy proposals. However, in nearly all cases the proposals concerned issues not requiring significant policy change. Effective management practices made TISCO an efficient and profitable steel company. Its accomplishments were clearly superior to those of the state-owned steel plants.[46] Its monopoly status reduced the incentive for TISCO to push effectively for a change in policy. The Ministry of Steel's attempt to protect the state-owned steel plants had the effect of creating a rental haven for TISCO.

The MSP owners had three primary interests, of which two were somewhat contradictory. First, they were eager to ensure that the price of basic steel, controlled by the Ministry of Steel (via the Joint Plant Committee), remained low. Second, they were interested in reducing taxes and duties levied on their products. Third, they wanted the state-owned steel plants to increase their production of basic steel—raw material for the MSPs.

The first two interests led the MSP owners to seek only piecemeal changes within the regulatory policy framework. They had an built-in interest in retaining the existing regulatory controls over the price and production. The third interest would have led the MSP owners to demand that the state-owned steel plants increase production of basic steel. This, however, would require changes in the management of the state-owned steel segment—its privatization or at least fewer regulatory controls—or an increase in state investment in the segment. The first option was ruled out because the MSP were interested in the maintenance of regulatory controls and especially price and production controls by the Ministry of Steel. The second option required collective action and lobbying.

The structure of the MSP segment precluded collective action. A protected and limited domestic market meant that the nearly 300 mini-steel plants competed against each other. Moreover, the MSP owners procured infrastructural facilities, which were under the administrative control of local authorities, not the Ministry of Steel, such as electricity and water, via local political patronage. Both electricity and water supply have been under the administrative control of local and state-level governments, not the Ministry of Steel. Thus, the nature of competition among the mini-steel plants and the absence of other incentives to come together precluded the MSP owners from lobbying the ministry for fundamental changes in investment. This, along with their interest in retaining specific aspects of the regulatory policy framework, led them not to push for change in steel policy.[47]

Labor in the steel sector could have been interested in policy change insofar as it potentially led to higher wages, benefits and employment levels. Labor could have influenced policy in two ways: via collective bargaining, and via political patronage and clientelistic politics. Of the two methods, collective bargaining was more likely to compel the state to alter its basic policy regarding investment in steel, management practices, and regulatory policy. Historical circumstances and labor laws have, however, led Indian steel workers to follow the second method. To achieve increases in wages, benefits and employment levels, they have drawn on ties of political patronage, not on the trade union structure.

Every Indian political party has a trade union affiliated to it, and all political parties claim to voice the concerns of the workers. As I argued in the preceding chapter, this arrangement of trade unions and political parties resulted in the marginalization of trade union interests within the political system. Local members of Parliament and political party officials, given their interest in grass-roots mobilization and the creation of vote-banks, have been the channels of communication between the workers at the steel plants and bureaucrats in the Ministry of Steel. The presence of vote-banks and their importance for election strategies and for communicating workers' interests clearly have been a factor in maintaining the status quo in steel policy. The unions have thus sought benefits through clientelism, not through an overhaul of steel policy.

Thus the three nonstate actors (TISCO, mini-steel plants, and trade unions) that could have potentially influenced the steel policy were either uninterested or unable to push for innovative and major changes. As a result, few changes were introduced in the steel policy framework. Further, initiative on the part of the political leadership has been inadequate to bring about a change.

In the face of declining performance, the Ministry of Steel responded only with organizational restructuring of the state-owned steel plants and limited encouragement of the mini-steel plant segment. At no point did steel policy address the problem of: lack of autonomy of SOE managers; the infrastructural shortages faced by mini-steel plants; TISCO's protected niche market, which allowed it to cream off profits; and more generally the problem of low productivity and the low quality of steel produced in India.

PHASE III: DECONTROLLING THE STEEL INDUSTRY

The turnaround in India's steel policy came with the economic reforms of 1991-92 when steel prices were decontrolled. Along with price controls, customs duties on imported steel and scrap were also reduced. Steel distribution was partially decontrolled. Allocation to the priority sector and small scale industries, however, was retained. The freight equalization scheme was abolished as well.

The decontrol of steel prices was expected to increase the profitability of the integrated steel plants. While the Steel Authority of India Limited (SAIL) and the Tata Iron and Steel Company (TISCO) were being offered a retention price of Rs. 11,000 per tonne for certain mild-steel items, similar products from the secondary steel sector whose prices were not controlled, used to sell at Rs. 14,000 per tonne. The partial decontrol of steel distribution meant that politicians' role in determining steel allotments and their resultant capacity to engage in corruption was undermined. Liberalization was also expected to enable SAIL to export its steel products rather than follow the diktats of the Ministry of Steel.[48] The decontrol of steel prices and the abolition of the freight equalization scheme, however, was expected to raise the cost of steel for consumers in northern, western, and southern Indian states (since all the integrated steel plants are located in the east).

During the period 1991-92 to 1994-95, SAIL's production of ingot steel grew at an average annual rate of 1.92 percent. During the same period

TISCO grew at 5.02 percent.[49] TISCO has begun to benefit from the modernization program it began in 1980, reaching its highest production of 2.81 million tonnes of saleable steel in 1996-97. The program has transformed TISCO from "a dusty fume-laden, antiquated steelworks using the open hearth-ingot casting route [into] an environmentally clean modern steel plant using primarily the BOF-continuous casting process."[50] And any significant long-term improvement is likely to be apparent only a year or so after the modernization project is completed.[51]

Production by the mini-steel plants has not improved significantly following liberalization. Their total steel production has been at around 4.0 million tonnes (1996-97). This production level is disturbing since the total annual capacity of the MSPs is 9 million tonnes.[52] Since the 1991 liberalization, a number of industrialists have either established or are considering establishing large mini-steel plants. (Sunflag, Essar, Lloyds, Jindal, and Malvika Steels are the prominent ones). These plants also use the electric-arc furnace method, but unlike the other mini-steel plants, they have substantially larger capacities, use sponge iron rather than steel scrap, and produce steel products traditionally produced by integrated steel plants. These features allow them to produce steel more efficiently than the smaller mini-steel plants.

Changes in steel policy during the 1990s have had consequences for the performance of state-owned enterprises whose steel inputs had earlier been subsidized by the price and distribution controls. State-owned enterprises, which use steel inputs, are clearly hurt by the higher cost of steel. This, added to the generally poor performance of most state-owned firms, has pushed these firms further down. Due to the budgetary constraints following the 1991 crisis, the government has been unable to bankroll these losses. As a result, a number of these firms are in the process of privatizing. But even if the cost of steel had not increased, most of these loss-making plants would have had to privatize. Their losses have been accumulating for many years.

As noted earlier, the policy changes have led entrepreneurs to enter, or consider entering, the integrated steel plant sector. Interestingly, the new entrants are increasingly turning to the IAS bureaucrats for help and advice in establishing and developing their firms. As one senior bureaucrats in the ministry noted, "they [i. e., the industrialists] are asking me for help in negotiating with financial institutions, and opening markets abroad, . . . but I know very little about how to negotiate with financial institutions, or how to enter international markets. . . . I did not anticipate this. . . . I need to learn more in these areas."[53] Steel industrialists believe the support and help of the Ministry of Steel is particularly important to enable them to enter the international markets. Thus rather than seek only a level-playing field, industrial actors are expecting the bureaucrats to provide the industry with the help necessary for their growth in an open economy. The Ministry of Steel, as a whole, has yet to respond adequately.

SAIL's problems and needs are compounded by its subordinate position to the bureaucrats within the Ministry of Steel. The chairman of SAIL, Arvind Pande, observed in 1997 that the "steel sector in India, particularly the public sector enterprises, need the support of a flexible and responsive policy environment to remain competitive. This calls for a review of the issue of autonomy to the [SOEs] with respect to corporate governance, investment decisions and joint ventures options."[54] And this issue has not been addressed so far.

In addition to this, SAIL, TISCO, and the larger mini-steel plants face serious infrastructural problems. Coordination between the Ministry of Steel, Shipping and Transport, and Power are urgently required. The state needs to formulate more responsive policies regarding India's infrastructure. Power in India costs 8 to 10 cents per kilowatt-hour (kwh); it costs only 3 to 5 cents in other steel-producing countries, including China. Infrastructure problems at India's ports has rendered imported coking coal more expensive. Coordination between the Ministries of Steel and the Shipping would help. However, for such coordination and responsiveness to occur, the bureaucrats in the Ministry of Steel need to understand their industry more closely. Short tenures, a generalist training, and few channels of communication with the steel entrepreneurs all make this impossible. Political encouragement for the growth of the steel industry is present, although it has yet to translate into effective policy responses.

THE INDIAN STEEL INDUSTRY IN COMPARATIVE PERSPECTIVE

The policy approach and strategy toward the state-owned steel plants established decades ago continued until 1991. Three factors have been responsible for this. First, the absence of organizational incentives discouraged IAS bureaucrats from introducing policy innovations. Second, although a push for change from managers might have countered the lack of internal incentives, this was absent as well. Differences in professional (and social) backgrounds between IAS bureaucrats and the managers ensured that few informal channels of communication existed between them. Thus, few informal channels of communication countered the constraints in the formal channels of communication introduced by the higher authority of IAS officials in the Ministry of Steel.

Third, the push for change might also have come from labor/trade unions. The close ties of patronage between the trade unions and the political parties ensured that the workers were not involved in a corporatist arrangement. Intense competition between the various trade unions at the plant level compelled union leaders to outdo each other in their demands for increases in wages and prerequisites. These demands were largely met via the established political patronage ties. As a result, there was little interest on the part of the trade unions to seek improvements in the company's performance. The permanent character of the jobs also reinforced a preoccupation with marginal gains in wages and prerequisites, not with the profitability or productivity of the steel plants. Declining profits and performance were of little consequence to the trade unions and consequently they were not involved in pushing for changes in policy.

The close ties between the trade unions and the political parties also dissuaded both managers and bureaucrats from attempting policy/strategy changes. Maintaining the status quo was considerably safer and more attractive. The pattern of relations among bureaucrats, managers, trade unions, and politicians therefore ensured that few policy changes were introduced.

Policy with regard to TISCO and mini-steel plants also did not change substantially until 1991. The regulatory environment offered TISCO a protected market. The low efficiency of the state-owned steel plants meant that TISCO was guaranteed profits if its operations were more efficient. In the absence of bureaucratic interference of the type SAIL was subjected to, TISCO was able to manufacture specialized steel and other products not subject to price controls.

TISCO's management also contributed to the company's success. The Tata Administrative Service is highly regarded for its abilities. The policy of TISCO leadership to retain cordial relations with politicians from all parties also helped the company successfully survive the license-permit-quota-raj. It would be wrong, however, to suggest that these relations involved patronage. Finally, TISCO's profitability enabled the company to, as one labor leader put it, "co-opt trade unions" and ensure an excellent record of industrial relations. TISCO's workers are among the highest-paid in India. Unlike SAIL, TISCO has only one recognized trade union, the Tata Workers Union (TWU). The absence of interunion rivalry made labor negotiations straightforward (not something appreciated by national trade union leaders). These factors together ensured that TISCO was able to overcome any restrictions imposed by the policy regime and that its operations were substantially more profitable than SAIL's.

Policies for mini-steel plants did not change during the 1970s and 1980s for a different reason. Granted protection from imports and a liberal entry policy, competition in this segment was high. By the 1990s there were almost 300 MSPs. However, stiff competition and poor infrastructural facilities (water and electricity) ensured that more than half were operating at less than 50 percent capacity and suffering losses.

Requests from MSP owners for policy change concerned only reductions in duty and taxes. Collective action problems ensured that the Steel Furnace Association of India (SFAI) made few requests to the Ministry of Steel for improvements in infrastructure, technological upgrades or export help. At the same time, the frequent transfer of the Ministry of Steel bureaucrats ensured that few informal channels of communication were established between them and the MSP owners. Consequently, while the Ministry of Steel did reduce duties and taxes occasionally, little else was done to improve the lot of the mini-steel plants.

For these reasons steel policy was retained more or less unchanged until 1991. While the bureaucrats were not predatory, they clearly were acting in a nondevelopmental manner. The continued poor performance of the industry did not spur IAS officials in the Ministry of Steel to change policy. This, lack of willingness and ability to change on the part of the bureaucrats is best explained by the structure of the ministry, the organization of industry, and the pattern of relations between the bureaucrats and the industrial actors.

Despite the liberalization of steel policy in 1991, the industry continues to be plagued by uneven growth rate, low rates of capacity utilization, and poor product quality. The larger mini-steel plants established since the 1990s appear to be performing better, but they constitute only a portion of India's steel industry.

According to the sectoral argument, the inability of the Indian state to address the needs of steel industry while promoting the software industry is not surprising. Such an inability, the proponents of sectoral arguments contend, is particularly noticeable in sectors with high capital intensity, high economies of scale, high production inflexibility, and asset/factor inflexibility, and is a consequence of these organizational and economic imperatives.[55] However, while the experience of the Indian steel might appear to fit this model, the Japanese and South Korean experiences do not. A review of their steel industries during the 1960s, 1970s, and 1980s indicates that the state's ability to modify its policy and respond to the needs of the industry has been a critical factor promoting growth in the Japanese and South Korean steel industries.

Following the steel crisis of 1974-75 the Japanese government, in contrast to governments in other steel-producing nations, responded quickly and successfully to help the steel industry adjust to the new circumstances. In cooperation with the leading producers, the Japanese Ministry of International Trade and Industry (MITI) "implemented a succession of joint production cuts to stabilize and raise domestic prices. At the same time the Japanese mills ran their facilities at a high rate, exporting the surpluses at steeply discounted prices. Concurrently, the Japanese government implemented a series of policy measures to enable the industry to adjust to new world competitive circumstances, providing assistance for the acquisition of overseas raw materials, conversion from oil to coal energy, and a variety of forums of steel-making research and development."[56]

Such proactive and responsive action on the part of the Japanese government is visible not only at times of crisis. MITI and the leading steel producers have had a collaborative relationship since World War II. The weekly meeting forums between MITI officials and steel producers are informally known as the Monday Club, and issues on the agenda include the exchange of market data, appropriate production levels, and other "market countermeasures."[57]

This collaborative relationship enabled the government, during the 1960s and the early 1970s, to help "the steel industry increase production and select the best technology for its expansion. The merger of Yawata and Fuji into Nippon Steel in 1970 reduced price competition so that the industry could continue to invest in new plants without worrying about profits."[58] And following the fall in demand for steel in the late 1970s and 1980s, these industry-state relations made the state willing and able to help "the industry adjust to slackened demand in the late 1970s and 1980s, by shifting many of the adjustment costs by responding more quickly to the decline."[59]

The relations between the Japanese steel manufacturers and the state have been close, informal, and cooperative. This interaction between MITI and the leading industrialists has been accompanied by considerable bureaucratic autonomy, from both the political elite and societal/industrial interests. As Chalmers Johnson observes, the Japanese political system "separates reigning and ruling: the politicians reign and the bureaucrats rule."[60] In other words, the Japanese political system enabled politicians to "create space for bureaucratic initiative unconstrained by political power."[61] Autonomy from societal/industrial actors, as Richard Samuels notes, "was induced through a process of reciprocal consent – that is, the Japanese state has a strategic role less because it leads than because it negotiates its authority."[62]

The South Korea steel industry is widely regarded as the most competitive steel industry in the world today.[63] A relative recent entrant into the steel industry, South Korea became a leading producer and exporter of steel by the mid-1980s, displacing Japanese exports in many of the East Asian markets. South Korea's steel industry has been dominated by a state-owned enterprise, Pohang Iron and Steel Company (POSCO). POSCO was established in 1968 and was headed until 1992 by Park Tae Joon, a confidant of Presidents Park Chung Hee, Chun Doo Hwan, and Roh Tae Woo. Park Tae Joon also was "a powerful politician, a member of the National Assembly and, from 1990 until 1992, the co-chairman of the ruling Democratic Liberal Party."[64] As a result of his political position, not only did Park Tae Joon have close and informal relations with members of the political elite, but his political connections and stature helped ensure that POSCO's senior management had close relations with the technocrats and bureaucrats in the concerned ministries, Trade and Industry, Commerce, and Finance.[65]

Such relations have been present not only in the case of POSCO and the government, but also between the government and business leaders more generally. In a study of business-government relations in South Korea, Leroy Jones and Il Sakong note that these relations are "facilitated by a network of personal ties between businessmen and bureaucrats, and by the interchange of personnel between the two sectors. . . . In these respects, there is . . . a similarity between Japan and Korea."[66] As Yoon Je Cho also observes, "close consultation between government and business and the government's risk partnership with business made what could have been a very distorted investment approach into a quite effective development strategy."[67]

While the South Korean state had these close relations with industrial actors, it was also autonomous from societal interests. What lent bureaucrats autonomy from societal pressures were the state's authoritarian roots and the presence of a coherent bureaucratic structure. Authoritarian roots alone do not necessarily result in state autonomy. Ruling elites in the bureaucratic-authoritarian regimes of South America tended to restrict the autonomy of the state bureaucracy, using the bureacracy as a tool to further their interests. South Korea, beginning with Park Chung Hee's presidency, was however, different. Explaining this difference, Evans notes that, "in general the [South Korean] military used the leverage provided by their own corporate solidarity to strengthen that of the bureaucracy rather than to weaken it."[68] The relationship between politicians and bureaucrats in South Korea came to resemble the Japanese pattern identified by Johnson, although "it never fully escaped the danger that the particularistic interests of individual firms might lead back in the direction of unproductive rent-seeking."[69]

Business-state cooperation along with the autonomy of the state from societal interests has enabled the state in South Korea to be remarkably flexible and responsive in dealing with the steel industry's needs. Bureaucrats were also helped by political encouragement. Promoting industry, and especially heavy industry, was a cornerstone of the political leadership's agenda beginning in the mid-1960s.

One question remains. Given the current economic troubles of South Korea, will the reasons for the success of its steel industry turn out to be its undoing in the long run, or are the current troubles transitional and temporary?[70] We will, of course, know the answer in the coming years. However, it should be clear from this discussion that the success of the South Korean steel during the take-off stage has a great deal to do with the presence of the developmental ensemble.

Thus, in both Japan and South Korea, what appears to have enabled the state to act in a responsive manner during the take-off stage was the presence of an autonomous state, close state-industry relations, and political encouragement. In other words, while the specific solutions/policy responses each state developed varied, what is similar is the flexibility with which they responded and their ability to identify and adopt appropriate policy measures, and this appears to depend on the presence of the developmental ensemble. The lack of such institutions with regard to the steel industry in India has been responsible for the lack of effective policy responses by India's Ministry of Steel, undermining the performance of the industry, both before and after 1991.

Unfortunately, the poorly performing steel industry has had a negative impact on industrial growth as a whole. The high price of Indian steel, its poor quality, and the restrictions on steel import have been major factors in the inability of the Indian manufacturing industry to compete in world markets. And in the absence of a more proactive and responsive steel policy, despite liberalization in 1991, the steel industry continues to perform poorly and undermine Indian industry as a whole.

Pressure from new entrants into the steel industry and from the large established steel manufacturers may be effective in transforming the Indian steel industry. However, for this to occur, the Ministry of Steel needs to redefine its role. Changes in its organizational structure will help alter the pattern of relations between the ministry and steel entrepreneurs. Close, informal relations foster the development of responsive steel policies. As the following two chapters demonstrate, such relations were present in the software sector and to a lesser extent in the automobile industry. This enabled the former to perform very well and the latter to perform moderately well.

4.

The Automobile Industry

L ike the steel sector, India's automobile sector has been regulated by a complex web of licensing and trade policies. The policy framework governing the automobile industry virtually eliminated foreign competition and severely restricted domestic competition in the commercial vehicle, passenger car, and two-wheeler segments between 1947 and 1984. Automobile policy was modified in the 1980s to allow greater domestic competition and also permit limited foreign participation.

Thus, unlike steel policy, which endured unchanged for nearly four decades, automobile policy was modified periodically. The various policy changes were, however, particularistic in nature, granting privileges to some firms over others. These policies did succeed in spurring entrepreneurship in some automobile firms, although they have yet to make the industry internationally competitive. Compared to their counterparts in the Ministry of Steel, Ministry of Industry officials did respond to some of the industry's needs. Why were bureaucrats in charge of automobile policy *willing and able* to respond to some needs and promote the growth of some firms and not others? How did the pattern of relations between the different actors in the industry influence the policy shifts? How did the industrial structure and the organization of the Ministry of Industry influence this and also the growth of the automobile industry?

To answer these questions I review the development of the automobile industry as well as the various changes in automobile policy. As with my analysis of the Indian steel industry, I relate this to the pattern of relations between bureaucrats, automobile manufacturers, labor leaders, and politicians. I conclude that ties between bureaucrats and the managers of the state-owned enterprise played a positive role. From the late 1980s onward especially, these ties played a crucial role not only in promoting the state-owned automobile firm but also in spurring the growth of the entire industry. However, ties between politicians and industrialists and between politicians and labor leaders have undermined the overall growth of the Indian automobile industry.

The automobile industry in India consists of four segments: commercial vehicles, passenger cars and jeeps, two- and three-wheelers, and automobile components. While automobiles were assembled in India from the 1940s on, their indigenous production began only in the 1950s. The total production of vehicles has increased from 4,112 annually in 1950 to 3,949,631 in 1996.[1]

From a grand total of 7 automobile assembly units in 1947, the industry now consists of over 25 units, with over 200 automobile component manufacturing units. Increasing domestic competition since the mid-1980s has improved the quality of Indian automobile products to a limited extent. The entry of nearly all the large international automobile manufacturers into the Indian market in the 1990s has improved the quality of Indian automobile products further.

However, the industry continues to be plagued by uneven growth rates and is yet to be a serious player in the international arena. Growth-restricting policies and a lack of an export focus for 40 years after independence have meant that only a few of the automobile units approach minimum economic scales of production. Capacity utilization remains uneven and indigenous technological development has been slow.

The Indian automobile industry can be divided into three phases of development. The first phase, from 1947 to 1966, was marked by the emergence of indigenous automobile production. The second phase, from 1966 to 1980, saw the decline of the passenger car segment but the growth of commercial vehicle and two-wheeler manufacturing. The establishment and growth of a state-owned passenger car enterprise and of four new commercial vehicle firms, and their effect on other automobile manufacturers are the central features of the third phase, from 1980 to 1993. Apart from these three phases, my analysis examines development prior to 1947 and, finally, the changes in the sector after delicensing in 1993.

The Origins of the Indian Automobile Industry

Automobiles were introduced into India in 1898. Cars and heavy vehicles were imported from Europe and America by British officials, Indian princely families, and prominent industrialists such as Tata, Birla, and Hirachand. Responding to domestic demand, General Motors (GM) and Ford entered the Indian market during the 1920s and 1930s. General Motors set up an automobile assembly plant in Bombay, where, by 1928, completely-knocked-down trucks and cars were assembled. Two years later Ford established similar assembling units in Madras and in Bombay and a year later in Calcutta.

Military requirements as well as the difficulties surrounding the import of automobiles by World War II led the government to encourage domestic manufacture. A panel was constituted in 1945 to examine the possibilities for the manufacture of automobiles and tractors in India. The report, presented in 1947, proposed the creation of incentives for Indian manufacturers. Two Indian industrial houses established automobile assembly plants in the 1940s. Hindustan Motors, set up in 1942 by the Birlas, assembled Studebaker Trucks, and Premier Automobiles, founded by the Walchand Group in 1944, produced Dodge Trucks. Competition from the already established Ford and GM slowed the growth of these two assemblers during their initial years.

The Tatas set up their automobile manufacturing and assembly plant close to the TISCO plant in Jamshedpur in 1945. The Tata Engineering and Locomotive Company (TELCO) initially manufactured steam locomotives for the Indian railways. Automobile manufacture at the TELCO plant began only a decade later. Commercial vehicles were produced following a collaboration with Daimler-Benz in 1954.

The industrialists behind these three automobile companies, G. D. Birla, Walchand Hirachand, and Jamshedji Tata, were prominent figures in the economic and the political arena during this period. As Frankel observes "Gandhi . . . [enjoyed] cordial personal relations with the major industrialists, including the Tatas, and Birlas, and with scores of lesser businessmen, merchants, and millowners in Calcutta, Bombay, and Ahmedabad," the leading industrial centers in India during the independence struggle.[2]

Apart from the Birla and Walchand groups, Ashok Motors (commercial vehicles, 1948) and Mahindra and Mahindra (jeeps, 1949) also entered the automobile sector. Thus by the late 1940s, the Indian automobile industry consisted of these Indian assemblers, two foreign-owned assembly plants (GM and Ford), and a number of automobile import dealers.[3] The industry, which was defined primarily by assembling units rather than manufacturing firms, altered its character almost totally in the years following independence.

PHASE I: IDEOLOGY, INTERESTS, AND PROTECTIONIST POLICY

As might be expected, the planning process promoted by Nehru and the Congress party shaped the overall character of the Indian automobile policy. Unlike the steel industry, however, automobile production was not regarded as the cornerstone of India's industrialization by the political leadership. This granted automobile policy substantial autonomy. Second, due to the considerable interaction between Congress party leaders and India's industrialists during the independence movement, automobile magnates exerted considerable influence over the shape of automobile policy during this phase.

In this section I first examine the position of the automobile industry in the Industrial Policy Resolutions. I then discuss the bureaucratic regulations and the implications of the Industrial (Development and Regulation) Act (1951) for the automobile industry. I also review the specific automobile policies adopted and the performance of the industry during this period. Finally, I explore the pattern of relations between bureaucrats, automobile industrialists, and politicians.

The first Industrial Policy Resolution, which was passed in 1948, specified the role of the state in industrial development. As discussed in chapter 2, the resolution divided industrial units into two categories. The first category consisted of industries which were reserved for the exclusive monopoly of the state. The second category covered industries in which private enterprise was permitted although regulated and controlled by the state, and the state was granted the right to intervene "whenever the progress of an industry under private enterprise is unsatisfactory."[4] The automobile industry was included in this category.

The manner of state regulation over industries was specified by the 1951 Industrial (Development and Regulation) Act. Under this act, all automobile companies were required to obtain a license for establishing a new unit, manufacturing a new automobile product, increasing production capacity, and changing the location of an existing plant. The bureaucratic process required to obtain such a license was also specified. While policy changes were introduced periodically, the overall process was maintained between 1951 and 1993. All applications for industrial licenses from automobile manufacturers had to be received by the concerned administrative ministry—the Ministry of Industries in this case. Upon the recommendation of the ministry, the application was forwarded to the Inter-Ministerial Licensing Committee. This committee was set up in 1952; and its members included the Secretaries of the various ministries such as Finance, Commerce, Labor, and Industry. Licenses were granted only after the Inter-Ministerial Licensing committee gave its formal approval.

In addition to the approval of this committee, all applications had to be cleared by the Directorate General of Technical Development (DGTD). Located within the Ministry of Industry, DGTD was assigned the task of examining all applications for industrial licenses from a technical angle. The Directorate examined whether: (1) the capacity expansion proposed by the applicant was required; (2) the additional capacity was commensurate with the applicant's installed capital goods; (3) the proposed changes would undermine the process of indigenization; (4) the proposed machinery and process is "modern and economic"; and (5) the location promotes the factory's economic viability.

As discussed in chapter 2, the various ministries in New Delhi are staffed by members of the Indian Administrative Service. To assist the generalist IAS officers with the technical aspects of policy making and implementation, each ministry had at least one technical department under it staffed by non-IAS bureaucrats. The key technical department in the Ministry of Industry was the DGTD. The technocrats in this department had considerably longer tenures than IAS officials in the Ministry of Industry and were usually career DGTD officials (i. e., not IAS members). Their interaction with industry usually was limited to company liaison officers who were concerned primarily with pushing their applications through the bureaucratic labyrinth. DGTD officials possibly did meet with the CEOs of small manufacturing companies. The automobile companies were, however, some of India's largest companies, and their CEOs certainly did not meet the DGTD officials. In addition, little periodic training had ensured that the DGTD officials lacked the capacity to generate policy initiatives designed to lead rather than restrain the automobile industry.[5] As a result of the composition of the Ministry of Industry, no informal channels of communication were established between the bureaucracy and the industrialists.

In line with the objectives of the Industrial Policy Resolution-48, the Ministry of Industry presented India's first automobile policy in 1949. With the aim of encouraging domestic manufacture of automobiles, the state banned the import of all fully built vehicles. Automobile firms engaged in assembling vehicles from completely-knocked-down units were, however, permitted to operate.

This policy was followed by a report of the Tariff Commission in 1953. Acknowledging the importance of the automobile industry for industrial development, the commission recommended that the manufacture of automobiles should be reserved for firms willing to manufacture components and complete vehicles with a phased manufacturing program. The closedown of assembling units was recommended. With regard to regulating the price of automobiles, the report advised against price controls "as long as the prices maintained by the manufacturers were reasonable. The Government were advised only to keep a watch on prices."[6]

The adoption of the recommendation of the Tariff Commission by the Government of India led to the exit of foreign automobile assemblers from

India. General Motors and Ford chose to close their operations in the country rather than establish plants for domestic manufacture. The exit of these firms led Premier Automobiles and Hindustan Motors, which had thus far assembled commercial vehicles, to enter the now-protected passenger car segment.

By the mid-1950s, the manufacturing programs of five automobile companies were approved. In addition to Premier Automobiles and Hindustan Motors, Mahindra and Mahindra, Ashok Motors, and TELCO were granted licenses. While Mahindra and Mahindra manufactured jeeps, Ashok Motors entered into a collaboration with Leyland to manufacture buses and trucks, and TELCO joined with Daimler Benz to produce bus chassis and trucks. Two new firms entered the two-wheeler segment as well. Automobile Products of India and Enfield competed with Bachraj Trading Company for this market. Automobile Products of India and Bachraj manufactured scooters, Enfield produced motorcycles.

In an effort to encourage domestic production and keep automobile prices down, the state lowered the rate of import duties on components still being imported. Nevertheless, automobile prices increased considerably during the early 1950s. As a result, in 1955 the Tariff Commission was requested to examine the pricing mechanism and recommend a price policy. The commission recommended against price controls and reiterated the other recommendations presented in its 1953 report. It also recommended that protection granted to the automobile manufacturers ought to be renewed after 10 years following a review of the of the industry's performance

The 1956-57 balance-of-payments crisis, however, altered the situation fundamentally. In an attempt to control the outflow of foreign exchange, the three passenger car manufacturers were permitted to produce only one model each. In addition, the cuts in foreign exchange allocated to them limited the quantity of components they imported and hence, the number of cars they produced.

The cuts in production of passenger cars led to a two-year backlog of orders and a steep increase in prices. In response, the state imposed informal price controls. People interested in purchasing a car had to place their order with the car dealers and deposit a partial payment at the Indian Postal Savings. Manufacturers were required to deliver cars to the dealers in the sequence in which the purchase orders were placed.

Throughout the 1950s, the state continued to provide the automobile industry with a protected market. The ban on the import of fully built vehicles in 1949 and the 1953 policy requiring all automobile assemblers to adopt a phased manufacturing program led to the exit of foreign automobile assemblers from the Indian market. Foreign competition had been effectively eliminated by the mid-1950s. Following their exit, Indian automobile companies entered all segments of the industry. Domestic competition was regulated via the licensing system. By requiring licenses for the entry of new firms, the expansion of existing ones, and for changing the product mix, the state was able to regulate the extent of domestic competition. Further, given that all firms depended on the import of components, the state was able to influence production rates via its control over foreign exchange allocation.

The state was, in effect, able to pick winners and losers from among the firms with licensed capacity. During the early 1950s, for example, the state encouraged production by Premier Automobiles and Hindustan Motors via relatively liberal foreign exchange allocations.[7] With their entry into the passenger car segment, both firms cut back their production of commercial vehicles. Meanwhile, TELCO, which had been established as a locomotive manufacturer in the 1940s, was granted a license for the manufacture of commercial vehicles. It entered into a collaboration with Diamler-Benz for the production of 3 to 5 ton diesel commercial vehicles (initially only trucks) in 1954. A year after commencing the production of commercial vehicles, TELCO began manufacturing components as part of its phased manufacturing program.

The other commercial vehicle manufacturer, Ashok Motors, was initially engaged in the assembly of Austin cars and Leyland commercial vehicles. With the adoption of policies requiring all automobiles companies to implement a phased manufacturing program, Ashok Motors was reorganized. Its managing agency agreement with Leyland was terminated, and it was instead incorporated as a manufacturing subsidiary of Leyland in India. The company also ceased to assemble Austin cars. Following these organizational changes, Ashok Motors was renamed Ashok-Leyland (India) Limited (ALL).

Finally, Mahindra and Mahindra, which had been incorporated in 1945, began production of jeeps in 1955. Before this, the company had been a sales representative of the American automobile manufacturer Kaiser Jeep Corporation. From 1955 onward Mahindra and Mahindra was the sole manufacturer of small utility vehicles (i. e., jeeps) until Maruti Udhyog's entry in 1984. The company achieved significant growth rates largely as a result of being the only supplier of jeeps to the Indian military and various paramilitary agencies.

The performance of automobile companies during the 1950s was below expected levels. In addition to the poor quality of the cars manufactured, there was widespread criticism from the press, the public, and from within the state about the high prices being charged by the protected firms. In response to this criticism, the state appointed a committee headed by L. K. Jha (a senior member of the

IAS/ICS) to examine these issues. In its report, presented in 1960, the Jha committee addressed these issues and problems. In order to lower costs and improve quality, the committee recommended the development of the ancillary industry within the regulatory licensing regime. During the 1950s indigenization had been interpreted as production of components and parts by the assemblers themselves, which had further reduced competition. The new focus on the development of the ancillary segment was expected to increase competition and generate improvements in quality and lower prices. The committee also recommended the continuation of the price controls adopted after the 1956 balance-of-payments crisis, so as to lower the final cost to the consumer. The various recommendations were subsequently adopted.

Thus, by the late 1950s, automobile policy consisted primarily of import restrictions, domestic content requirements, and price controls countering the effects of protection to some extent, administered via the complex licensing regime. Automobile policy initiatives had ensured the exit of foreign car makers. While this policy was clearly in line with the overall development approach of the 1950s and with the ideological inclinations of the political leadership, it undoubtedly suited the interests of Indian automobile manufacturers at that time.

The close relations established between the political leadership and India's leading industrialists during the independence movement proved to be a crucial factor in the shaping of automobile policy. The emphasis on indigenous development and state regulation accommodated rather than obstructed their interests. Automobile manufacturers frequently accused the government of bias and favoritism toward other firms. Premier Automobiles, for instance, charged that TELCO's entry into the commercial vehicle segment was the result of political favors granted to the Tata Group.[8] However, historical accounts as well as interviews with bureaucrats, industrialists, and politicians suggest that what nurtured these relations during the 1940s, 1950s, and 1960s was the common ideological goal of freeing India and ensuring rapid industrialization. This is not to suggest that "favors" were not granted to the companies owned by Tata, Shri Ram, Birla or Hirachand. The favors granted were, however, not the consequence of rent-seeking but of common political/social/economic interests of these industrialists and the political leaders. These common interests and ties provided a basis for the informal exchange of information.

Despite the collaborative nature of the politician-industrialist relations, a degree of tension persisted. It was perceptible, for instance, in a meeting between Tata and Prime Minister Nehru: While discussing the performance of state-owned enterprises, Jamshedji Tata told Nehru that a greater emphasis on profits was necessary. After a long period of silence, Nehru brusquely informed Tata to never again mention the word "profit" in his presence.[9]

During the 1950s, then, the regulatory automobile policy accommodated the interests of both the political elite and the automobile manufacturers. And the close relations established prior to independence between the two sets of actors were partly responsible for the specific shape of the policy. The collaborative experience of the Bombay Plan also played a key a role. During this phase, bureaucrats played only a minor role. Industrialists had little or no contact with senior bureaucrats. It was through their interactions with politicians, not bureaucrats, that automobile manufacturers sought to influence policy. Further, the presence of strong relations between industrialists and politicians had the effect of, if not discouraging, at least not encouraging the formation of bureaucrat-industrialist ties.

While the ties between these two sets of actors enabled the growth of the large Indian houses primarily by ensuring protected markets, it also, in time, worked to the disadvantage of the industrialists.[10] The presence of these ties did not encourage interaction between the industrialists and the bureaucrats, and so when changes in political circumstances undermined political leadership-industrialist ties, the automobile industrialists were left without allies. As I discuss later, this hurt the interests of the automobile firms during the late 1960s, 1970s, and 1980s.

The Components Segment

The automobile components segment consists of two parts—large and medium-size firms, and small companies falling under the small-scale industries classification. While the former firms have been governed by the Industrial (Development and Regulation) Act, as have other manufacturing industries, the latter have been regulated by the small-scale licensing regime.

The growth of the components segment took off following the adoption of the Jha Committee report of 1960. The report divided ancillary production into three categories: components in which India was self-sufficient;[11] components whose production had begun in India but demand as yet was not satisfied;[12] and components whose production had been licensed.[13] The Jha Committee argued that the frequent and steep rise in the price of automobiles, particularly cars, was a consequence of the lack of competition in the ancillary segment and of the high degree of vertical integration in the industry as a whole. This industrial structure was, of course, a direct result of the 1950s emphasis on the adoption of a phased manufacturing program by all the automobile manufacturers and the simultaneous lack of encouragement of the ancillary segment.

Following the recommendations of Jha Committee, the development of the ancillary segment began. Reviewing the growth of the ancillary industry during this period, Krueger observes that "there was a four-fold increase in ancillary production in an eight year period [1961 to 1968] and the growth in ancillary output was spread across all varieties of components."[14] She notes that the rapid growth was possible "partly because of the growth in final demand for the ancillary's output (both O. E. and replacement) but mostly because the industry was able to increase its share of the Indian market as it replaced imports."[15]

The Indian industrial development strategy has consistently sought to encourage the growth of small-scale industrial-units. Besides being protected from foreign producers and large/medium domestic manufacturers, small-scale units have been provided easier credit facilities and infrastructural support and considerably less onerous licensing requirements. Although a large number of small-scale components units has mushroomed in the past 40-odd years, the strategy has led to a fragmented structure with inefficient units, whose production levels almost never reach minimum economic scales, that never engage in product specialization, or invest in research and development, that have high production costs, and whose product quality is substandard, to say the least.[16] This organization of the components segment continues until today. And the problems resulting from a fragmented structure, uneconomic production levels, high production costs, low investment in Research and Development, poor quality and low product efficiency have remained as well.

The strategy toward the automobile industry through the 1950s and the early 1960s thus emphasized indigenous manufacture of automobiles and increasingly the development of small-scale units for the manufacture of components. Unlike the case of the steel industry, political rhetoric did not actively promote the development of the automobile industry.

This relative lack of prominence given to the automobile industry in political/ideological debate increased the autonomy of the process of automobile policy strategizing. Close historically grounded relations between the political leadership and the industrialists influenced the pattern of automobile policy, ensuring that the implementation of the licensing policy accommodated the interests of the existing automobile manufacturers. At the same time, the organization of the Ministry of Industry discouraged the development of ties between bureaucrats and industrial actors.

The automobile policy framework developed during the 1950s continued, with few modifications, through the 1960s. The emphasis on indigenous production and regulated private sector involvement was retained. The modification was primarily in terms of the relative importance given to the various segments of the automobile industry. Toward the end of the 1960s, passenger cars came to be regarded as luxury products. Consequently, automobile policy acquired an explicit bias against them. As discussed in the next section, this bias along with the absence of well-established relations between the bureaucracy and the industry and the deteriorating relations between the industry and the political leadership undermined the development of the entire industry.

PHASE II: RULES, REGULATIONS, AND POLITICS

From the late 1960s onward, Indian automobile policy was perceptibly altered. The populist wave led by Mrs. Gandhi affected the automobile industry. The populist wave was accompanied by deteriorating relations between automobile manufacturers and the political leadership. The breakdown in the informal relations between these two sets of actors undermined industrialists' ability to work the licensing system. While the licensing system had been promoted by the industrialists during the 1940s, 1950s, and the first half of the 1960s, they variously critiqued and condemned it during the remaining years of the 1960s and the 1970s.

Two wars (with China in 1962 and with Pakistan in 1965) as well as poor agricultural production (due to successive severe droughts) created a financial crisis by the mid-1960s. In an apparent attempt to appease donor countries and international financial institutions, Mrs. Gandhi devalued the rupee in 1966. Politicians from across the ideological spectrum attacked the devaluation. They regarded it as an abandonment of India's national integrity. India's leading industrial and business groups were uncomfortable with both the 1966 devaluation and the populist economic strategy proposed by Mrs. Gandhi. Industrialists had been hit hard by the devaluation. The devaluation had increased the rupee costs of repayment obligations on foreign exchange credits provided by foreign collaborators by more than one-third.[17]

Changes were also occurring on the political front. Nehru's death in 1964 led to leadership struggles cloaked in ideological guise within the ruling Congress party. And following Shastri's short tenure as prime minister, dissatisfaction and struggles within the party increased. The growing political and social dissatisfaction arising out of the economic crisis of the mid-1960s offered convenient issues around which the Congress party clashes were framed before and after the 1967 general elections.

These changing political circumstances and economic problems led India's industrialists to attack the economic strategy, the planning process in general, and Mrs. Gandhi in particular. G. D. Birla, for instance, critiqued both Mrs. Gandhi's economic policies and the process of planning in place.[18] He threatened that the business community would make a major issue of the failures of planning in the 1967 elections and prophesied that the Congress party would not do well in the polls—which, incidentally, was the case.

In an effort to counter political threats from within the party, Mrs. Gandhi asserted that "her differences with [the other party factions] had all along centered around issues of social change."[19] These pronouncements gained popularity and undermined the political power of the Congress party members opposing her, who were increasingly identified as having colluded with vested interests, particularly with prominent industrialists. With this Mrs. Gandhi's government had truly entered a populist phase.

The increasingly dominant populist ideology with its anti-big industry emphasis within the political leadership had led to a third inquiry by the Tariff Commission into the development of the automobile industry in 1966. The commission consisted of senior IAS bureaucrats and members of the erstwhile ICS. It was expected to examine the question of continuance of protection for the automobile and ancillary industry and the informal pricing system. Two reports were presented, one on each of the two issues. The commission made the following recommendations: that in an attempt to ensure that all automobile manufacturers attained minimum economic scales of production, the number of models in any category of automobiles ought to be kept to an absolute minimum; and that the system of informal price controls on passenger cars be retained.

The first recommendation did not result in any significant policy changes. The licensing system that was concerned with regulating the expansion and entry of automobile firms continued to do so, although with added firmness.[20] The second recommendation, however, led to changes. The Tariff Commission suggested a controlled price for passenger cars, which at least for Premier Automobiles was below its estimated unit cost of production.

Premier Automobiles responded by raising prices, and the Ministry of Industry imposed statutory price controls on the passenger car segment. Premier Automobiles challenged the imposition of statutory price controls in court.[21] The court ruled in favor of the firm in 1975. At the same time as the state imposed statutory price controls on passenger cars, it removed informal price controls with regard to jeeps. Thus, while automobile policy aimed at encouraging the commercial vehicle, two-wheeler, and component segments, the growth of the passenger car segment was not encouraged and even blocked. Charges of bias against the segment were countered by the assertion that Indira Gandhi's populist ideology did not permit the allocation of scarce foreign exchange or domestic resources for "luxury industries." Both the political leadership and the senior bureaucrats in the Ministry of Industry reiterated this claim during the late 1960s and the 1970s.

The political leadership argued that this automobile strategy was in line with the industrial development strategy adopted by Nehru and, to some extent, Mahatma Gandhi. However, as the preceding analysis of the automobile strategy during the 1950s and 1960s suggests, the bias against the passenger car segment emerged only in the late 1960s. The state in the 1950s and in most of the 1960s clearly did not prevent the growth of the passenger car segment. Further, the development of various automobile firms, especially Premier Automobiles and Hindustan Motors, had been fostered with a combination of protection, production licenses, and government purchases.

By leaving the segment open to private Indian entrepreneurship since the 1950s, and by ensuring its protection, the passenger car segment had, in effect, been nurtured. And if the automobile manufacturers had not formally demanded this policy, they had certainly been comfortable with it. In a 1965 brochure the Association of Indian Automobile Manufacturers noted that the "protection given to the industry in 1953 enabled the young sapling [the Indian automobile industry] to take firm root in Indian soil. The bold, imaginative and farsighted policy then adopted had been fully recognized and appreciated by the pioneers [of the Indian automobile industry]."[22]

The interests of the automobile manufacturers and the political leadership had coalesced during the 1950s into a protected market for domestic producers. The rules and regulations securing the protected market had been administered by the bureaucrats in the Ministry of Industry. And the automobile manufacturers had used their political connections to circumvent the bureaucratic regulations at various times during the 1950s.

The economic crisis of the mid-1960s, the accompanying devaluation of the rupee, Indira Gandhi's political inclinations, and the constellation of interests within the Congress party had, however, altered this pattern of interaction. A new policy regime consisting of statutory price controls, higher excise taxes, and duties was now in place. With the informal ties undermined, the policy changes transformed the relatively pliable and "workable" licensing framework into a restrictive and rigid one.

As noted in chapter 2, the Indian Parliament passed the Monopolies and Restrictive Trade Practices Act (MRTP) in 1969. The act grew out of concerns expressed by the political leadership that the licensing regime had been ineffective in encouraging the growth of small and medium-size industrial establishments. A Ministry of Industry study in the late 1960s noted that "the licensing system not only failed to prevent the growth of capacity in less essential industries, but actually had worked to provide a disproportionate share of the new licensed capacity to the few firms belonging to the larger business houses."[23] The study further observed that "the share of total approved investment allocated to the four largest business houses—the Birlas, Tatas, J. K. Singhania, and Shri Ram —actually increased."[24] The report singled out the Birla group and argued that the industrial house had "submitted such a multitude of applications in almost every product as to prompt serious questions that they were trying to 'foreclose' licensable capacity to other potential entrepreneurs."[25]

While the MRTP Act appeared to be limiting the monopolistic position of the Birla group, it affected other automobile manufacturers as well. Firms in the components segment (which were primarily small-scale and medium) escaped the restrictions of the Act.[26] While the passenger car segment was clearly targeted, large automobile manufacturers in the other segments were also not spared.

The populist policies were further strengthened in 1973 with the adoption of the Foreign Exchange Regulation Act (FERA).[27] The act forced automobile companies with foreign collaborators to change the terms of their agreements. Companies such as TELCO, which had established a significant level of technological and research capability, and others such as Premier and Hindustan Motors, with high levels of indigenous production, were not seriously hurt by FERA. Other manufacturers, however, now faced additional obstacles with regard to collaborating with multinationals and importing components.

The oil crisis of 1973 brought forth new concerns regarding the automobile industry. India's petroleum requirements have always been met primarily by crude oil imports. While India has, since independence, established substantial crude oil refining capability, domestic oil reserves supplement rather than substitute imports. The demands of an industrializing economy and of a growing population have meant that crude oil accounts for a substantial portion of India's total imports. Consequently, the oil crisis of 1973 sharply affected the country's economic and fiscal well-being.

The crisis led to an evaluation of the growth pattern of the Indian automobile industry and especially the low fuel efficiency of Indian automobiles by bureaucrats in the Ministry of Finance (who were concerned about the foreign exchange expenditure on crude oil) and the Ministry of Industry. This study led to the division of the automobile industry into two: luxury and nonluxury.[28]

With regard to the nonluxury segment, the Ministry of Industry adopted a policy framework that sought to encourage growth and improve technological levels. To enable the commercial vehicle and the two-wheeler manufacturers to upgrade their technology, modernize their plants, and achieve economies of scale in production, the Ministry of Industry placed them on the Appendix I list. This ensured that all applications by companies within these two segments for production and capacity expansion, modernization requiring foreign exchange, and even foreign collaborations would be treated more favorably than before.

The policy toward the components segment remained more or less the same. The manufacture of a majority of components was reserved for the small-scale industries. As a result, the segment continued to be beset with problems of fragmentation, inefficiency, abysmal levels of investment in research and development, high production costs, and substandard product quality.[29] While a few components were added to the list of those reserved for small-scale industries and a few others were removed, the overall policy framework and the licensing regime remained the same.

In 1975 the commercial vehicle and two-wheeler segments received further encouragement, when the non-MRTP and non-FERA companies in these segments were permitted to expand their production capacity and production without limit. These policy changes, as anticipated by the Fifth Five Year Plan, led to a boom in the two-wheeler segment.[30] The relative liberalization of commercial vehicle policy was followed by an increase in production of commercial vehicles, especially diesel vehicles.

Although the limited policy liberalization with regard to manufacturing capacity had led to the growth of these two segments, the largest companies in these areas had benefited disproportionately. The intended effect—the widening of the industry—had not occurred. According to a World Bank report, "concentration levels were high in many segments of the automobile industry, particularly utility vehicles, where [Mahindra and Mahindra had a] monopoly, and MHCVs [medium and commercial vehicles] and cars, where virtual duopolies prevailed. Effectively, this implied lack of competition in these sectors. Concentration was lower in LCVs, [light commercial vehicles] but even in this case effective competition was limited by consumer preference for the Matador [a Bajaj Tempo product]. A similar comment applies to scooters."[31]

In 1975 the Supreme Court finally arrived at a verdict in the suit filed by Premier Automobile's regarding the imposition of statutory price controls on passenger cars. To assess the validity of the claims made by Premier Automobiles in its suit, the Supreme Court had appointed the Car Prices Inquiry Commission. The Commission consisted of a senior technocrat from the Ministry of Defense, a chartered accountant, and was headed by a former High Court judge. Based primarily on the report presented by this Commission, the Supreme Court ruled in favor of Premier Automobiles. Statutory price controls on passenger cars were subsequently abolished.

Commenting on the inflexibility of the policymaking process in the late 1960s and early 1970s, Premier Automobiles noted that if "the Government had accepted the industry's plea much earlier [regarding price controls, and] if the Government had revised the prices adequately in time (which it did after the Supreme Court Judgment), the industry would not have landed into a financial morass. It will require many years more for the industry to come out of this near financial ruin which it had faced for no fault of its own."[32]

As noted earlier, the Ministry of Industry, with its generalist bureaucrats with short tenures had been unable to establish formal and informal channels of communication with the automobile manufacturers. The historical roots and the structural features of the Indian Administrative Service dissuaded the bureaucrats from developing strong ties with industrial actors. At the same time, the pattern of relations between the manufacturers and the political leadership had not pushed the industrialists to seek the development of such channels of communication. When the bureaucratic regulations, initially proposed by the industrialists, became cumbersome, political intervention had come to the rescue.

Changing political circumstances, however, had made this impossible by the late 1960s. The new political alignments had continued into the 1970s and passenger car manufacturers got no reprieve. By the early 1970s, additional constraints were imposed on the manufacturers of passenger cars as a result of the oil crisis. Manufacturers of commercial vehicles and two-wheelers, however, received limited policy support.

Growth during the 1970s

The 1970s were clearly "a disastrous period for the car industry."[33] After growing at an annual rate of 30.06 percent in the 1950s and at 14.05 percent in the 1960s, the passenger car industry did not increase its production during the 1970s. The statutory price controls led to negative profits for all three car manufacturers during at least some of these years. The oil crisis also had led to a fall in demand for passenger cars. During the period 1950 to 1980, the production of passenger cars had increased from 2,221 to 30,538, after rising to a high of 39,937 just prior to the 1973 oil crisis. In addition to falling profits, declining demand, and increased controls, all three car companies were plagued by labor problems throughout the 1970s.

Consider the performance of the car manufacturers. Standard Motors, which had manufactured 274 cars in 1950, produced only 6 cars in 1980. While production at Premier Automobiles and Hindustan Motors began to decline during the mid-1970s, both companies experienced little or no growth in the rate of production from the late-1960s onward. By 1969 Premier Automobiles had reached a production level of 12,218. During the 1960s, production at the company had grown by an annual rate of 9.56 percent. During the 1970s, by contrast, production growth was down to 0.13 percent a year. Production at Hindustan Motors also followed a similar pattern. Production of passenger cars had increased by 18.7 percent annually in the 1960s. During the 1970s, on the other hand, car production at Hindustan Motors increased at an annual rate of only 2.91 percent.

Of the two companies, Hindustan Motors performed somewhat better in terms of profits. This was partly a consequence of the different levels at which prices were set for the cars produced by the two companies (higher prices for Hindustan Motors' cars relative to Premier Automobiles' cars) and the greater (and relatively stable) demand for Hindustan Motors' cars. Cars produced by Hindustan Motors were larger than the model manufactured by Premier Automobiles and were purchased by state agencies for official use.

In the medium and heavy commercial vehicle segment, TELCO grew by 10.13 percent a year during the 1960s; Ashok Leyland Limited, by 8.41 percent. Between 1970 and 1973, both companies experienced declining and even negative growth rates. However, unlike the passenger car companies, the growth rates in the medium and heavy commercial vehicle held more or less steady during the 1970s as a whole. While TELCO's production declined to 6.24 percent a year, ALL's annual growth rate dipped precipitously during 1971 and 1972 but rose rapidly during 1973 and 1974 and again in 1978 and 1979, and achieved an average annual growth rate for the decade of 11.09 percent.

Increased production during the late 1970s was a consequence of the introduction of liberal policies with regard to capacity expansion of commercial vehicle manufacturing units in 1978. Both TELCO and ALL took advantage of these policy changes. TELCO established a new plant at Pune in 1978, and ALL expanded its capacity during the period 1976 to 1982. The demand for commercial vehicles rose following an improvement in agricultural and industrial production during the late 1970s. In addition, the poor performance of the Indian Railways, due to management and labor problems, promoted the demand for commercial vehicles. In 1971 TELCO manufactured 24,665 commercial vehicles, while ALL produced only 5,472. By 1976, TELCO had increased its production level to 26,444 and ALL to 9,179. And by the end of the decade, ALL manufactured 12,315 vehicles, a little under half of TELCO's figure of 31,685 vehicles.[34]

Bajaj Tempo Limited, a company within the Bajaj group, began the production of medium and light (petrol) commercial vehicles in 1958. Ten years later, the company diversified and started manufacturing diesel commercial vehicles. During the 1960s, Bajaj Tempo grew at an average annual rate of

17.66 percent. By the end of the 1970s, the company produced only diesel commercial vehicles, manufacturing 9,801 in 1980. Its rate of growth of production during the 1970s was 13.16 percent, making it one of the fastest-growing automobile companies during this decade. Bajaj Tempo gradually emerged as the leader in this segment, with a declining contribution from Premier Automobiles (1,235 in 1980) and Hindustan Motors (4,880 in 1980), and limited competition from Standard Motors (3,491 in 1980).

As discussed earlier, production of two-wheelers in India had begun in 1955. The segment grew rapidly, with 113,047 produced by 1970 and 417,602 by 1980. Automobile Products of India and Enfield India were granted licenses for the manufacture of scooters and motorcycles respectively. Bajaj Auto Limited entered the scooter segment in 1960 and was followed by Ideal Jawa in 1961 (mopeds), Escorts Limited in 1962 (motorcycles), and Mopeds India Limited in 1965.

While Automobile Products of India (API) was the leading producer of scooters through the 1950s, it faced stiff competition from Bajaj Auto by 1965. And by the end of the 1960s, Bajaj had emerged as the leader with a production of 26,431 two-wheelers by 1969. The company continued to thrive during the 1980s and became the third largest two-wheeler manufacturer in the world, after Honda and Yamaha. One of the few Indian automobile companies to have achieved minimum economic scales of production, Bajaj is also India's leading exporter of automobile products.[35] Only in the mid-1990s did Bajaj Auto experience uneven growth rates and even negative growth rates. Unfortunately, Bajaj Auto has not been able to significantly upgrade its product technology, and as a result, its dominant hold is increasingly challenged by two-wheeler manufacturers with access to foreign technology via their joint venture partners. Bajaj Auto is also facing pressure to upgrade its technology as a result of tighter emission standards.

In the motorcycle segment, both Enfield and the newer manufacturer Escorts had about a 50 percent share of the market from 1966 until 1974. From then on Escorts began to dominate the segment, and by 1980 it produced more than double the number of motorcycles made by Enfield. While superior performance and better management may have been responsible for the increasing dominance of Escorts, the close ties between its owner/CEO, H. P. Nanda, and Indira Gandhi clearly did not hurt.[36]

The relatively fewer restrictions on entry in the two-wheeler segment during the 1970s resulted in the establishment of several new scooter, motorcycle, and moped firms by the mid-1970s. Of the new entrants only Scooters India (a state-owned enterprise) was permitted to have foreign collaborators. However, Scooters India did not emerge as a leader in its field. Local politics, labor problems, and poor management ensured that this state-owned enterprise was not on the road to success. Persistent problems led to the plant's closure in the 1990s. And by 1993 the Ministry of Industry was considering the possibility of privatizing the plant by selling it. No decision has yet been taken, largely as a result of labor/political interests.

Thus, the development of the Indian automobile industry during the 1970s was influenced by (a) the oil crisis of 1973 (and of 1979), (b) the changing political alignments accompanying Mrs. Gandhi's accession to power, and (c) the organizational characteristics of the Ministry of Industry.

The oil crises compelled the state to reconsider its automobile and transportation policy, insofar as a greater emphasis was placed on the development of the two-wheeler and commercial vehicle segment. Policies regarding production capacity in these segments were liberalized. At the same time, macroeconomic constraints (insofar as it reduced foreign exchange resources for import of components and for the import of oil) in conjunction with the existing regulatory framework reinforced the state's tendency to pick winners and losers from among the various Indian automobile manufacturers.

The macroeconomic constraints and the financial crisis accompanying the oil crisis led to restrictions on the import of components by car manufacturers and hence limited their growth. With fewer resources at its disposal, the state was increasingly compelled to favor one company over the other in the allocation of import licenses. This, in turn, helped reinforce the emergence of patronage relations between politicians and specific industrialists. A shrinking resource pool (i. e., declining financial resources for imports) made import licenses that much more valuable, especially to the car manufacturers.

If the oil crisis had sidelined the passenger car segment, the changing constellation of political interests altered the relations between the political leadership and the car manufacturers. The informal channels of communication between the two actors were seriously undermined. This decreased the ability of the automobile industry as a whole to influence policy formulation. Its declining influence might have been countered by the development of channels of communication between industry and bureaucrats in the Ministry of Industry. However, ties between the bureaucracy and the industrial actors had not developed. The structure of the Indian Administrative Service and the organization of the Ministry of Industry did not facilitate the emergence of such ties.[37]

The ability of bureaucrats, to generate policy changes was undermined by their lack of informal knowledge about the needs of the industry, by the lack of bureaucratic incentives, and by the presence of close patronage relations between politicians and a few industrialists. The IAS bureaucrats in the Ministry of Industry during this period were clearly not willing to push for innovations in policy to spur the automobile industry. If the incentive structure of the IAS cadre did not quite discourage them from being policy entrepreneurs, at least it did not encourage them. At the same time, neither the politicians nor industrial actors pushed bureaucrats to implement change. The absence of informal ties between automobile manufacturers and bureaucrats ensured that the former did not pressure the bureaucrats to modify policy. The presence of close relations between certain industrialists and India's leading politicians also acted as a disincentive for innovative bureaucratic action. Eager to avoid taking risky action, bureaucrats tend to tread lightly in the face of close politician-industrialist ties. If there is one thing IAS officials are more uncomfortable with than adopting innovative policy decisions, it is attracting political ire.

Thus, the growth of the automobile industry during this phase had been dependent on the political leadership's picking of winners and losers. Changing political inclinations, the oil crises, and the accompanying macroeconomic constraints, however, altered this. And in the absence of close ties with bureaucrats, industrialists without close ties with politicians were left at sea.

PHASE III: THE EMERGENCE OF NONCONTRACTUAL RELATIONS

The success of the Congress party in the 1980 election led to the reappointment of Indira Gandhi as prime minister, an office she held until her assassination in 1984. Her return to power marked the beginning of the third phase in the development of the Indian automobile industry. Two fundamental changes occurred during this period. First, policies regarding the commercial vehicle segment (especially concerning entry of new firms) were liberalized, and as a result four new light commercial vehicle companies were set up. Second, a state-owned automobile manufacturing plant, Maruti Udhyog Limited (MUL), was established with Japanese collaboration. Of these two initiatives, the establishment of MUL led to fundamental changes in the structure of the industry. First, however, I discuss the policy initiative that permitted the entry of four new commercial vehicle manufacturers in the early 1980s.

The Commercial Vehicle Segment

Political obligations induced Mrs. Gandhi to grant four new entrants licenses for the manufacture of light commercial vehicles.[38] All the new entrants established plants with the help of foreign collaborations involving both technical and financial agreements. Another characteristic the four manufacturers had in common was the absence of prior experience in the automobile industry. Given that the licensing process reviewed the past performance/experience of an applicant before granting licenses, the allowances made in these four cases were clearly unusual. The licenses permitted each of the new manufacturers a production capacity of 12,500 light commercial vehicle per year.

Delhi Cloth Mills (DCM), part of the Shri Ram group, entered into an agreement with Toyota (with 26 percent equity) for the manufacture of light commercial vehicles. Production began in 1985 with a production capacity of 12,500 units. Since the very beginning productivity and profits at DCM Toyota have been undermined by the low production capacity, which is well below minimum economic capacity. The three other new commercial vehicle companies established during the early 1980s were Swaraj Mazda, Allwyn Nissan, and Eicher-Mitsubishi. Swaraj Mazda had been established by a prominent Indian industrialist (based in London), Swaraj Paul, who was one of Indira Gandhi's conspicuous supporters. As the name of the company suggests, Swaraj Paul entered into a collaboration with Mazda.

The third new entrant into the segment was Allwyn. Allwyn (Pvt.) Limited, a leading engineering corporation, manufactured household appliances such as refrigerators and electrical products. The company set up its first automobile manufacturing unit in collaboration with Nissan. The fourth company to enter the light commercial vehicle segment was Eicher. A manufacturer of mechanized agricultural implements and vehicles, Eicher joined with Mitsubishi to produce light trucks. All four new companies manufactured automobiles that were in direct competition with each other. All faced rising costs due to the escalating yen, problems of low productivity, and it is not surprising that profits have been hard to come by for these companies.

As these four new plants entered the market, a policy aimed at increasing the production capacity of existing commercial vehicle plants was introduced. The capacity permitted by the firm's industrial license could now be reendorsed up to 133 percent provided the firm had achieved a capacity utilization of at least 94 percent during any of the previous five years. Both MRTP/FERA and non-MRTP and non-FERA commercial vehicle manufacturers could to avail themselves of this opportunity to increase their capacity.

The liberalization of policy with regard to production capacity of existing commercial vehicle firms was followed by policies that liberalized the process of introducing new models of commercial vehicles. These policy changes together with the policy changes of the 1970s that had placed the commercial vehicle segment on the Appendix I list, and removed MRTP and FERA restrictions, led to the introduction of new models by the existing commercial vehicle producers.

TELCO introduced new models of its light commercial vehicles in 1984 and 1986. It also brought out a pickup van (to be later converted into a car) in 1988. The technology for each of these new models was developed internally by the company. In addition to developing new models, TELCO introduced significant improvements (including fuel injection engines, fail-safe parking brakes, and power-assisted steering) in its existing automobile products.

Like TELCO, Mahindra and Mahindra and Bajaj Tempo also introduced technical improvements. However, initiatives at both of these firms depended on technical collaborations. A collaboration with Peugeot enabled Mahindra and Mahindra to manufacture a diesel engine and a four-speed transmission. Bajaj Tempo Limited, a division of Bajaj that manufactured three-wheeler commercial vehicles, also introduced a new model. A technical collaboration with Diamler-Benz enabled the company to upgrade its automobile technology.

While Premier Automobiles Limited remained uninterested in commercial vehicles, Hindustan Motors attempted to revive its commercial vehicle segment in the 1980s. A technical agreement with General Motors' Japanese collaborator Isuzu led to the production of the basic Hindustan Motors' commercial vehicle with an Isuzu engine.

During Mrs. Gandhi's second tenure as prime minister, improvements in quality and technology partly transformed the commercial vehicle industry. The relative liberalization of policy toward the commercial vehicle segment since the mid-1970s, along with the immediate threat of competition from the four new entrants with their Japanese collaborations, had compelled TELCO, M&M, Hindustan Motors Limited, and Bajaj Tempo to introduce technological improvements. While TELCO did so with the help of its internal R&D capability, the other three were permitted under the somewhat liberalized licensing procedures to seek technical assistance from abroad.

Maruti Udhyog Limited (MUL)

The second action taken by Indira Gandhi after her reelection that significantly altered the face of the Indian automobile industry was the establishment, in 1983, of a state-owned passenger car enterprise with Japanese collaboration—Maruti Udhyog Limited. Its history is a complicated one, enmeshed in political conflicts and power struggles, and it all began with Mrs. Gandhi's younger son, Sanjay, in the mid-1970s.

Sanjay Gandhi was interested in manufacturing small passenger cars in India drawing on indigenous research capabilities. A company, Maruti Limited, was established and eager businessmen seeking Mrs. Gandhi's patronage helped support the venture. Along with acquiring financial support, the company was also successful, not unexpectedly, in receiving a license from the Ministry of Industry for the manufacture of 50,000 cars. The project was a fiasco; not a single vehicle was produced, charges of embezzlement and fraud were leveled against the promoters, and several suits were filed by creditors. The problems were, of course, exacerbated after Mrs. Gandhi's ouster from power in 1977. The company's financial and managerial problems and, more important, the scent of a political scandal lingered after Mrs. Gandhi returned to power in 1980. And in the midst of the business debacle and unfolding political crisis, Sanjay Gandhi died in a plane crash.

With the help of her considerable political resources, Prime Minister Gandhi decided to salvage both her image and the company, by nationalizing it. In 1981, Parliament with its Congress majority passed the Maruti Limited (Acquisition and Transfer of Undertaking) Act and thus nationalized the firm. Maruti Udhyog Limited (MUL) was placed under the administrative control of the Ministry of Industry and senior bureaucrats were selected to supervise its development. At the time of MUL's establishment, existing private sector car manufacturers were not alarmed at the emergence of a rival company. Given the dismal, and at best, uneven record of Indian state-owned enterprises (consider the performance of SAIL), the automobile manufacturers "appeared to watch the developments with [a] somewhat amused concern."[39]

After examining the possibility of collaborations with various European, American, and Japanese automobile manufacturers, MUL entered into a partnership with Suzuki and signed a memorandum of understanding in April 1982. According to Maruti's evaluation team, Suzuki offered the best terms regarding product mix, technology transfer, and equity participation. MUL began production of three kinds of vehicles: a front-wheel drive, 800cc car; a rear-wheel-drive minivan; and a jeep.

The project report stated that MUL would achieve a little over 95 percent indigenization by 1988-89. MUL asserted that a "Japanese automobile that would initially be assembled largely from imported components was to be transformed within a short period of five years into an almost completely "home made" product of equal quality."[40] The process of indigenization was, however, significantly slower. MUL claimed that the delays were the result of the inability of component manufacturers to meet its requirements. By 1988-89, the 800cc car was indigenized up to 86 percent and only 58 percent of the jeep was indigenous.[41]

Despite these delays, MUL's growth performance was not insignificant. Within only a few years of its establishment, the company had attained productivity levels and had reached minimum economic scales of production far superior to the other two Indian car manufacturers. Within five years of beginning production in 1984, MUL's output had reached 115,048 vehicles, out of which 105,826 were cars. All the other automobile manufacturers together had an produced only 71,364 cars. This production structure, however, is not at all surprising given the protection and preferential treatment granted to MUL.

The partnership with Suzuki contradicted all previous statements by the Ministry of Industry that claimed that the introduction of new technology for the development of the passenger car segment via foreign collaborations would not be permitted. Requests for technical collaborations by Premier Automobiles and Hindustan Motors had always been turned down. The adoption of FERA in 1973 also reinforced this feature of the Indian automobile policy. Further, while Premier Automobiles and Hindustan Motors were prevented from increasing their production levels and struggled with less-than-minimum economic scales of production, MUL, from the very beginning, was licensed a production capacity that ensured economies of scale of production and efficiency.

If preferential treatment for MUL began with the partnership agreement with Suzuki, it clearly gained in strength through the 1980s despite periodic declarations to the contrary. The minister for industry, N. D. Tiwari, asserted, for instance, that MUL was being promoted only with the intention of modernizing the entire automobile industry by introducing competition. He reiterated that the "Government will do unto Maruti only what it would do unto the rest of the industry."[42] Only a few months later, however, the Ministry of Industry reduced customs and excise duties on automobiles with a capacity of less than 1000cc. Of the three major passenger car makers, Premier Automobiles and Hindustan Motors produced cars with a larger capacity, while Maruti produced cars of less than 1000cc capacity.[43] Excise and customs duties on components for "small and fuel-efficient" cars (which applied only to Maruti and Sipani) were also reduced substantially.

The private car manufacturers reacted strongly to these developments and argued that the new duty structure was aimed at promoting only Maruti. The fact that an insignificant car maker (in terms of production capacity) like Sipani was included in the list of beneficiaries fooled no one.[44]

To promote MUL sales, the government also increased the extent of car loans available to bureaucrats and other senior officials employed by the state. While the earlier loan amounts usually enabled bureaucrats to purchase only used cars (either Premier or Hindustan Motor), the new loan regulations were clearly designed to encourage bureaucrats to buy new MUL cars. It is, however, unclear whether this regulation emerged from the ranks of the IAS officials interested in purchasing a new car or from the political leadership eager to ensure its sale, or from both. In any event, the interests of these two actors had the effect of promoting MUL products over those of Premier Automobiles and Hindustan Motors.

If the establishment of Maruti Udhyog Limited in 1982 evoked little concern among the private car manufacturers, the growing list of benefits given to the state-owned car company clearly generated considerable alarm. In an attempt to address this concern, the Ministry of Industry issued new regulations regarding technological upgrading, collaborations, and capacity expansion. However, the process of obtaining an industrial license remained cumbersome. The only change was a limited assurance that the bureaucrats in the ministry would consider the applications for license "more favorably" than before.

In 1984 passenger car makers were offered fiscal incentives to enable them to import technology, and improve the fuel efficiency of their vehicles. Premier Automobiles and Hindustan Motors both used this opportunity to enter into limited technical agreements with Nissan and Isuzu respectively. Following the collaboration, Premier Automobiles introduced a new car, the Premier 118NE, with a relatively fuel-efficient Nissan engine. Hindustan Motors put together a car, Contessa, with a Vauxhall body and an Isuzu engine. Mahindra and Mahindra was also permitted in upgrade its technology via a technical collaboration with Peugeot.

A scheme of "broad-banding" was introduced in 1985. Under this scheme, automobile manufacturers were permitted to change their product mix and utilize the installed capacity. Thus, automobile firms could alter their product mix among the four-wheeler category or the two-wheeler category in an attempt to utilize their installed capacity more efficiently. This initiative was followed by the exemption for two-/three-/four-wheelers from the provisions of sections 21 and 22 of the MRTP Act. In other words, large industrial houses no longer had to submit proposals for substantial expansion or for setting up of a new unit under the MRTP Act and could simply seek approval under the Industrial Development and Regulation Act (1951).

At the same time, however, the Ministry of Industry placed all segments of the automobile industry under Schedule IV. Schedule IV covered industries likely to face a raw material shortages or infrastructural constraints, or which generated high levels of pollution. This meant that all automobile industries required an additional clearance. While they could obtain licenses to increase their production capacity or upgrade their technology, under the broad-banding scheme, for example, they were not assured of such a license given the Schedule IV restrictions.

Despite the additional restrictions, 16 applications for foreign collaborations and expansion were received by 1988. Only the 3 applications for technical collaborations alone were approved. The Ministry of Industry delayed taking decisions on all the technical-cum-financial collaborations. Two sets of factors influenced this delay. First, there were concerns within the Finance Ministry regarding the foreign exchange demands of the potential collaborations. Second, concerns about undermining MUL increasingly dominant position in the passenger car segment also encouraged the Ministry of Industry to delay taking a decision.

The classic civil service method for postponing a decision—creating an expert committee to investigate the matter—was adopted. A "high-powered" committee led by the Finance Secretary was assigned the task of examining the criteria for approving technical-cum-financial collaborations and for outlining a new automobile policy. No policy outline was, however, presented until the early 1990s. And the various applicants for technical-cum-financial collaborations gradually withdrew their proposals. Changes in automobile policy were finally introduced in 1991 as part of the overall economic liberalization following the balance-of-payments crisis.

Why did the Ministry of Industry adopt the approach that it did toward the state-owned passenger car company? This question is puzzling, given the approach of the Ministry of Steel toward SAIL. Why did SAIL not benefit from similar nurturing disposition on the part of its administrative ministry?

Part of the reason why the Ministry of Industry sought consistently to promote MUL may have been due to Indira Gandhi's personal interest in ensuring the realization of her son's dream. Comparison with the steel industry suggests that this reason, however, could only be partly true. Nehru was personally very interested in promoting HSL (SAIL's precursor). However, his interest did not automatically translate into growth-promoting relations between the Ministry of Steel and HSL.

The variation in the relations between the Ministry of Steel and SAIL and the Ministry of Industry and MUL was partly the consequence of the internal organization of SAIL and MUL. Unlike SAIL, the senior management at MUL (and its CEO as well) were former (or current) members of the Indian Administrative Service. Bureaucrats in the Ministry of Industry were also drawn from this civil service cadre. The esprit de corps among the members of the IAS helped promote MUL over the other automobile companies.

The absence of a hierarchical relationship between IAS bureaucrats and senior MUL management (given that both belonged to the same civil service) meant that noncontractual ties between the two were able to overcome any restrictions on the latter's autonomy and restriction in day-to-day operations. These noncontractual ties cut bureaucratic rigidities and eased regulations. More important, however, the increased autonomy of MUL managers enhanced their willingness and ability to innovate with regard to corporate strategy and industrial relations.

MUL has responded to industrial disputes and labor problems not with a short-term policy of appeasement but by creating a "productive work culture."[45] At the same time, the ability and willingness of MUL management to respond has effectively undermined trade union-political party ties. Faced with a strike in the late 1980s, MUL management responded with programs aimed at increasing worker participation. In sharp contrast to SAIL's appeasement policy, MUL's response to labor's demands was founded on a long-term policy. And the response clearly paid off. Following negotiations, the largest trade union at MUL introduced a number of changes in its structure, including breaking its affiliation with the Indian National Trade Union Congress. And since this strike MUL has had no significant labor problems.[46]

Aside from preferential treatment in terms of policy, the management at MUL was able to utilize the Indian administrative network to get faster and more favorable licenses and clearances (for production, foreign exchange, and the necessary infrastructure) from the Ministry of Industry and from other ministries as well. Private automobile manufacturers, and especially passenger car manufacturers who had established at best few ties, both formal and informal, with the Ministry of Industry bureaucrats were consequently at a disadvantage. In the absence of close relations with the political leadership and faced with a competitor who had strong ties with the bureaucracy, the private passenger car manufacturers struggled to retain their hold on the Indian market.

The revisions in the automobile policy framework continued under Rajiv Gandhi's tenure as prime minister (1984-1989). Unlike the changes in policy during the 1970s and the first half of the 1980s, which were introduced in a capricious manner, the automobile policy initiatives adopted under Rajiv Gandhi were presented in a relatively less arbitrary way. The Seventh Five Year Plan, which was prepared and adopted at this time, noted that the "automotive sector is expanding rapidly and major changes in product quality and technology will be effected during the Seventh Plan period."[47]

Apart from changes in the policy toward the commercial vehicles and passenger cars, modifications were also introduced in the policy for the components, heavy commercial vehicle and two-wheeler segments. In 1985 the non-MRTP/FERA components manufacturing segment was effectively delicensed.

While the policy initiatives were less biased than before, their implementation by the Ministry of Industry was not. Compare the broad-banding policy and the earlier price control policy. The price control policy had been biased against one car segment (passenger cars) and also against one specific manufacturer (Premier Automobiles Limited). In other words, the source of the bias was the price control policy statement itself, not the manner in which the bureaucrats implemented it. In contrast, the broad-banding policy statement was clearly nonbiased, insofar as it simplified regulations and licensing procedures and sought to apply identical rules for all segments and companies. However, the manner in which the IAS bureaucrats in the Ministry of Industry implemented policy statements, clearly was biased.

Growth during the 1980s

With the establishment of MUL, production in the passenger car segment grew from 30,538 in 1980 to 176,609 in 1990. During this period, Hindustan Motors increased its production level from 21,752 to 26,204, growing at a annual rate of 5.67 percent for the decade. The increase was primarily as a result of the introduction of a new model. Production of the basic Hindustan Motors model had declined by 255 units between 1970 and 1990.

Premier Automobiles produced cars at the rate of 17. 86 percent during the 1980s. This was, in fact, the company's fastest period of growth since its first years following its establishment. In 1990, the company manufactured a total of 42,737 cars, which was five times its production in 1980. While Premier Automobiles was manufacturing nearly 8,000 of the new-model cars (introduced following the broad-banding scheme), production of the older model had grown to respectable levels by the end of the 1980s. The increase was a function of growth of production within the existing production capacity.

In only six years MUL had increased its production of cars and minivans from 12,087 to 106,956. Between 1986 and 1989 MUL's manufacture of cars and vans grew at the annual rate of 22.40 percent. Cars accounted for almost two-thirds of its 1990 production. By 1991 the licensed capacity granted to MUL (140,000) was more than that granted to both Hindustan Motors and Premier Automobiles.

Meanwhile, Standard Motors, which also had introduced a new car model under the broad-banding scheme, closed down in 1989. Labor problems were the primary factor responsible for the ending of production. Under the labor laws (outlined in chapter 2), Standard Motors was not permitted to lay off workers and dispose off its assets, and was instead required to follow the advice of the Bureau of Financial Restructuring (under the Ministry of Labor) with regard to formal exit.

In the commercial vehicle segment, TELCO remained the leading manufacturer of trucks, buses, and light commercial vehicles. Between 1980 and 1990, TELCO increased its production of buses from 7,936 to 11,514, trucks

(8 ton and above) from 23,832 to 52,080. In addition, TELCO introduced an indigenously developed light commercial vehicle in 1986, and by 1990, the company was rolling 18,235 such units off its assembly line.

Ashok Leyland, which was manufacturing 6,230 buses and 6,553 trucks in 1980, increased its production figures to 8,759 buses and 15,037 trucks by the year ending 1990. Both TELCO and Ashok Leyland are among the world leaders in the specific class (in terms of size) of commercial vehicles they manufacture. In 1988, TELCO ranked first, while Ashok Leyland was fifth.[48]

The light commercial vehicle segment, however, was beset by problems. Inefficient scales of production, high import content, and low demand led to declining profits and even losses for the manufacturers. The new entrants faced the brunt of the difficult market. In the early 1980s, the 20,000-unit market was divided among: Bajaj (50 percent), Hindustan Motors (11 percent), Standard Motors (18 percent), Mahindra (18 percent), and Premier (2 percent). By the late 1980s, the market had doubled but it now was divided among nine manufacturers: Bajaj (34 percent) , Hindustan (3 percent), Standard Motors (3 percent), Mahindra (23 percent), TELCO (16 percent), Swaraj (4 percent), Eicher (5 percent), Allwyn (3 percent), and DCM Toyota (7 percent).

Factors Underlying the Changes of the 1980s

Three factors account for the decisions regarding the establishment of the new automobile firms. First, the political leadership clearly played an important role. It is unlikely that the state would have nationalized MUL without Mrs. Gandhi's personal directive. Her interest in MUL survival ensured the establishment of the state-owned enterprise. Second, the ties of patronage between Mrs. Gandhi (and her political colleagues) and industrialists led to the licensing of the four commercial vehicle firms—Eicher Motors, DCM Toyota, Swaraj Mazda, and Allwyn Nissan. Third, close relations between the bureaucrats in the Ministry of Industry and the senior managers at MUL, and the absence of informal channels of communication between the bureaucrats and the CEOs/management of the private automobile firms, helped ensure that measures securing a protected market for the state-owned car firm were adopted and implemented.

Up until the 1980s, the political leadership had introduced changes in the policy framework; in the continued absence of any incentives or contact with the industrial actors, bureaucrats in the Ministry of Industry had merely administered those changes. With the establishment of Maruti, with its IAS management, however, the role of the bureaucrats in the Ministry of Industry dramatically changed. The esprit de corps within the IAS cadre now offered new incentives prodding the bureaucrats to modify policy in favor of MUL. As the same time, informal channels of communication between the bureaucrats and the IAS management at Maruti ensured that the Ministry of Industry was aware of the modifications required/preferred.

In the absence of channels of communication between private industry and the Ministry of Industry, and with the shift in political patronage ties away from companies such as Premier and Hindustan Motors, the biased modifications introduced by the bureaucrats were only reinforced.

Why then did the state introduce broad-banding—a policy measure intended to benefit all the automobile manufacturers? Two arguments have been offered in response to this question. According to Atul Kohli, broad-banding was part to the larger attempt by the Rajiv Gandhi government to liberalize the overall industrial policy framework.[49] Bureaucrats in the Ministry of Industry also offered this argument, stating that broad-banding was implemented solely as part of the wider policy reforms adopted by the political leadership. The second argument offered by Narayana contends that broad-banding was introduced primarily to give the appearance of even-handedness to automobile policy.[50]

Evidence appears to support the second argument. The policy modification sought to encourage automobile-product diversification. However, to introduce new products, nearly all the automobile firms required foreign technical collaboration, an issue not addressed by the policy. This left decisions about foreign technical collaborations in the hands of bureaucrats, to be decided on a case-by-case basis.

That the bureaucratic decisions were biased is clear when one considers that while only one passenger car company (MUL) was allowed to enter into a foreign technical collaboration, numerous entries were permitted in all other segments. The bureaucrats in the Ministry of Industry were clearly not interested in increasing competition in the passenger car segment.

Interestingly, while policies regarding most industries (including steel) were liberalized in 1991 as part of the International Monetary Fund/World Bank restructuring program, the automobile policy for passenger cars was left untouched. Interviews with journalists suggested that this was largely as a result of pressure from MUL, and the bureaucrats' attempt to protect the state-owned enterprise. Little else explains why when "core" industries such as steel were delicensed, and only critical ones such as defense and nuclear energy were still licensed, passenger cars remained a licensed industry. Passenger cars were delicensed in 1993 after the IMF/World Bank programs were introduced in 1991. Private automobile manufacturers were permitted to enter into collaborations with foreign firms. FERA and MRTP no longer applied to the automobile industry.

Premier Automobiles, HML, Mahindra & Mahindra, and TELCO have all entered into partnerships with international manufacturers. Premier entered into a partnership with Peugeot to manufacturer cars which would be in direct competition with MUL's products. GM entered into an agreement with Hindustan Motors to manufacture cars. Rather than import components, Hindustan Motors was to begin with the production of automobile components and then move to upstream to the manufacture of automobiles. Mahindra & Mahindra has a joint venture with Ford to assemble the Ford Escort and has plans to manufacture a second car. Diamler-Benz/Mercedes, which has had a long association with TELCO, has established a new joint venture with it. Others in the fray include Fiat, Honda with Hero Motors, Toyota with Kirloskars, Daewoo with DCM, and Mitsubishi with Hindustan Motors. Hyundai has set up a 100 percent owned subsidiary in India.

With regard to performance, the Indian automobile industry found itself in the midst of a recession following the economic crisis of 1991. The passenger car industry recovered during the next few years, and by 1993-94 the industry grew by 20 percent, by 25 percent during 1994-95, by 19 percent in 1995-96, and by 16 percent in 1996-97.[51] The decline in the growth rate by 1996-97 reflects the poor performance of especially Premier and HML. Both firms had negative growth rates that year. Increased competition, management difficulties, and labor tensions have been cited as the reasons for their declining growth. Other automobile manufacturers, including MUL, DCM Daewoo, GM, and Mercedes Benz, all performed well.

The light commercial vehicle segment grew by 13.81 percent in 1996-97, as compared to 39.19 percent in 1995-96 and by 23.24 percent in 1994-95. The heavy and medium commercial vehicle segment grew by 20.09 percent in 1996-97, by 27.10 percent in 1995-96, and by 54.60 percent in 1994-95. The two-wheeler segment grew by 12.16 percent in 1996-97, by 20 percent in 1995-96, and by 25 percent in 1994-95. The recent decline in growth has been attributed to a hike in petroleum prices, reduced government spending, and a sluggish economy.[52]

The entry of foreign automobile companies and the establishment of joint ventures in the 1990s has helped spur the components industry. Foreign car manufacturers entering India also have set up joint ventures with component manufacturing firms. The industry is thus in the midst of establishing a large number of joint ventures. The industry grew by 25 percent in 1995-96 and by 14 percent the following year. Component exports grew by almost 25 percent in 1996-97, maintaining a trend begun in the late 1980s. And as the president of the Automotive Component Manufacturers Association (ACMA) noted, "the new vehicle manufacturers from abroad are also attracting their existing component suppliers . . . to set up manufacturing bases in India."[53] Echoing sentiments similar to those expressed by Arvind Pande (chair, SAIL), automobile manufacturers and ACMA argue that the state needs to develop more responsive policies to enable the firms to increase exports, and prevent the emergence of a fragmented market structure (especially in the case of component manufacturers).

THE INDIAN AUTOMOBILE INDUSTRY IN COMPARATIVE PERSPECTIVE

The first phase of the Indian automobile industry was marked by the introduction of measures eliminating foreign competition, greatly reducing domestic competition and creating rental havens. Protectionist policies were adopted as a consequence of demands from the automobile manufacturers for a protected market and the ideological (Fabian-Socialist) inclinations of the political leadership. What enabled the manufacturers to retain a protected market and thus grow and what enabled the political leadership to maintain its ideological stance against the automobile industry and retain the support of the large manufacturers were the close relations that had developed between them since before independence.

The protectionist policies evolved (in the second phase) into a complex licensing regime, which granted Ministry of Industry bureaucrats considerable discretionary power. At the same time, changes in the constellation of political interests altered the pattern of ties between the political leadership and the industrial actors. With political patronage ties gradually undermined, the automobile manufacturers were increasingly at the mercy of the licensing regime administered by bureaucrats.

Bureaucracies that are relatively autonomous from the political leadership can and do utilize this discretionary power to introduce new and innovative policy measures. From the mid-1980s on, the Department of Electronics did precisely this.[54] Granted autonomy, and aided by its interaction with the industrial actors, the Department introduced changes within the computer policy framework. When compared to previous policies as well as to the overall industrial policy framework, these policies were clearly innovative.

However, the Ministry of Industry bureaucrats who were granted autonomy from the political leadership with regard to policy fine-tuning adopted an obstructionist approach to innovative policy formulation and industrial development. During the 1960s and the 1970s these bureaucrats were, in effect, offered incentives to obstruct rather than develop new policy initiatives regarding the automobile industry. In the absence of organizational incentives, political encouragement, and channels of communication between industry actors and bureaucrats, and in the presence of close relations between a few automobile manufacturers and the political elite, Ministry of Industry bureaucrats were neither *willing* nor *able* to respond to the needs of the sector and to foster entrepreneurial perspectives among the automobile industry elite.

By all accounts, political calculations led to the establishment of four new light commercial vehicle manufacturers and a state-owned passenger car unit in the early 1980s (the third phase). With the establishment of MUL, especially, a new dynamic was introduced in the process of automobile policy formulation. For the first time in the automobile industry, bureaucratic ties held the key to success, although only for MUL. While political encouragement (in the absence of organizational incentives) was an essential factor in promoting MUL, it was not a sufficient one. Nehru and his colleagues, promoted Hindustan Steel Limited to a similar extent, yet HSL was not as successful as MUL.

Ministry of Industry bureaucrats attempted to develop innovative policy initiatives. Unlike the Department of Electronics officials, however, they adopted this approach only with regard to the state-owned automobile company, MUL. While the Department of Electronics officials adopted policy initiatives helpful for the private firms (and even hindering the performance of the state-owned firm, Electronics Corporation of India Limited), and the Ministry of Steel bureaucrats failed to adopt such policy initiatives entirely, Ministry of Industry bureaucrats did so only with the intention of promoting the state-owned firm.

The analysis of MUL suggests that state-owned enterprises do not necessarily perform poorly. Successful performance is, however, dependent on the presence of channels of communication between the bureaucracy and the state-owned enterprises. In the case of MUL, such ties grew out of cohesiveness (and esprit de corps) of the IAS cadre. In other words, esprit de corps offered incentives that made bureaucrats willing and able to introduce policy changes. In the absence of industry-bureaucracy channels of communication, industrial actors sought political patronage ties. This, of course, further discouraged bureaucrats from being willing and able to be policy entrepreneurs. Further, while the success of the state-owned enterprise was based partly on policies restricting the growth of the private companies in the industry, in the long run the policies encouraged private automobile companies to push collectively for liberalization regarding the import of technology and capacity expansion.

What started out as a particularistic automobile policy framework acquired a broader developmentalist perspective by the early 1990s. With the delicensing of the industry, the emphasis was less on protecting one firm over the other and more about examining how the entire industry might grow. As with steel policy, the final push toward a liberalized policy framework was a result of the economic reforms of 1991. However, the initial move in this direction was established with MUL's entry.[55] Surely, without MUL's entry the private firms would not have pushed for liberal policies. Without MUL the protective niche market had substantially greater appeal. Intrabureaucratic ties and bureaucratic autonomy played a crucial role in introducing automobile policy innovations. The presence of the developmental ensemble with regard to MUL proved critical not only for MUL's success but for the transformation of the entire industry.

Consider three alternative explanations for the development of the Indian automobile industry. According to the neoclassical economic perspective, the industry during the first and second phase offers a clear illustration of the negative effects of state intervention. Automobile firms were merely responding to the constraints and incentives of the regulatory regime. But what about MUL's role? The change in the late 1980s and the early 1990s followed MUL's successful establishment. It spurred the other manufacturers to focus on improving the quality of their products, to demand lesser protection, and to be more efficient. Faced with competition and unable to counter it with the help of either political patronage ties or rent-seeking bureaucrats, private industrialists were left only with the option of improving their firms' performance. Where formerly the private manufacturers had been eager to maintain a protected market and produce substandard automobiles, they are now rapidly improving in terms of efficiency and quality in an effort to stave off competition from MUL. Thus, MUL's entry and successful performance were agents of change. State intervention in the form of a state-owned enterprise appears to have succeeded in introducing dynamism and entrepreneurship into the industry.

It does appear that under specific circumstances, state-owned enterprises can and do act as agents of economic growth. Even a recent World Bank report notes that "MUL's presence also has generated significant spillover benefits for Indian industry, particularly the auto components sector."[56] But according to the neoclassical economic perspective, state intervention via state-owned enterprises is inefficient and counterproductive. Evidence from the Indian automobile industry appears to prove this belief wrong.

The principal-agent argument offered by positive political economists is also unable to explain MUL's success. According to them, the poor performance of state-owned enterprises is a consequence of an inefficient incentive structure, which is a result of public ownership.[57] Since public managers and employees allocate resources that do not belong to them, they do not have to bear the costs (positive or negative) of their decisions. At the same time, the "owners" of the state-owned enterprises, the taxpayers, lack strong incentives and, more important, effective mechanisms to monitor the performance of the employees of state-owned-enterprises. This incentive structure for managers of state-owned enterprises and other state agencies is said to lead to inefficiencies in management and production.

Positive political economists thus argue that the below-par performance of state-owned enterprises is a consequence of the inability and unwillingness of the management of state-owned enterprises and of the state bureaucrats to adopt practices that lead to growth, productivity, and efficiency. This, is turn, is a consequence of public ownership of property. The state bureaucrats are unable to regulate the state-owned enterprise managers and provide them with appropriate inducements. In other words, problems inherent in the principal-agent relationship undermine the efficient working of the state and state-owned enterprises.[58]

The applicability of principal-agent arguments for understanding the performance of state-owned enterprises is unclear at best. Unlike the transaction cost argument offered by positive political economists, the principal-agent argument recognizes that the incentives and constraints acting upon a bureaucrat are not identical with those acting on a private economic actor or entrepreneur. The problem with the view, however, is that it does not recognize nonrational incentives and constraints that might moderate and even counter the effects of the rational incentives and constraints. The esprit de corps among bureaucrats and among bureaucrats and the state-owned enterprises managers can and does alter the incentives and constraints that each face, as demonstrated by MUL's experience. The principal-agent model, which focuses on the contractual relations between the concerned actors, needs to be supplemented with an analysis of the noncontractual relations between them.

The third counter argument is offered by the sectoral perspective. According to this view, reform of "high/high" industries is unlikely since the constellation of interests generated in such sectors tends to promote stasis over change.[59] However, while the absence of reform and change in the Indian steel industry supports this claim, change in the automobile industry does not. Both industries are high/high industries, yet one industry was easier to reform than the other. And what ensured successful reform in the automobile industry was the informal noncontractual ties between bureaucrats and MUL. While it is surely the sectoral characteristics of the automobile industry that shaped the nature of constraints, and consequently the specific kinds of policies adopted, it appears to be the case that what gave the state the ability to overcome these constraints were the organizational characteristics of the bureaucracy, the state-owned enterprise (MUL), and the relations between them. The absence of noncontractual relations between the bureaucrats and SAIL obviated the possibility of policy changes.

MUL's experience offers interesting insights into the role of labor in industrial transformation. Its experience helps us refute the argument based on South Korean and other East Asian models of growth that labor repression is an important component of states effective at promoting industrial transformation. With the state as its ally, MUL was better able to deal to with its labor. Support from the state enabled it to successfully counter the largely destructive role of national labor leaders (discussed in detail in chapter 2), to satisfy the demands of its workers without tension and acrimony (which existed in other Indian automobile firms), and to develop a corporatist firm-level arrangement. The absence of any dabbling in MUL's affairs by national labor leaders clearly helped. Thus while transforming India's labor laws is not essential for improving industrial performance, any changes in those laws that increase the voice of Indian workers rather than those of national politicians masquerading as labor leaders will help the workers.

The developmental ensemble appears to have played a key role in promoting MUL. MUL's success had the effect of injecting a much-needed dose of competition into the Indian market. Other automobile manufacturers were forced to improve their products and production efficiency even prior to the 1991 liberalization. Since 1991, the product quality and efficiency of the industry has improved, and while growth rates have picked up they remain uneven. Political encouragement for the industry is present, and bureaucrats are autonomous. What is needed, however, is the development of close relations between industrialists and bureaucrats, so bureaucrats are informed of the needs of industry. And as the next chapter argues, the developmental ensemble was present in the Indian software industry and helped promote growth not only of a few firms but of the industry as a whole.

5.

The Computer Software Industry

If the performance of the Indian steel industry has been below par and that of the automobile industry has been somewhat better, Indian computer software firms have performed phenomenally. While steel policy was retained unchanged for over four decades and automobile policy was guided by particularistic politics, computer policy has moved from being restrictive and regulatory to developmental. In other words, computer policy, and software policy in particular, now fosters "long-term entrepreneurial perspectives among private elites by increasing incentives to engage in transformative investments and lowering the risks involved in such investments."[1]

This chapter examines why bureaucrats in charge of the computer software industry were "willing and able" to act in a developmental manner, unlike those in the Ministry of Steel and Ministry of Industry. How did the relations between the different actors in the industry influence the policy changes? How did the organization of the computer industry and the organization of the Department of Electronics influence the pattern of relations?

The computer industry emerged in India during the early 1960s, and software firms took root only in the mid-1970s. In 1975 the industry exported software worth Rs. 8.5 million, a figure that increased to Rs. 30 million by 1978. Software production for domestic consumption has also grown fast, from Rs. 2.295 million in 1981 to Rs. 76.920 million in 1985. During these years software exports increased from Rs. 44.048 million to Rs. 279.93 million. The growth has been especially phenomenal since the mid-1980s; the software industry has grown by leaps and bounds. Between the years 1987 and 1997, Indian software export increased from Rs. 710 million to Rs. 39 billion. In 1996-97 the software industry earned total revenues of Rs. 64 billion.[2]

The development of the computer software industry may be divided into three phases. The first phase began with the presentation of the Bhabha Committee Report in 1966 and lasted until the late 1970s. During this period, the focus of the electronics/computer policy was on the hardware segment. The software industry was encouraged only insofar as it was essential for hardware production and development. The computer industry was dominated by state-owned enterprises and multinational companies, such as International Business Machines (IBM) and International Computers Limited (ICL). The second phase began with the adoption of the 1978 computer policy. This phase was marked by the entry of private manufacturers into the hardware and to a more limited extent into the software industry. The state-owned computer firms thus lost their monopoly status during this period. The Indian software industry entered its third phase in the mid-1980s. Since then the state has adopted a relatively developmentalist approach toward the software industry. And it is during this phase that the software industry "took off."

The basic conclusion that emerges from this chapter is that the organizational structure of the Department of Electronics facilitated the formation of noncontractual relations between bureaucrats and industrial actors. The development of these ties was also promoted by the characteristics of the industry, such as the small size of the firms, the firms' focus on the international market, and a strong industry association. In conjunction with the cohesiveness and autonomy of the Department of Electronics, these noncontractual ties encouraged bureaucrats to be "willing and able" to act in a developmental manner.

This analysis focuses on three specific issues. First, it considers the role played by the political actors in the policy formation process, examining the extent to which they have influenced the policy framework. Second, it deals with the organizational structure of the Department of Electronics, the Electronics Commission, and other related government departments. Finally, the chapter examines the effect of any interaction between senior state managers and software entrepreneurs both via formal and informal channels.

Given that the development of software policy is closely associated with the overall computer policy, this chapter examines the latter policy framework as well. I begin my discussion by reviewing the origins of the Indian computer policy and the structure of the state agencies created to develop the industry. The next section examines the development of the software industry and software policy and the factors underlying these changes. The final section focuses on inter- and intra-organizational factors influencing the shifts in both software and computer policy.

THE ORIGINS OF INDIAN COMPUTER POLICY

The origins of any concerted effort by the government of India to develop the electronics industry in general, and the computer industry in particular, can be traced to the early 1960s. India's humiliating defeat by China in the 1962 war forced a serious examination of India's defense capabilities. In particular, attention was focused on the military's electronic and information technology support systems. This review led to the development of an electronics and information technology policy.

Prime Minister Nehru's approach to the electronics and computer industry echoed his approach toward industrialization and especially toward the steel industry. The bedrock of his approach was an emphasis on centralized planning, creation of an apex planning agency, and extensive controls over private initiative. One of Nehru's first actions was the establishment of the Electronics Committee. Like the Planning Commission, which helped formulate steel policy during the 1950s and 1960s, the Electronics Committee was a committee of experts. It was assigned the task of advising the Planning Commission, the cabinet, and other ministries on issues regarding the electronics and informatics industry.

It is worth noting here that despite similar initial patterns of state intervention in the steel and computer software industries, the results have been remarkably different. While few would argue that the Indian steel industry has been a success, the software industry has clearly performed well.

Senior scientists and distinguished technocrats with academic and research backgrounds were nominated as members of the Electronics Committee. Dr. Homi Bhabha, the director of Tata Institute of Fundamental Research (TIFR), was appointed chairman.[3] With his induction into the policymaking process, other scientists at TIFR and other leading scientific institutions also became increasingly involved. Prominent scientists who followed Dr. Bhabha included: Professor Narsimhan (member, Electronics Committee); Dr. Vikram Sarabhai (second chairman); Dr. M. G. K. Menon (third chairman and first secretary of the Department of Electronics).

PHASE I: THE FOCUS ON COMPUTER HARDWARE

The Electronics Committee presented its first policy statement on electronics and computers in 1966, as part of the Bhabha Committee Report. Its main thrust was on attaining self-sufficiency while catching up with the developed countries in information technology. The Committee proposed "an all-out effort not only to design and produce the small and medium scale computers but also the components and subsystems."[4] The emphasis on indigenous production was reiterated in the 1968 report. The Committee noted that all of India's computer needs aside from large systems ought to be met through indigenous manufacture.

Apart from defining the outlines of Indian computer policy, the Electronics Committee was also concerned with developing projections of India's requirements of computers and electronics, and establishing and regulating the state-owned computer enterprises. In its 1966 report, the Committee projected, for instance, that between the years 1966 and 1976, India would require 6 large, 500 medium, and 5,000 small computers.[5]

The task of manufacturing these computers was assigned to the state-owned enterprise Electronics Corporation of India Ltd. (ECIL). ECIL was established in the late 1960s, and in its early years it was involved in the manufacture and development of electronic and computer components and systems. By the end of the 1960s, ECIL was also entrusted with the development of software packages and the manufacture of computer peripherals. The managerial cadres at ECIL consisted almost entirely of scientists. Financially supported partly by the Electronics Committee, ECIL was expected to work closely with it. ECIL, however, was placed under the administrative control of the Atomic Energy Department. This organizational structure led to considerable intra-bureaucratic struggle between the Electronics Committee and the Atomic Energy Department, over the control of ECIL. And these battles helped undermine ECIL's performance.[6]

Apart from ECIL, two multinational electronic/computer companies, IBM and ICL, operated in India in the mid-1960s. IBM had sold its products in India since the 1950s, but only in 1963 did the company begin manufacturing and assembling computer systems there. In addition, IBM was also involved in leasing, reconditioning, and renting out its products.

Operations in India, especially its rental and leasing division, turned out to be profitable for IBM.[7] In a review of the electronics industry, a Parliamentary Committee noted that "[with] regard to machine rentals . . . thousands of machines [are rented] at fixed rates . . . [and] while IBM recovers for most of the machines depreciation based on four years' life, such machines last for years and years [in India]. Another interesting feature of these rental machines is that most of them have already served elsewhere . . . the best part of their useful lives. When they became obsolete in those countries and therefore scrapped, they were being imported into India . . . refurbished and circulated, as rental machines earning revenues at fantastic rates."[8]

If IBM was criticized for supplying Indian users with outdated machines at a high price, it was also charged with leading to a net outflow of foreign exchange. A Parliamentary report noted that rather than contribute to India's self-reliance as anticipated, IBM's operations were weakening the country's foreign exchange position.

ICL also was involved in the manufacture and refurbishing of computer systems. While IBM's activities in India attracted considerable debate and comment in the political circles, ICL's smaller position in the industry enabled it to escape the harsh criticisms.

By the end of 1966, a total of 42 computer systems were set up in India. Of these, IBM had installed 31 (refurbished/new) systems. ICL and the Soviet Union had sold 2 each, and 5 systems had been purchased from other foreign manufacturers. IBM increased its sales considerably in the next five years, selling over 100 computer systems out of a total of 145. This enabled IBM to retain a market share of around 73 percent. ECIL had a 8.5 percent market share, Honeywell had 8 percent, Digital and Hewlett-Packard both had 0.7 percent. The Soviet Union had 0.7 percent market share, and other foreign companies had 1.4 percent.

During the 1960s, the Electronics Committee, which was organized in a manner similar to the Planning Commission, centralized decision making. By functioning like a "think-tank," the Committee was effective in institutionalizing the position of the electronics industry within the planning process. Its close association with the Planning Commission and the cabinet helped ensure that the interests and requirements of scientific research institutions and technical agencies within the state apparatus were accommodated in the planning process.

However, while the policymaking process was centralized, the process of policy implementation remained fragmented. Although the Electronics Committee had a central role in the policy planning process, it was not entrusted with policy implementation, given the original reasons behind the development of this industry. Rather, the task of policy implementation was assigned to the Department of Defense Supplies within the Ministry of Defense. One state agency, thus, was concerned with policy formulation and the other with implementation, and neither had control over the other. This division of labor led to considerable inter-bureaucratic tension and necessitated organizational changes by the late 1960s. According to C. R. Subramanian, the input from the Electronics Committee "did not seem to influence the bureaucrats in the Department of Defense Supplies. The Department did not take the views of the Electronics Committee seriously and considered them academic."[9]

By the end of the 1960s, this tension reached a fervent pitch. And in an attempt to mobilize support for the Electronics Committee, the chairman organized a national conference on electronics. At the conference, two critical arguments were made. First, Electronics Committee member Professor Narsimhan argued for the creation of state agencies that promoted interaction between user industries, research and development laboratories, teaching institutions, and small entrepreneurs. Second, the performance of IBM and the protected market granted to it led Professor Sarabhai, also of the committee, to argue that while international companies can contribute to the development of the Indian computer industry, they ought to be permitted to operate in India only insofar as they do not harm the national goals of self-reliant, indigenous development. While Sarabhai's views formed the core of India's regulatory computer policy for nearly two decades, Narsimhan's proposals led to the creation of the Department of Electronics and the Electronics Commission in 1970.

The Department of Electronics and the Electronics Commission

The Department of Electronics and the Electronics Commission were expected to work in conjunction with each other and were granted greater autonomy insofar as they were not placed under the control of any administrative ministry. This autonomy vis-à-vis other state agencies was expected to enhance their planning and regulatory abilities. Most of the scientists in the Electronics Committee were appointed to senior positions within the two new agencies.

The Department of Electronics differs from other administrative ministries, such as the Ministry of Industry and the Ministry of Steel, in three significant ways. First, the Department of Electronics (and the Electronics Commission) is not dominated by members of the Indian Administrative Service but by technocrats and scientists. These technocrats and scientists play a significant role in process of policy formulation. In the Ministry of Steel, for example technical specialists are decidedly subordinate to the IAS officials.

Second, unlike the Ministries of Steel or Industry whose officials (i. e., IAS members) are transferred out every five years, the technical specialists in the Department of Electronics have longer tenures. A substantial number of scientists who were inducted into the Department at the time of its establishment in 1970 continue to work there. As a result, most members of the department have developed considerable technical expertise. This is, of course, in sharp contrast to the generalist IAS bureaucrats.

Third, the long tenures of the technocrats and scientists has also fostered intradepartmental cohesiveness, which is further enhanced by the similar educational backgrounds of the officials. While such an organizational structure has allowed the Department to act in a cohesive manner, it has prevented the establishment of collegial ties with other departments and ministries.

Computer Policy of 1973-1974

The first head of the Department of Electronics and of the Electronics Commission was Professor M. G. K. Menon. Under his tenure the department retained the autarkic approach introduced by Homi Bhabha and Vikram Sarabhai of the Electronics Committee.[10] Like them, Menon emphasized indigenous development and the encouragement of the industry via close state guidance and involvement.

Menon also favored the reorganization of the state agencies concerned with the computer industry in line with Narsimhan's views presented earlier at the National Conference. He emphasized that the administration of high-technology industries ought to be placed in the hands of scientists. Menon's views, therefore, reinforced the Department of Electronics' organizational character as a scientific department staffed by technocrats and electronics specialists.

Menon's policy approach closely followed the proposals outlined by the Bhabha Committee Report and those presented at the National Conference. Under his leadership, the Department of Electronics presented its first computer policy in 1973-74. This policy specified that: (a) the requirements for large computers will be essentially met by imports during the Fifth Five Year Plan period; (b) the program aimed at self-sufficiency with regard to mini-computers and medium-size computers by the end of the Fifth Plan period; (c) the program also aimed at rapidly building up a self-sufficient industry with regard to computer peripherals, including import of know-how where required; (d) the software demand should essentially be met by an indigenous base that would be actively built up with the further aim of generating an export potential to ensure that the country would be self-sufficient with regard to the maintenance of extant computer installations.

The software policy of 1974 further specified the role of the state in this industry. In the policy statement, the Department of Electronics observed that, "the Software Industry [had] considerable potential for being developed as an indigenous industry with export potential."[11] Thus, for the first time, the software industry was recognized for its export potential. The 1974 policy went on to state that all companies entering the industry ought to be incorporated as a firm under the guidelines laid out by the Ministry of Industry.

In an attempt to promote the industry, the Department of Electronics agreed to offer time on its computer hardware facilities on a no-profit basis. The 1974 policy also permitted the import of additional hardware and software, with five provisions: (a) it is used entirely for software export-oriented activities; (b) software to the extent of 100 percent of the total cost of the system, including maintenance costs, is exported; (c) the required hardware is purchased, not rented or leased; (d) the entrepreneur would not require additional foreign exchange for maintenance and other upkeep; (e) and if the firm was unable to export the necessary software, the government retained the option to take over the hardware. In addition, the 1973 policy required all interested companies to "provide satisfactory proof of their experience and ability to make the venture a viable one" to the Department of Electronics.[12] Finally, the policy statement banned all forms of foreign collaboration.

Apart from these two industry specific policies, two other policies played an important role in shaping the computer industry: the MRTP Act (1969) and FERA (1973). As discussed in chapter 2, these acts sought to restrict large private corporations and especially multinational corporations. The adoption of FERA required all international computer firms operating in India either to dilute their equity or to leave India.

Even prior to the adoption of FERA, the Parliamentary Public Accounts Committee (PAC) had expressed strong concerns about IBM's and ICL's activities in India. As noted earlier, the PAC argued that given that IBM's operations were leading to a net outflow of foreign exchange and India's primary concern was to develop an indigenous industry, IBM's activities ought to be better regulated. The recommendations made by the PAC report were reflective of the changes in the political climate in the direction of populism.

In a memo to the PAC, the Department of Electronics stated that the FERA "required that the trading activities of foreign equity companies be severely restricted. Therefore based on the guidelines for implementing the relevant sections of the Act announced by government in late December 1973, the Department of Electronics has further reviewed the activities of IBM and ICL. This review has resulted in the Department of Electronics recommending to the [Government] that both IBM and ICL should terminate the trading and service activities within the next two years."[13] This recommendation was subsequently accepted.

After almost four years and many meetings and negotiations later, ICL gave in to the Department's demands. The Department of Electronics accepted ICL's offer to merge its two Indian subsidiaries and dilute its equity to 40 percent. The new company was called ICIM (International Computers Indian Manufacture). ICL also gave the Department of Electronics assurances regarding its proposals to assemble hardware in India and to a lesser extent export hardware from India. This seemed particularly attractive to ICL since IBM (its main competitor in India) was still in the process of negotiating its position and was likely to leave the market.

IBM did indeed opt to leave India rather than dilute its equity. IBM's decision was also the culmination of a protracted process of negotiation. Following a petition to the government, IBM continued to operate in India until 1978. Meanwhile, frantic negotiations were held between the IBM senior management and various politicians and ministers to resolve the issue. In an article in a computer magazine, a former IBM employee discussed the final meeting between the Chairman of IBM and the Indian Prime Minister, Desai: "[the] meeting was very brief, wherein the chairman of IBM . . . told . . . Desai that 'the only way we can operate is [as a] 100 per cent [owned company].' And, Desai . . . told him, 'It is your decision, if you want to close down, go right ahead. '"[14] IBM withdrew from India in 1978.

Meanwhile Burroughs, which had operated in India since the 1960s via a distributor, decided to form a partnership with 50 percent equity with a Tata company—Tata Consulting Services (TCS). The new company, Tata-Burroughs, began production in 1979 as a software exporting unit.

As noted earlier, the reorganization that led to the establishment of the Department of Electronics in 1970 granted technocrats and scientists greater authority and autonomy with regard to both policy formulation and implementation. Entrepreneurs and companies seeking to enter the industry now dealt with only one technical department—Electronics. The process of obtaining a license was simplified insofar as entrepreneurs were now required to interact with only one technical department, which, given that it was responsible for framing the policy, was in a better position to interpret it. Earlier, getting a license or permit required interaction with both the Electronics Committee and the Department of Defense Supplies.

What remained unchanged, however, was the requirement that all entrepreneurs obtain export-import permits (from the Ministry of Commerce), foreign exchange clearances (from the Ministry of Finance and the Reserve Bank of India), and an industrial license (from the Ministry of Industry). These permits and licenses had to be obtained after the approval of the Department of Electronics was received. The reorganization thus left untouched the myriad of bureaucratic rules and regulations.

As both computer entrepreneurs and IAS officials in the Ministries of Finance, Industry, and Commerce indicated, the bureaucrats in these agencies were unfamiliar with the emerging field of computers. As one IAS official put it: "We knew nothing about computers: how were we expected to evaluate applications and proposals?"[15] Granting them the ability to issue permits and licenses only complicated and delayed matters.

However, if IAS officials lacked technical knowledge, the technocrats in the Department of Electronics lacked awareness of industrial dynamics. For one, the technocrats had little practical knowledge of and interaction with the "real" industrial world. Prior to 1970 this lack of knowledge was not significant, since the focus at that time primarily was on serving the computer requirements of the defense industries via state-owned enterprises.

The 1973 and 1974 policies, however, had altered this. The focus now was on the development of private computer firms catering to more than just defense needs. And this required knowledge not just of the technical aspects of computer development or defense requirements but also of industrial dynamics and market trends. The Department of Electronics, and Professor Menon personally, were criticized for formulating policies from within an ivory tower.[16]

This problem was further compounded by the appointment of senior technocrats as CEOs of state-owned enterprises such as ECIL. While this could have helped bring technocrats closer to the real world, the opposite occurred.[17] The widespread consensus within the scientific community regarding indigenous and state-led development was partly responsible. Also responsible were the scientists' relatively comprehensive power over the policy process and the lack of competition from either domestic or international computer manufacturers. The technocrats, as a result, managed the state-owned enterprises more like research institutions than like internationally competitive firms.

The reorganization and subsequent establishment of the Department of Electronics reduced conflict among the electronic/computer policymaking and implementing agencies (insofar as it granted control over both policy formulation and implementation[18]), but it increased the extent of inter-bureaucratic conflict between the various ministries. The financial and trade aspects of the computer industry's development had to be approved by the Ministries of Finance and Commerce. Unlike the personnel of the Department of Electronics who are mostly technocrats, the Finance and Commerce Ministries are almost completely staffed by members of the Indian Administrative Service. The absence of communication networks between the Ministries of Finance and Commerce on one hand and the Department of Electronics and the Electronics Commission on the other coupled with their different agendas, led to inordinate delays in policy formulation and implementation.[19] Thus, the organizational changes, although they partly addressed the issues encountered by the state while intervening in the computer industry, also created additional problems.

The policy changes and the organizational restructuring had the following consequences: first, a market protected from international competition was created for ECIL, ICIM and Tata-Burroughs; second, technocrats who had considerable technical expertise, although they lacked familiarity with industrial dynamics, were granted greater autonomy with regard to computer policy making; third, while the "computer bureaucracy" (i. e., the agencies in charge of computer policy) were somewhat simplified, the industrial licensing requirements remained byzantine, in effect creating a market protected from domestic competition as well; and fourth, the restructuring left untouched the relationship between ECIL and the Department of Electronics. ECIL continued to be under the authority of the Atomic Energy Department. The bureaucratic battles between these two agencies over control of ECIL clearly helped undermine its performance.

Between the years 1973 and 1977 a total of 317 computer systems were sold to Indian users. Of these, 167 were developed by the state-owned ECIL. IBM's market share had fallen to 6 percent from a high of 73 percent five years earlier. Sales of ICL computers, meanwhile, increased to 21 (from 17 in the period 1967 to 1972). Other international computer companies that sold their systems in India included: Burroughs (1.9 percent), Digital (15 percent), and Hewlett-Packard (3.1 percent).

The restrictions on the import of technology and the regulatory compulsions to use indigenous technology, along with the licensing requirements encouraged few entrepreneurs to enter the industry. As a result, during the 1970s state-owned enterprises dominated the computer industry.

Despite the lackluster performance of the computer industry, the 1973 and 1974 policy framework endured largely unchanged until the late 1970s. Five factors ensured the stability of this policy. First, Prime Minister Indira Gandhi (during her first stint from 1966 to 1977) reinforced the Nehruvian emphasis on self-reliance and indigenization. The ideology of the national political leadership continued more or less unchanged.

Second, Indian scientists involved with electronics policy were very familiar with the science of computers and electronics but lacked knowledge of its industrial dynamics: how to do business, how to innovate, how to strategize, and generally how to play the game. Without the capacity to combine technical expertise and business acumen effectively, they were unable to come up with non-autarchic alternatives. Moreover, these scientists were also adherents of the Nehruvian ideology. Current Department of Electronics officials remark that they had been "brainwashed" by this ideology at that time. The ideology and knowledge of the computer policymakers was thus clearly conducive to the maintenance of the status quo in policy approach.

Third, the relationship between the Department of Electronics and other ministries, such as Finance and Commerce, created another barrier. Because of its financial and trade implications, any policy change introduced by the department required the approval of the Finance and Commerce Ministries. The technocrats of the Department and the bureaucrats at the Ministries however, came from different career backgrounds, as discussed earlier. Channels of communication between the two sets of actors were few and far between. From the perspective of the Department of Electronics getting a policy proposal through the Ministries of Finance and Commerce was an arduous task. Inter-bureaucratic obstacles thus worked against change in policy framework.

Fourth, larger financial investment by the state might well have helped the industry, but during this period the state was financially unable to make the large investments in this or any other industry. Last, the state faced little pressure from private entrepreneurs to modify the 1973 policy. The private entrepreneurs in the industry were very few and very small. The state-owned enterprises had a monopoly status, which meant that apart from Tata, none of the politically connected large Indian business houses had or considered it worthwhile to have a stake in the industry.

PHASE II: THE EMERGENCE OF THE EMPHASIS ON COMPUTER SOFTWARE

Despite these obstacles, computer policy and especially software policy was transformed significantly by the mid-1980s in a series of incremental steps. The first movement toward the transformation of policy framework may be traced to the 1978 computer policy.

Computer Policy of 1978

The 1978 Computer Policy permitted private entrepreneurs to enter the mini/microcomputer industry. Small- and medium-scale entrepreneurs were especially invited to enter. The 1978 policy noted that qualified nonresident Indians "wishing to return and invest in minicomputer related programs would be actively promoted."[20] ECIL, the state-owned enterprise concerned with the manufacture of computer systems, therefore lost its monopoly on the Indian market. The policy, however, required that applications for manufacturing computer systems and products from individuals and private groups had to be approved by the Department of Electronics and then by the Ministry of Industry, as required by the general industrial policies.

All applications for the import of computer hardware and software had to be channeled through the Department of Electronics. Following a review of the proposal, the Department would float a global tender for the computer equipment it deemed suitable. The Department would then negotiate on behalf of the actual user (e. g., a private commercial establishment, an individual, or a research institute) or hardware/software manufacturer and exporter with the international producer/seller. Finally, the Department would deliver the equipment to the applicant.

This policy approach incorporated many of the features of the overall license-permit raj. Where it differed from the Bhabha-Menon approach was with regard to the role of private entrepreneurs. While in the earlier phase, state-owned enterprises were given a monopoly over production, in the second phase of the industry's development private entrepreneurs were at best permitted to enter and at worst only tolerated. Under the 1978 policy private computer firms were, however, dependent on the technical expertise (as well as goodwill) of the officials in the Department of Electronics for their growth and operations.

The crucial consequences of the 1978 policy were neither expected nor immediate. By giving room to private entrepreneurs in the computer industry, the policy initiated a series of developments that profoundly altered the structure of the industry by the mid-1980s. And I discuss these changes in the sections below.

But first, what explains the shift in computer policy? The answer to this question lies in ECIL's abysmal production performance. ECIL was increasingly unable to meet domestic demand and was producing substandard equipment. According to Grieco, ECIL's performance was below par in three respects. First, ECIL's products were significantly more expensive than a comparable (or a technologically superior) foreign computer even after adding the various taxes and import duties. Second, ECIL's slow rate of production meant that it "was unable to make timely deliveries of [its] systems to Indian users."[21] Third, "ECIL failed to develop systems that were technically sophisticated."[22] Grieco concludes that "[a]s a result of these technical problems and high prices ECIL was unable to penetrate the Indian market deeply during the 1970s . . . in spite of all the regulatory efforts of the commission and department."[23]

In addition, the ECIL project failed due to its inability to develop adequate, especially commercial, software. In an attempt to ensure standardization of software available in India, ECIL computers were sold with software the company manufactured. The idea was to ensure that the computer industry did not develop a fragmented market structure dominated by small manufacturers and users of a wide range of computer systems, models, and software. Such a fragmented industry, it was argued, would be a greater drain on India's foreign exchange, insofar as a wider range of maintenance services and software systems would have to be imported. Thus, lack of competition, bureaucratic turf battles, and a lack of familiarity with industrial dynamics all ensured that ECIL software was of poor quality. And the policy of requiring buyers of ECIL hardware to buy ECIL software further hindered the sale of ECIL hardware to commercial buyers.

The policy of selling ECIL hardware with ECIL software had another consequence: it discouraged the growth of the private software industry. Non-ECIL hardware available at this time also contributed toward the discouragement of the private software manufacturers, since they too were sold with software packages. As a result, the 1973 computer policies fostered the slow growth of the hardware industry and by limiting the market for software, the policies also slowed the growth of the software industry.

Analysis of ECIL's buyers offers further evidence of the state-owned enterprise's lackluster performance. Statistics on the market share of the various computer firms during this period misrepresent ECIL's performance. By the 1970s ECIL had cornered around 40 to 50 percent of the computer hardware market. However, only four computer systems were purchased by private firms or other institutions between 1971 and 1978. The other institutions, state departments and universities, were compelled to buy ECIL's products by the Department of Electronics. Proposals to purchase computers by various state agencies and state-run research institutes/universities were sent to the Department of Electronics for review. Government guidelines that stipulated that all departments/ministries/state-owned enterprises purchase equipment from other state agencies wherever possible ensured that the Department of Electronics recommended ECIL products.

ECIL's poor performance led to considerable public criticism by the late 1970s, including questions in Parliament. At the same time, despite the obstacles for change within the Department of Electronics some murmurs of dissatisfaction had begun to appear. An internal panel set up by the Department had recommended that a few private computer manufacturing firms should be permitted to supplement ECIL's production. This recommendation was initially presented within the Department as a way of "reducing the burden" on ECIL rather than restricting its market. Given ECIL's inability to meet demand adequately, the improvement of the industry's overall performance became a concern especially as public criticism began to grow.[24] Internal self-examination and external criticism started coming together. It is important to note that the policy of permitting private entrepreneurs into the computer industry did not completely undermine ECIL's market. By restricting the private entrepreneurs to the microcomputer segment and by permitting the import of only large systems, the Department of Electronics was able to retain for ECIL a protected albeit limited minicomputer market.

While private manufacture of microcomputers and peripherals was encouraged, the aversion toward foreign participation remained. Permitting private Indian firms to participate was one thing; assigning a highly visible multinational corporation like IBM a role at this time was quite another. The latter was still not acceptable ideologically within either technocratic or political circles.

The 1978 computer policy began the process of transforming the software industry by encouraging private entrepreneurship. The policy changes led to the entry of small and medium-scale computer professionals/entrepreneurs from India and abroad (i. e., nonresident Indians) into the software and hardware industries. A large majority of software entrepreneurs were engineers and science graduates. And a "new environment came into being in India . . . when companies of Indian origin set up [shop]."[25] The Indian computer industry which had stagnated in terms of production and technology began to take off.

With regard to the hardware segment: ICL as discussed earlier, agreed to dilute its ownership as required by the Department of Electronics, down to 40 percent it was now renamed ICIM (International Computers Indian Manufacture Limited). Burroughs followed ICL's lead and entered the Indian market by teaming up with a Tata company to form Tata-Burroughs in December 1977. Unlike ICL and Burroughs, IBM decided to withdraw from the Indian market rather than either dilute its ownership or take on an Indian partner. And by the middle of 1978 IBM had closed its various operations in the country.

Four Indian companies took advantage of the 1978 computer policy and entered the industry. The former employees of IBM also established an independent company following IBM's departure from India. This company named International Datamatics (IDM) was, however, primarily concerned with servicing computer products (a task performed solely by ECIL until then) and also acted as a sales agent for other manufacturers. DCM Dataproducts, which had since the mid-1970s manufactured calculators entered the microcomputer segment in 1978. Hindustan Computers Limited (HCL), a company created by former DCM employees, began the production of microcomputers by the late 1970s as well.

Between 1970 and 1978, the market structure of the computer hardware segment had changed substantially. IBM's market share had decreased by a factor of ten. While ICL's market share remained more or less the same, ECIL's portion of the market had increased sixfold. The addition of four new Indian hardware manufacturers contributed further toward changing the market structure. Between 1960 and 1966 IBM had a market share of 73.8 percent and ICL had a market share of 4.7 percent. During the period 1967 to 1972, ECIL gained a market share of 8.5 percent IBM's share declined to 69.3 percent and ICL's share increased to 11.1 percent. By 1978 to 1980,

ECIL's share increased to 10.2 perecent while that of IBM and ICL declined to 0 percent and 2.1 percent respectively. The other major players by 1980 were: HCL with a 40.5 percent share of the market, and DCM with a 27.5 percent share.

The entry of Indian computer hardware firms increased the demand for domestic software products.[26] If private hardware manufacture was to be encouraged, then the availability of software had to be ensured. The 1981 software policy addressed this issue by recognizing the need to promote the software industry. However, the policy offered few new measures to promote software export and the development of the industry in general. Despite not introducing new policy measures, the very entry of manufacturers into hardware production, and the subsequent demand for software that was now required for the indigenously produced computer systems led to the growth of the software industry.

Private software manufacture had been mildly encouraged as far back as 1970. At the National Conference on Electronics, one participant proposed offering incentives to Indian computer scientists abroad to establish software firms in India. Later that same year the Department of Electronics called upon engineers and scientists to produce software for domestic production and export. Few entrepreneurs, however, took up the offer. And the software segment remained divided between international producers and ECIL.

Three factors explain why the software industry did not take off despite these offers during the early and mid-1970s. First, hardware produced by ECIL was loaded with ECIL's software and foreign computers likewise came with imported software. There was limited demand for additional indigenous software. Second, during this period software exports were the concern of a department in the Ministry of Commerce, which was staffed by bureaucrats unfamiliar with the international software industry or how to promote exports. Third, proposals for export had to be cleared by a variety of state agencies, including the Department of Electronics and the Ministry of Commerce. Complicated bureaucratic procedures, lack of incentives for export, and low domestic demand all ensured that the software industry did not boom during this period.

The circumstances, however, changed by the late 1970s. The change was primarily in terms of the growth of the private hardware segment and restrictions on the import of software ensured a growing demand for indigenous software. Further, since software exporters were permitted to import hardware at lower import duties in return for export targets, software entrepreneurs began focusing on both the domestic and international market.

Some of the entrants into the software segment following the 1981 software policy included: Applied Computer Sciences Organization, Dowell

Consultants, Infosys, Integra Micro Systems, International Systems Services, Kirloskar Computer Services, Mascon Technical Services, Mastek, Mostek Electronics, Softek, Software Research Group, and Softplus Computer Services.

These companies had to interact with the Department of Electronics to acquire a license to begin production and import the necessary hardware for software production and export. This interaction came to play a crucial role in the subsequent development of the computer software policy. Thus, apart from altering the market structure of the computer industry, the 1978 (and 1981 policy) introduced changes in the pattern of interaction between the technocrats in the Department of Electronics and industrial actors. No longer were these technocrats interacting only with other technocrats at ECIL or managers at multinational corporations. They were now interacting with small private entrepreneurs, a large number of whom had fewer than a dozen employees when they began.[27]

The policies and procedures, according to officials at the Department of Electronics, and the computer manufacturers, led to a pattern of interaction between them that was formal as well as informal. When asked what facilitated such interaction, both sets of actors identified their similar professional and class backgrounds as being central.

Interviews with both Department of Electronics' technocrats and software manufacturers suggest that the two are linked by educational and even social ties.[28] The new computer entrepreneurs were graduates of engineering colleges—such as the Indian Institutes of Technology, the Indian Institute of Science, and/or American and European universities—institutions where Department of Electronic technocrats also had been educated. Not only did this facilitate informal relations between the officials and entrepreneurs, but it also encouraged such relations among the entrepreneurs and it helped strengthen the industry association. This, as I discuss later, played a crucial role in transforming the process of policy formulation.

Both the entrepreneurs and technocrats also remarked that the long tenures of Department of Electronics officials ensured the emergence of noncontractual ties between the two. If the technocrats in the Department had been transferred frequently as the IAS bureaucrats in the Ministries of Steel, Finance, and Commerce were, it is doubtful whether such ties would have deepened.

The next crucial step in the evolution of the computer industry was the rise to power of Rajiv Gandhi in 1984. In light of his strong personal interest in the development of India's high-tech and especially its computer industry, as well as in economic liberalization, Rajiv Gandhi encouraged the Department of Electronics to change the computer policy framework further. Influenced by their interaction with the entrepreneurs and professionals on the one hand and with the push from above (i. e., the Prime Minister's Office) on the other, the Department of Electronics officials were willing and able to introduce the policy initiatives of the late 1980s.

Rajiv Gandhi's interest thus increased the autonomy of the Department of Electronics vis-à-vis other ministries and departments and reduced the extent of inter-bureaucratic tension in policy formulation. Having access to the Prime Minister was a great asset for the department. Finally, as already stated, the long tenures of the technocrats in the Department of Electronics as opposed to the transient assignments of the IAS bureaucrats encouraged long-term planning. Thus, by the mid-1980s, the institutional context in which the computer bureaucracy was placed had profoundly changed. And these changes in turn facilitated subsequent changes in policy, beginning with the 1984 and 1986 policies.

Computer Policy of 1984 and 1986

The computer policy statements of 1984 and 1986 delicensed the minicomputer manufacturing segment, reduced the restrictions on technology import by manufacturers of computer systems and subsystems, and reduced the rates of excise and import duty. The 1984 Computer Policy introduced a single-window clearance procedure. Manufacturers interested in acquiring a license for production, foreign collaborations, equipment import, and so on, would now be required to apply only to the Department of Electronics for all the relevant clearances and permits. An Inter-Ministerial Standing Committee (IMSC) met every 15 days to evaluate the applications. The IMSC was chaired by an Additional Secretary from the Department of Electronics and included a representative of: the Directorate General of Technical Development (the Ministry of Industry department, which evaluated all industrial licensing applications), the Ministry of Finance, the Ministry of Commerce, and the Planning Commission. In a further attempt to ease the bureaucratic process, the 1984 policy stated that all applications not decided after two months would be automatically cleared.

The micro/minicomputer segment was thrown open to all interested entrepreneurs. While the FERA restrictions on foreign collaborations applied, all other restrictions were eliminated. The computer industry was also exempted from the locational policy. This policy initially had been introduced to regulate the location of various firms so as to control environmental pollution, but it had increasingly been used to regionally distribute industries according to political interests.

The other major changes introduced during this period concerned hardware/software import. According to the 1973 and 1978 policies, all entrepreneurs interested in importing computer equipment for general use or software export were required to channel their purchases through the Department of Electronics. The Department was assigned the task of determining the most appropriate computer and also negotiating its purchase on behalf of the actual users. This process was, altered significantly. Applicants were now allowed to choose from a list of computer systems identified by the Department of Electronics, rather than have the selection made for them. In addition, applicants were permitted to negotiate directly with the international producer/seller. However, the Department offered to undertake the task of negotiating if the applicant so desired.

The 1984 policy modified the Department's role, reducing its regulatory activities. While an effort was made to ensure that cutting-edge computers alone were imported, users were permitted to select computers and purchase them directly. In easing the process and guidelines for computer import, the Department of Electronics moved away from its emphasis on a wholly indigenous computer industry dominated by state-owned enterprises.

If the 1984 policy indicated the shift in overall strategy, the process of its formulation reinforced this conclusion. Under Bhabha's and Menon's guidance, policies had been framed after much consultation exclusively with scientific "experts." In a significant departure, the 1984 policymaking process involved private computer manufacturers and users as well. If the various reports in the 1960s had touted the central role played by the scientific community, Department of Electronics officials were now highlighting the contribution of industrialists.

One key department of official involved in formulating the 1984 policy described the process as follows:

> ... there was a debate [in the department] whether or not [we] should float global tenders, evaluate and choose computers on behalf of every user in the country. Some of us sincerely felt that it was a nebulous task apart from being an activity which should not be taken up by the Government in an area like computers. This was discussed at the CSI [Computer Society of India] forum for two consecutive years where I had outlined possible alternatives and requested the reaction of the participants [computer manufacturers, large users, and scientists]. This interaction benefited us considerably and it turned out that there should be more competition instead of only patronizing the monopolistic trends. . . . We had framed a draft of such a policy by March 1984. [The next step was to consult senior economists in the government.] A number of computer industrialists were also consulted. Separate discussions were held by the DOE [Department

of Electronics] with them[.] . . . Discussions were also held with associations like MAIT [the Manufacturers Association for Information Technology]. In the final framework that was announced, . . . objections of MAIT and other such organizations were taken into account.[29]

The 1986 Software Policy further reflected this trend. It placed software imports under the Open General License category of imports. Imports under this category did not require a clearance or a permit. Actual users, hardware manufacturers, and software manufacturers could now import software without obtaining either a license or have the Department of Electronics "choose" the software for them. Software exporters and all other users had to pay a tax of 60 percent on imported software. Software imported by 100 percent software export units was not taxed. The import of hardware by software exporters was taxed at 60 percent. Again, 100 percent export units were not required to pay this tax.

In addition, in an attempt to stimulate exports, the Department of Electronics raised the export obligation on firms importing computer hardware for software export. While according to the 1978 policy approach firms had to export 100 percent of the cost when using their own foreign exchange resources to import equipment, they were now expected to export 150 percent of the costs. In a further attempt to encourage firms to accumulate foreign exchange via exports, the Department of Electronics specified that all firms borrowing foreign exchange from the state-run EXIM bank had an export obligation of 350 percent of the costs. The customs duty on products imported via this route were lowered from 60 percent to 30 percent.

By the late 1980s, the computer software industry had grown considerably. The list of software exporters increased from 50 companies in 1986 to 140 in 1990. The list of software exporting firms included small and large Indian firms as well as a few multinational companies. Foreign computer firms were allowed to operate in India under guidelines laid down by the Foreign Exchange Regulations Act of 1973. According to these guidelines, multinational firms could enter the Indian market only if they had an Indian partner (with at least 60 percent equity). However, 100 percent export multinational firms were permitted to operate without an Indian partner.

Among the first multinational companies to establish an Indian subsidiary was Texas Instruments (TI). The primary reasons behind this move was the easy availability of good software designers who were also inexpensive.[30] According to Richard Gall, managing director of TI (India), TI "couldn't hire enough software designers in Europe to meet demand, and India was producing more than it could use."[31] And what enabled TI (India) to optimize its use of the available talent was its ability to install its own electric generators and satellite dishes.

Thus unlike the indigenous software firms whose performance and growth was limited by the availability of datacom facilities, TI (India)'s production was not. TI (India) has grown from a company with a turnover of Rs. 41 million in 1988-89 to Rs. 128 million in 1992-93. However, the growth although substantial, has been below expectations and targets. This was due to internal management problems, not infrastructural shortages or limited resources for investment. Analyzing TI (India)'s performance, *Dataquest* notes that the "company's conservative approach in terms of dependency on the parent company, and lack of flexibility to the changing business scenario have been its major stumbling blocks."[32]

A large number of indigenous software firms have performed even better. A good example of an entrepreneurial indigenous software firm is Infosys. Infosys was established in the 1981 in Bangalore by an Indian computer scientist, N. R. N. Murthy, who after graduating had worked in France for over a decade. The initial capital base of the company was only Rs. 10,000. Infosys offers software services, turnkey projects, and packaged products. By 1993, 92 percent of the company's revenues came from exports. The company has carved a niche for itself, specializing in software for banking, manufacturing, and consumer services. Its turnover has increased from Rs. 25 million in 1988-89 to Rs. 143 million in 1992-93, an average annual growth of 50 percent. In the years since, Infosys has grown at a compound annual growth rate of over 75 percent. During the same period the company raked in net compound profits of over 75 percent as well. Infosys has played in key role in mobilizing the National Association of Software and Service Companies (NASSCOM). Its CEO was elected president of NASSCOM in 1991-92.

Patni Computer Systems (PCS) is another good representative of entrepreneurial software firms in India. PCS was established in the 1970s with the head office in Bombay and a branch in Boston, Massachusetts. Unlike Infosys, PCS is located in an 100 percent export processing zone—the Santa Cruz Export Processing Zone (SEEPZ)—outside Bombay, and hence caters only to the export market. Its location gives PCS privileged access to datacom infrastructure provided by the Departments of Electronics and Telecommunications. PCS's turnover, like Infosys's, has grown at an average annual rate of 50 percent, increasing from Rs. 41 million in 1989-90 to Rs. 168 million in 1992-93. Like Infosys, PCS has marketed itself as a developer of software for turnkey projects for CNN, General Electric, and Data General, among others.

Pentafour is yet another successful Indian software company. The company was started by Chandrasekaran upon his return from the United States. While in the United States he had worked for a software company and developed software for multimedia applications. Today, Pentafour Software is a leader in the area of computer animation in India, and is making its presence felt in the international market as well. Its turnover has grown at 80 percent annually in the past five years and profit after tax has risen by 88 percent.[33]

Future Software is another recent entrant into the software industry that has experienced high growth rates. Begun in 1985 by a computer scientist (formerly a resident of the United States), the company recorded growth rates of 50 percent in the early 1990s. Specializing in systems software and networking, Future Software has focused on exports. More than 90 percent of its total turnover comes from exports, most of which have been to the United States and Europe.

Apart from multinational and midsize companies, the industry also includes a few large indigenous companies (turnover above Rs. 200 million). One such company is a Tata group company, Tata Unisys Ltd. (TUL). Established in 1978, its products include both computer hardware and software. In recent years, however, the firm's software division has fueled its growth. TUL's turnover has increased from Rs. 331 million in 1988-89 to Rs. 910 million in 1992-92. And 80 percent of the total turnover came from software exports.

Another Tata company that is also a market leader is Tata Consultancy Services (TCS). Established in 1968, TCS is the oldest private Indian computer company. However, its growth rates have been remarkable only in the past decade. Products developed/offered by TCS include turnkey projects, software export, and packaged software. Software services export—which contributed 80 percent of the firm's turnover—increased by 37 percent in 1992-93, reaching Rs. 1.75 billion. As a result, TCS now leads Indian software firms in both overall revenue and software exports.

PHASE III: THE FINE-TUNING OF SOFTWARE POLICY

During the late 1980s and the early 1990s, additional computer policy reforms, which fine-tuned the policy framework, were introduced regularly. The changes in policies were of two kinds. On the one hand, the changes reduced the extent of regulations and licensing requirements. Import duties on computer systems were reduced. Minicomputer hardware importers are no longer required to get their purchase plans approved by the Department of Electronics. On the other hand, new measures designed to promote exports were adopted. In 1989, for instance, the Department of Electronics altered the export obligation in an attempt to further induce software manufacturers to enhance their export levels. The export obligation for the import of equipment was raised to 350 percent. The Department of Electronics became actively involved in identifying international markets and in providing marketing support.

Aside from these changes in the regulatory framework, programs aimed at offering computer entrepreneurs infrastructural support were introduced. Industrial parks with the necessary communication infrastructure for software manufacturers and exporters were established. Software Technology Parks (STPs) were started at seven locations throughout India. The export obligation for firms located in the STPs was lowered to 1.5 times the cost of the equipment imported. In addition, the Department of Electronics offered to provide core computer facilities as needed by the users.

The Department organized state visits that included computer manufacturers (and especially software entrepreneurs) to Europe, North America, and East Asia to promote the Indian computer industry. It also organized various promotion campaigns with help from Indian missions in Europe and the United States. In a report, the Department of Electronics noted that these campaigns "did succeed in helping the companies in overcoming the credibility problems [and] helped in establishing the contacts which later materialized into business deals."[34]

In 1990 the Department of Electronics and the European Commission signed a memorandum of technical cooperation. As part of the cooperation, the two agencies organized eight workshops in various European cities bringing together Indian software entrepreneurs, European businesspeople, and Department of Electronics officials. The participating Indian software firms were medium sized and included among others Mastek, Hexaware Infosystems, and Think Systems.

The Department of Electronics along with the European Union also established a center in India to promote software exports to Europe. A Department official noted that this "will be our window to Europe. It will help Indian exporters set their quality to match new European standards."[35] After the first year the software center was expected to be run by industrialists and manufacturers from both India and the European Union.

The Department has also lobbied, on behalf of the computer industry, with the Department of Telecommunications for the creation of the required infrastructure facilities.[36] In an interview the Electronics Secretary identified the Department's role as follows: "The industry has to deal with various agencies like customs and excise, commerce, and financial institutions. In these areas, we have been acting as friend, philosopher and guide of the industry. For example, there was a complaint that banks were not extending consumer finance for purchase of electronic equipment. [When this came to my knowledge I] immediately took up the issue. Banks have given a positive reply and this we have communicated to industry. Take the area of customs duty. We always take up the issue with the finance ministry."[37] The Secretary further noted that the fine-tuning of the policies "would not have been possible but for that alliance. The Department of Electronics acts as the champion of the industry and there is continuous interaction with other [government agencies]."[38]

In an address to NASSCOM in 1991, the Secretary of the Department of Electronics, N. Vittal, noted that the relationship between the state and industry has undergone a transformation in the past decade. He remarked that the relationship, especially in the software sector, is one of strategic alliance. And this alliance, he argued, has been essential for "getting the policies suitably tuned to meet the needs of the industry."[39]

During the early 1990s the Department of Electronics introduced further modifications in the policy structure. First, profits from software export were exempted from income tax. Second, customs duty on software imports for exports were significantly lowered. Third, to ensure the availability of trained personnel the Department of Electronics launched an accreditation scheme for private educational institutions. Fourth, such institutions are now permitted to import necessary computer systems for training with a low rate of customs duty. Fifth, the export obligation for hardware/software import by software-export firms was lowered to 300 percent and the import duty (or customs duty) was lowered to 25 percent. Sixth, regulations regarding the availability of foreign exchange for software exporters was eased. Seventh, the export obligation for units in STPs has been simplified. And finally, communication facilities for software units located in STPs have been improved.

As part of the new liberalization measures, the government introduced a new export-import policy that covered computers in April 1991. Unlike the software manufacturers, who had consistently been demanding fewer regulations and a more open market, the hardware manufacturers sought the extension of a protected market. The software manufacturers had all along welcomed multinational software firms, regarding them as a source of contacts, technology, and greater visibility. And since the 1991 liberalization, hardware manufacturers have frantically lobbied the government to retain the policy protections against imported assembled computer hardware products.

MAIT (the hardware manufacturers' association) called for: (a) restrictions on the import of computer systems; (b) a licensing policy for the import of circuit boards; (c) no restrictions on the import of components by manufacturing firms; and (d) competent manufacturers assigned as designated maintenance firms that would provide the comprehensive maintenance of imported computer systems.

While the 1991 export-import policy retained some restrictions on computer imports, recent policies have introduced more liberal measures. Under these policies restrictions were placed on the import of microcomputers alone, larger computers could be freely imported. Subsequent policies have lowered the value limit on microcomputers, which has enabled the import of smaller computers without restrictions.

According to Sharma, what ensured that at least some of the hardware manufacturer's demands were accepted was: "A series of representations and meetings, hours spent on discussions, and a cohesive voice of the industry chieftains. For once the industry held hands together, forgetting past differences and prolonged bickering that once marked its functioning."[40]

Two factors prevented the hardware firms from succeeding fully in their attempt to lobby the government. First, under Vittal the Department of Electronics had increasingly adopted an antiregulatory-protectionist stance. Given the success of the software industry, Department officials were loath to retain, let alone introduce, additional licensing requirements and regulatory policies. And this stance was also supported by the change in the national economic climate by 1992. Second, export-import policies are decided by the concerned administrative department (here the Department of Electronics) and the Ministry of Commerce. While long-term patterns of interaction had been established between the computer firms and Department officials, such ties had not quite developed between the firms and the IAS bureaucrats in the Ministry of Commerce.

Interestingly, while the Ministries of Steel and Industry tended to have an inward focus, and at best never exhibited an outward interest, the Department of Electronics, especially during the 1990s, appears to have been acutely aware of the performance of other countries in the software industry. This, of course, is in sharp contrast to the perspective adopted by the same department during the 1960s and early 1970s. Not only did the Department of Electronics examine the performance of industrialized countries, but it also studied the development of the software industry in competing countries.

The focus has also shifted with regard to domestic competition. While in the 1960s and 1970s computer hardware and software policy aimed at promoting a few firms (state-owned or private) in a protected environment, in the 1990s the aim has been to create a competitive industrial structure open to all firms. In a seminar organized by the United Nations in Delhi in 1991, Secretary Vittal argued that the "challenge before us . . . is: can we create a . . . situation of intense [competition] in our country?"[41]

Other changes during the 1990s have included a major reorganization of the Department of Electronics, with existing organizational structure being replaced by one more streamlined and industry-promotion oriented. The Department is now divided into four wings: Industrial Promotion, Infrastructure, Technology Missions, and Services. While the Industrial Promotion division is assigned the task of overseeing exports, interacting with the Ministries of Finance and Commerce, and customs issues, the Infrastructure division is concerned with software development, satellite communication, and the software technology parks.

To boost the performance of software exporters, income tax laws applicable to software entrepreneurs have been modified. As noted earlier, under the 1991 policy change, profits from software export have been exempted from income tax.[42] In 1993 the Reserve Bank of India and the Ministries of Commerce and Finance approved a software duplication policy under which no import duty is applied to software duplicated in the country. Until 1993, if a firm imported a software package and duplicated it for its employees use, the firm had to pay an import duty for every copy it made of the imported software.

This analysis suggests that four factors have enabled the fine-tuning of software policies since the mid-1980s. First, the pattern of informal interaction developed during the 1980s with software entrepreneurs helped Department of Electronics officials understand the needs of the industry and what it would take for the industry to grow. Second, this pattern of interaction was facilitated by the industry association, NASSCOM. Periodic meetings and seminars organized by NASSCOM offered a forum to exchange ideas and information between industry and the state.

Third, the presence of a few IAS bureaucrats in the Department of Electronics facilitated interaction with various ministries, such as Finance and Commerce. For the first time since its creation, a member of the Indian Administrative Service was appointed as the head of the Department in 1987. His preexisting ties with his colleagues in the Ministries of Commerce and Finance helped interbureaucratic interaction. Impossible in the past, the channels of communication made fine-tuning policy much easier.[43] With an IAS member (the Secretary of the Department) lobbying on behalf of industry, proposals for policy change were accepted much more easily by other ministries.

Finally, the lack of constraints on the bureaucrats' autonomy also played a crucial role. Restrictions on the autonomy of Department of Electronics officials' to act in a developmental manner could have come from three sources: trade unions, political leadership, and industrial actors. Since there are no trade unions in the computer software industry, the possibility of the trade union federations influencing Department of Electronics technocrats/bureaucrats does not arise.[44]

As the discussion earlier indicates, the political leadership, rather than constraining developmental action by the Department of Electronics, was actively encouraging such action. Especially under Rajiv Gandhi, the political leadership was interested in promoting the computer industry. Political interest in micromanaging industrial policies arises when either the politicians can use the policies to gain financial support for their party from large industrialists, or when the industry is a large employer whose workers can potentially be mobilized for electoral purposes. The computer software industry had neither large industrialists nor was it a large employer. Consequently, the political leadership's interest in the industry, apart from the encouragement Rajiv Gandhi offered, was almost nil.

Software entrepreneurs could have restricted bureaucratic autonomy by developing clientelistic ties with the bureaucrats, but they did not for three reasons. First, the industry was dominated by small firms that lacked the resources to capture all or even one of the bureaucrats/technocrats in the Department of Electronics.[45] Second, even if computer software firms had the resources to capture Department officials, they were uninterested in doing so. The public goods (i. e., satellite facilities) that these entrepreneurs sought could not be provided on an individualistic basis. It made sense for any software firm requiring these facilities to seek them collectively rather than capture individual bureaucrats. And, of course, given the overwhelming focus of the firms on the international market, capturing bureaucrats was not the right way to go, since what they sought were policies that nurtured growth, not protected markets and particularistic bureaucratic largesse. Finally, the presence of a strong, relatively coherent, and successful industry association also preempted any interest on the part of software entrepreneurs to capture bureaucrats. The industry association was able to obtain the necessary response from the Department of Electronics. The existence of noncontractual ties between the industrialists and Department of Electronics bureaucrats provided an additional avenue for interaction, discussion, and persuasion. With little interest in a protected market and having channels through which their demands could be articulated successfully, the software manufacturers had little interest in establishing clientelistic relations with Department of Electronics bureaucrats/technocrats.

Given that nearly all computer software firms were small and hence could not capture Department of Electronics officials; that even those that could afford to capture them, did not want to do so; and that the computer software industry association was able to obtain most of the help and benefits they sought, they (i. e. the software firms) placed no restrictions on bureaucratic autonomy. For these reasons, Department of Electronics officials did not develop clientelistic ties with industrial, political or trade union actors.

While the autonomy resulting from Rajiv Gandhi's leadership and interest had aided policy changes in the mid-1980s, the enhanced embeddedness—more ties and channels of communication—of the Department of Electronics within the state apparatus facilitated the changes thereafter. A push from the political leadership was instrumental to begin with. The sustenance of policy change, however, depended on the autonomous bureaucrats having noncontractual ties with software entrepreneurs.

Growth of the Industry during the 1990s

Between 1992-93 and 1996-97 the software industry grew at an average annual rate of 52.61 percent. The export segment grew by 53.20 percent, while domestic software grew just a little slowly at 51.88 percent.[46] During this period the industry's base widened considerably. While the industry's leading companies are indeed large firms with turnovers in the Rs. 500 to 1,000 million range, the number of small- and medium-scale companies has been growing. About two-thirds of all software firms are classified as small-scale firms under the India's licensing laws. As of 1992 there were 324 domestic software companies. Of these, 57.5 percent had less than 20 employees, 72.5 percent under 30 employees. Only 8 percent employed more than 100 employees.[47] Of the 223 software export firms, 46.5 percent have less than 20 employees, 71.6 percent have fewer than 40 employees. Only 7.5 percent have more than 100 employees.[48]

In the past few years a growing number of firms in the software industry have been established by nonresident Indians. One firm established during the 1990s was American Systems International Inc., a firm owned by a nonresident Indian. American Systems International Inc. entered into a tie-up with an indigenous firm, NELCO (an electronics manufacturer), to develop software. Another Indian software exporter, Andhra Pradesh Technology Services Ltd., formed a joint venture with two nonresident Indians in 1991-92. The firm is engaged in software export.

Multinational firms, including IBM, have entered the Indian market. Motorola, Hewlett-Packard, Apple Computer, Sun Microsystems, Intel, and Dell Computer have all either set up wholly owned export units or joint ventures (for both the domestic market and for export) or are in the process of doing so.

Identifying the advantages of the Indian market for multinational corporations, the *Wall Street Journal* noted that

India is a springboard to several markets. There is India's small but growing personal computer market. . . . Annual PC sales are expected to more than double in the next five years. . . . There's also the export market: Skilled labor is relatively cheap, so hardware companies can assemble their products here for shipment abroad. Finally, there's the fast-growing international software market: Indian engineers are among the world's best at meeting the complex programming needs of big computer companies.[49]

By 1996-97, there were 425 domestic software firms and 360 firms in the export segment. And continuing the trend, a large number of companies in both segments are small, employing under 10 people. The industry's high rate of growth established in the late 1980s continues. It grew by 53.84 percent in 1996-97; exports grew by 45.09 percent. These rates of growth of production and of export are expected to continue.

Large industrial houses, other than Tata, have entered the software segment in recent years. Given the low capital required and the high returns, business groups such as Parry's, Bangur's, Parle, and Duncan's set up their own software division catering to exports. They are expected to do well, especially since most of them already have offices in a number of countries.

In another development, software exporters are increasingly focusing on niche markets rather than working on turnkey projects (i. e., complete projects involving multiple tasks). Firms have increasingly moved away from on-site services to offshore services located in India. The improved availability of communications links at reduced prices has been one factor in this shift. It has also led to a spurt in the number of software exporters establishing offices and marketing alliances abroad. Setting up "offices or subsidiary companies abroad [has] contributed actively to the revenues, and investing in them has become a major growth strategy for companies [such as Infosys]."[50]

There has also been an increase in the sales and development of Indian packaged and semi-packaged software as opposed to "bodyshopping," which involves not the manufacture of software in India, but rather, Indian scientists and programmers traveling abroad to the client's workplace to develop software on-site. Examples of packaged software include: Executive Desk from Soft Plus, Marshall by Ramco, COSL's Finware, DMAP and Bancs2000 from Infosys, and Indus Software's uBridge Synthesis. Infosys, for example, has projected that most of its earnings of $120 million by 2000 will come from its products rather than its services. To develop an internationally competitive technological base, Infosys has launched the largest ever flotation of American Depository Receipts by any Indian company. It is the first Indian company to be listed on an American stock exchange.[51]

The Indian software industry has clearly moved along. In an interview a Pakistani bureaucrat indicated that Pakistan's tiny software industry has taken off because India's is moving away from bodyshopping; Pakistani software firms are picking up the bodyshopping work that Indian companies are turning down.[52]

Reviewing the performance and prospects of the Indian software industry, N. N. Sachitanand notes that conditions "seem to be right for the growth of the Indian software industry. Import of contemporary platforms is easier and customs duties are going to be brought down. The number of satcom data links is going up. Export demand is increasing. [And] project management skills are improving."[53] The software industry has performed very well during the 1990s (it has the fastest growing export rates in India), and it is beginning to move up on the technological scale.

The hardware segment has been less successful. The easier import procedures and lower duties during the early 1990s made state-of-the-art hardware available at prices comparable to the older-generation products manufactured domestically. Although the segment achieved sales of $2.03 billion in 1996-97, an increase of around 29 percent, the industry does not appear particularly poised to advance technologically or to become independently internationally competitive. The high growth rates reflect a booming domestic hardware market thanks to a declining product prices and an expanding Indian middle class.

The liberalization of entry regulations has meant that most personal computer manufacturers have entered into various kinds of partnerships with Indian hardware firms. Multinational corporations account for around 40 percent of the Indian market share, and estimates indicate that this is likely to increase rapidly in the coming years. The entry of multinational corporations along with the elimination of tariffs on computer imports, as Anand Parthasarathy notes, is likely to reduce "the computer [hardware] industry . . . to an efficient screw driver operation."[54]

The hardware industry, led by MAIT, had, as noted earlier, called for a reduction in tariffs on computer components so as to spur India's computer assemblers. In response, the government has further reduced duties on computer hardware to 10 percent for computer components, such as populated boards, storage devices, and monitor tubes. The duty on complete assembled computer systems has been maintained at 20 percent. The industry is less happy about the adoption of the World Trade Organization's (WTO) recommendations for zero duty by 2002. This has prompted Indian hardware firms to enter into joint ventures or partnerships rather than remain competitive independently. All but one of India's hardware companies have found it viable to jettison "their own brands and [sell] internationally well known brands."[55] In addition, smaller hardware firms have become importing computer components, purchasing monitors, keyboards, power supplies, and containers locally and assembling cheaper PCs.

The result of these developments in the computer industry is that, while the software industry appears closer to be establishing itself as a product developer, the hardware industry has almost stopped focusing on product development and has shifted to the development of marketing techniques.

INDUSTRY ASSOCIATIONS

In addition to the individual interaction between software entrepreneurs and Department of Electronics officials, the two industry associations have come to play a central role in the process of policy formulation. NASSCOM (the software manufacturers association) and MAIT (the computer manufacturers organization) have interacted frequently with the Department of Electronics. Annual industrywide meetings, monthly discussion groups, and seminars have been organized (often jointly) to inform both the entrepreneurs and the bureaucrats.

By the late 1980s, the two computer manufacturers associations had become powerful cohesive actors playing a central role in policy formulation. They displayed remarkable capacity for collective action. In an article the executive director of NASSCOM noted that industrialists regard the cooperation between the Department of Electronics and the industry in the formulation of policies as an important factor behind the growth rates of the industry.[56]

In a report prepared in 1992, NASSCOM made the following recommendations to the Department of Electronics: (1) Ensure that the software companies, and marketing firms are able to offer trained graduates the "best" work environments so as to dissuade them from seeking jobs abroad. (2) Provide the software industry with adequate communications facilities. It noted that with "good communications, companies . . . need not make massive individual investments on computer hardware/software but prefer to share these resources wherever required."*(3) The Department of Electronics ought to focus on building up the image of the industry abroad, by organizing delegations, participating in seminars and exhibitions, and issuing advertisements.

Interestingly, while the recommendations made by Association of Indian Automobile Manufacturers or Steel Furnance Association of India often fell on deaf ears in the Ministries of Industry and Steel, the recommendations made by NASSCOM have received wide support within the Department of Electronics. In a recent article, for example, a Joint Secretary in the Department echoed the recommendations made earlier by NASSCOM.[57] He noted that to promote the software industry, the Department of Electronics ought to focus on strengthening the educational and training facilities, providing high-speed datacom links, and helping companies that are entering the international arena market themselves.

---

* NASSCOM, *The Software Industry in India-1992,* New Delhi: NASSCOM, 1992.

What explains the successful collective action on the part of the computer manufacturers? After all, in steel, the many mini-steel plants never became a collective force.

Three factors help explain this. First, unlike steel producers, computer manufacturers were not concentrating on the domestic market alone. Their focus on exports meant that every producer could participate in a growing market without feeling threatened. There was room for cooperation. Second, the manufacturers also needed the Department of Electronics for specialized infrastructural support, such as satellite facilities and telecommunication links. Given the costs and nature of these facilities, they could not be provided for some manufacturers and not for others. If, however, a large number of manufacturers demanded them, the likelihood of their provision by the state increased. Standing alone, the new entrepreneurs could lose; standing together, they benefited a great deal. This realization facilitated collective action. The mini-steel plants did not require the intervention of their administrative ministry, the Ministry of Steel, to the same extent. There was nothing comparable to satellite facilities, for example. The infrastructure required by the mini-steel plants, electricity and water supply, was under the administrative control of local authorities and also could be provided on a particularistic basis. Providing one mini-steel plant with adequate water and electricity did not require the state to provide other plants with the same facilities. To the contrary, doing so generally meant cuts for other users. Hence there was no incentive to lobby the central government collectively.

Finally, computer manufacturers, given the small size of their operations, depended on the state and in particular the Department of Electronics to help them enter new international markets. The organizing of a variety of state visits, international seminars, and trade fairs enabled the computer firms to extend and strengthen their operations. Of the two associations, NASSCOM was relatively more successful in influencing computer policy. Dominated by exporters, and dependent on the communication links provided by the Department of Electronics, its members saw relatively greater value in having the Department as an ally in international markets.[58] The absence of an export focus among the mini-steel plants was yet another factor precluding their collective organization.

THE INDIAN SOFTWARE INDUSTRY
IN COMPARATIVE PERSPECTIVE

From a policy that all but discouraged private entrepreneurship and had been dominated by state-owned computer firms during the 1960s and 1970s, computer software policy moved to one that actively sought private investment, and presented itself as being very private industry friendly (during the 1980s and 1990s). These policy changes succeeded in altering the structure of the software industry. The industry, which was dominated by slow growing state-owned computer firms and had few private Indian entrepreneurs, is now dominated by private entrepreneurs and has been growing at a compound annual rate of around 52 percent since 1992-93.

A number of factors have contributed to the transformation of software policy: autonomy of the technocrats from industrial interests; informal ties between the technocrats and software entrepreneurs; a few IAS officials within the Department of Electronics; the small size of the majority of firms; a strong and cohesive industry association; and political encouragement from above.

The bureaucrats/technocrats in the Department of Electronics are relatively autonomous. What has prevented their capture by entrepreneurs was the small size of most firms. Most firms are too small to afford to capture Department of Electronics officials. Meanwhile, the informal ties between the bureaucrats and the entrepreneurs helped inform the former of the policy changes required for development.

Since the technocrats in the Department of Electronics were not members of the IAS, they were unable to avail themselves of intra-IAS ties to get the required approval of the policy changes from the Ministries of Finance, Commerce, and Industry. The presence of a few IAS bureaucrats within the Department of Electronics, however, helped ensure that the proposed policy changes were approved and adopted relatively easily.

The presence of a strong and cohesive industry association also enabled the Department of Electronics to fine-tune software policy. This association helped inform the technocrats/bureaucrats of the industry's dynamics and the changes necessary for growth. The industry association was strong and cohesive as a result of three interrelated factors. First, software manufacturers were not concentrating on the domestic market alone. Their focus on exports meant that all firms could participate in a growing market without feeling threatened by each other.

Second, the firms' required state support with regard to the provision of other collective infrastructural facilities by the Department. Since these facilities could not be provided for only some members, strengthening the industry association and demanding the infrastructure collectively helped. Third, the firms needed the state to help them enter new international markets. In the relative absence of competition among themselves and unable to capture the technocrats individually, the software firms were left with no alternative but to strengthen their association and thus gain the Department's support.

Thus, autonomous technocrats, having informal ties with software entre-preneurs, were willing and able to act in a developmental manner. The pres-ence of a few IAS officials within the department, a strong and cohesive industry association, and political encouragement from above further rein-forced the Department of Electronics ability and willingness to respond to the needs of the entire industry.

Two counter explanations need to be considered. First, the neoclassical argument: the software industry in India took off from the 1980s onward be-cause the level of state intervention declined. In other words, did fewer reg-ulations lead to growth? The analysis presented in this chapter indicates otherwise. A review of software policy clearly suggests that the level of state intervention in the industry did not decline substantially until the reforms of 1991; and that the Department of Electronics' policies played an important role in facilitating the growth of the industry. Keeping the state out of the in-dustry would not have worked. While private telecommunication companies could have provided the infrastructural facilities, private firms are unlikely to have organized international trade missions. The state's helping hand was present and essential. A close examination of the policy changes, especially during the late 1980s and early 1990s, indicates that the policies were not so much liberalized as fine-tuned. In other words, the policy framework was not eliminated but frequently modified. Given this, it seems inappropriate to ar-gue that policy liberalization led to growth.

The second explanation is the sectoral explanation. According to this ex-planation, software is more likely to perform better than either steel or auto-mobiles because the sectoral imperatives of the industry generate politics conducive to policy change and reform. Politicians in the software industry, the argument goes, face fewer restrictions when it comes to modifying policy.

This explanation, too, is inadequate. If the sectoral imperatives of the software industry enabled growth in the mid- through late 1980s, why did it not do so earlier? And the explanatory framework certainly cannot explain the reforms in the Indian automobile industry. Here was an industry that, ac-cording to the sectoral explanation, was less amenable to reform than say the software industry. Yet by the late 1980s, it had been significantly altered.

We also need to consider a third, popular explanation for the success of computer software and Maruti Udhyog Limited (MUL), and the failure of the steel industry in India. According to this view, political encouragement and support was present for MUL and for the software industry but was absent in the case of steel. Indira Gandhi and Rajiv Gandhi took a personal interest in MUL, and Rajiv Gandhi took a personal interest in high-tech industries. It is this interest that ensured that the state would promote them. While this explanation has a popular appeal, it is clearly an inadequate one. It ignores the extent to which Nehru and his colleagues promoted steel. Interviews with MUL officials and Ministry of Industry bureaucrats suggests that Rajiv Gandhi in fact did not take a personal interest in MUL.[59] It was, after all, a firm founded by his brother Sanjay, and the two did not get along too well. Second, Rajiv Gandhi took a personal interest in the entire computer sector, not just in the software industry. Yet India's computer hardware industry continues to be a weak performer. Political encouragement cannot be the entire explanation for the success of the software industry. As this chapter has argued, political encouragement played a key role in making bureaucrats willing to adopt policy changes. It cannot also make them able to adopt effective policies. What enabled bureaucrats to do this was the pattern of interaction between them and industrial actors. Informal relations between them acted as a conduit for the transfer of useful information about industry needs. What appears to have emerged in the software arena are overlapping circles of trust. The technocrats/bureaucrats in the Department of Electronics were held together by an esprit de corps that generated shared understandings and trust. The IAS members of the department were part of the wider IAS community within the state. Software manufacturers united to form NASSCOM. And much more than in the case of the steel or the automobile industry in India, software manufacturers together with the members of the department formed a community. Close, informal relations within each of these communities helped develop bonds of trust, which translated into more responsive policy. This, then, is key lesson that the Indian software experience offers for understanding how entrepreneurial bureaucrats emerge and how states can promote industrial transformation.

Understanding the Japanese experience is important here.[60] The developmental ensemble appears to have helped the Japanese software industry perform well not only during its initial years but later on as well. As Japan specialists and comparativists have documented, the state in Japan was at once autonomous and had close and informal ties with industry leaders.[61] Politicians encouraged bureaucratic innovativeness, and the state apparatus has been cohesive with a strong esprit de corps. In the discussion below I reinterpret the evidence gathered by these scholars using the concept of the developmental ensemble.

Japan is the third-largest producer of software in the world today (after the United States and the European Union). And as with most other Japanese industries, the large conglomerates, or the *zaibatsus,* dominate the software industry. Over 80 percent of software produced in Japan is proprietary, software developed by Japanese firms such as Fujitsu, NEC, and Hitachi. The software industry in Japan emerged as the *zaibatsu*-established software divisions to develop in-house software necessary for high-tech scientific and entertainment products. "The original software industry consisted of spin-offs of [the *zaibatsus*]. These spin-offs are organized into software factories to develop custom software for these operating systems and to meet particular business' needs, often using custom programming languages."[62] As a result, Japan is not a large exporter of software products; and "most Japanese software exports are entertainment or game software" and are exported as part of other products.[63]

Consequently, to understand the role of the Japanese state in promoting the software industry, we really need to understand how the state intervened in the electronics and semiconductor industry. According to Hart, the Japanese state "played a key role in the late 1970s in bringing the firms up to internationally competitive standards in technology and prices by subsidizing R&D [research and development] and organizing R&D consortia."[64] During this period MITI "sponsored a 10-billion-yen program to develop a super high-performance computer at the Electro-Technical Laboratory (ETL). Hitachi was chosen as the lead firm in this program. Hitachi, Fujitsu, and NEC were responsible for developing mainframe hardware; Toshiba, Oki, and Mitsubishi were to develop optical-character-recognition hardware, *kanji* displays, and high-quality cathode ray tubes (necessary for displaying the more complex *kanji* characters); Hitachi and Fujitsu were to develop new disk drives; a software consortium of major firms, the Japan Software Company, was to develop software."[65] The Japan Electronics Computer Corporation (which MITI established in 1961) also brought together computer industry actors and the state and was used to channel state subsidies to the firms.

Thus, as a result of the dominance of the *zaibatsus* in the software industry, the pattern of relations between industry actors and the state discussed in chapter 3 applies to the software industry as well. The relations between the Japanese software manufacturers and the state have been close, informal, and cooperative. This interaction between MITI and the leading industrialists has been accompanied by considerable bureaucratic autonomy, from both the political elite and societal/industrial interests. The Japanese political system enabled politicians to encourage bureaucratic action and to "create space for bureaucratic initiative unconstrained by political power."[66] Autonomy from industrial actors, as Richard Samuels clarifies, "was induced through a process of reciprocal consent—that is, the Japanese state has a strategic role less because it leads than because it negotiates its authority."[67]

Considering the Japanese software industry is useful for understanding the Indian software industry. It suggests ways in which the developmental ensemble may be strengthened in the Indian software industry so as to promote the industry not just in its early years but later as well. The central lesson for India from the Japanese experience is that the continued presence of the developmental ensemble matters. These institutions emerged in India in a rather fortuitous manner. The challenge for both the Indian state and the software manufacturers association is to maintain them. The adoption of structural adjustment policies in 1991 has fostered a climate critical of state intervention.

However, as the Japanese experience suggests, it would be a mistake for the Department of Electronics and NASSCOM not to maintain the close informal pattern of interaction they have had. This lesson is, of course, applicable not simply for the Indian software industry but for the steel and automobile industries as well. The responses of the industrialists in the latter two industries indicates that they would more than welcome closer interaction with ministry bureaucrats. Industry-specific associations also need to be strengthened. Interactions between industry associations and bureaucrats are more likely to lead to policies benefiting the industry as a whole than are interactions between individual industrialists and bureaucrats.

6.

Rethinking the Developmental State

U nder what circumstances is the state likely to foster long-term entrepreneurial perspectives among the industrial elite and thus promote
development? In the context of the development of the steel, automobile, and
computer software sectors, this question can be disaggregated into three specific questions. First, why did the state not change its policy response to the
steel sector given its poor performance? Second, why did the state-owned automobile firm perform well while the state-owned steel plant did not? Third,
why did the state adopt a developmentalist approach with regard to computer
software and not for steel and automobile.

Answering these three questions is critical for understanding the factors
underlying the performance of the three Indian industries studied, and it
also contributes towards the debate about the state and industrial development. By extension, it helps to explain why Japanese and South Korean bureaucrats so often have been developmental, and their counterparts in
countries as diverse as India, Venezuela, Brazil, and Nigeria so often have
not. My aim has been to rework recent explanations in the context of a different set of empirical cases. Via their comparison, old arguments may be
refined and insights gained.

First I answer the three comparative questions just raised. Next I review the theoretical framework developed in chapter 1. The last section
examines the implications of my comparison of the Indian steel, automobile, and software industries for the debate about the role of the state in industrial development.

ANSWERING THE THREE COMPARATIVE QUESTIONS

Indian steel policy remained more or less unchanged for over four decades. During this period the performance of the steel industry declined. The rate of growth of steel production declined, and in some years the absolute production level fell as well. Levels of capacity utilization remained low. The state-owned steel plants administered by the Ministry of Steel were, in particular, poor performers. And the industry as a whole was not internationally competitive. Why did the poor performance of the state-owned plants not induce the Ministry of Steel bureaucrats to modify steel policy? Why, in the face of the overall declining performance, did steel policy remain more or less unchanged?

The answer partly lies with the structure of the bureaucracy and the inability of the elite Indian Administrative Service (IAS) bureaucrats in the Ministry of Steel to act in an entrepreneurial and innovative manner. The structure of the IAS, with its frequent transfers, generalist training, and few organizational incentives to introduce policy changes, ensured that the IAS officials who occupied a dominant position in the Ministry of Steel had limited ability and interest in introducing responsive policies.

What also appears to have inhibited policy change was the absence of channels of communication between the managers at the Steel Authority of India Limited (SAIL) and the IAS policy formulators, together with the greater authority of latter over the former. The greater authority of the IAS bureaucrats, along with their frequent transfers and their cohesive cadre structure, discouraged the transfer of information from managers at state-owned enterprises to the IAS bureaucrats in the Ministry of Steel. Without the necessary information, the bureaucrats lacked the knowledge of which policy changes would be effective. Thus, the pattern of relations between the managers at SAIL and the IAS bureaucrats—in particular, the absence of noncontractual relations between them—hindered the transfer of information from SAIL to the Ministry of Steel.

Moreover, the pattern of relations also had the effect of restricting the autonomy of SAIL managers. These constraints on their autonomy undermined SAIL managers' willingness and ability to manage the company more efficiently, which compounded SAIL's problems. Neither its managers nor the IAS bureaucrats overseeing the firm had the incentives to modify steel policy and improve SAIL's performance.

The unwillingness and inability of SAIL managers to be effective was also exacerbated by the nature of industrial relations at the firm. The multiplicity of trade unions at SAIL created a climate of union rivalry and industrial tension. In response, constrained by IAS bureaucrats from above and contentious unions from below, and with few incentives to improve production, SAIL managers followed a policy of labor appeasement rather than attempting to motivate workers to improve productivity. The close historical association between the unions and politicians only made both managers and bureaucrats less willing and able to manage effectively and/or modify policy. The pattern of relations between SAIL managers and the Ministry of Steel thus not only restricted the transfer of information between the two but also undermined incentives that might have induced management to push successfully for policy change.

Pressure for policy changes might have come from private industrialists in the sector (TISCO, mini-steel plants). However, both TISCO and the mini-steel plants were either unable or uninterested in demanding a policy change. The potential threat of nationalization (which forced TISCO to toe the political line) and its ability to work the licensing regime effectively guaranteed that TISCO made few attempts to change policy. Having a rental haven ensured that TISCO had little interest in major policy changes.

The story with the mini-steel plants is different. A liberal entry policy during the 1970s led to the mushrooming of the segment. Most of the companies have less-than-minimum economic scales of production and face serious infrastructural problems and input shortages. These in-built inefficiencies, along with the competition among the plants has undermined collective action on their part. The primary concern of the mini-steel plants, consequently, has been to get marginal tax and duty relief and not to push the Ministry of Steel bureaucrats to address the fundamental problems afflicting the segment, such as the problems of inferior technology, low production capacity, and input scarcity.

Finally, politicians could have pushed for policy changes—and they did so, three times. The first effort led to the growth of the mini-steel plants segment in the early 1970s, and the second led to the establishment of SAIL. While SAIL got quagmired by IAS bureaucrats, the mini-steel plants came to be dominated by patronage politics and cannot be regarded as a success on the whole. The third attempt at reforming the steel industry and injecting dynamism during Rajiv Gandhi's tenure as prime minister in the mid-1980s resulted in little improvement.

For these reasons steel policy was retained unchanged until 1991. Despite the industry's poor performance, IAS officials in the Ministry of Steel were not driven to change policy. While the organizational structure of the IAS (discussed in chapter 2) ensured that its bureaucrats were not acting in a predatory manner, that same organizational structure along with the pattern of relations between the Ministry of Steel and steel sector actors discouraged developmental action.

Given SAIL's poor performance, it is particularly surprising that Maruti Udhyog Limited (MUL), the state-owned automobile firm, performed so much better. A comparison of the two firms suggests that the MUL's superior performance can be attributed to the presence of informal channels of communication between the company and the Ministry of Industry, channels absent in the case of SAIL. Why did the state-owned automobile firm perform well while the state-owned steel firm did not?

Part of the reason why the Ministry of Industry sought to promote MUL consistently may have been due to the interests of the political leadership—that is, Indira Gandhi's personal interest in establishing MUL. Comparison with the steel industry suggests that this, however, could only be partly true. Nehru and other political leaders were similarly interested in promoting SAIL and its precursor, Hindustan Steel Limited (HSL). However, interest on the part of the political leadership did not automatically translate into growth-promoting relations between the Ministry of Steel and SAIL.

The relations between the Ministry of Steel and SAIL, and between the Ministry of Industry and MUL were a consequence of the internal organization of the four organizations. Unlike SAIL, the senior management at MUL (and its chief executive officer as well) were former (or current) members of the Indian Administrative Service. Bureaucrats in the Ministry of Industry were also IAS members. The esprit de corps among the members of the IAS discussed in chapter 2 helped promote MUL over the private passenger car and other automobile companies.

The absence of a hierarchical relationship between the IAS bureaucrats and senior MUL management (given that both belonged to the same civil service) meant that noncontractual ties between the two were able to overcome any restrictions on the latter's autonomy and day-to-day operations. Thus, although the Ministry of Industry "controlled" MUL, noncontractual ties between them cut bureaucratic rigidities and eased regulations. Aside from preferential treatment in terms of policy, the management at Maruti was able to utilize the Indian Administrative network to get faster and more favorable licenses, and clearances (for production, foreign exchange, and the necessary infrastructure) from the Ministry of Industry, and from other concerned ministries as well.

More important, however, the increased autonomy of the MUL managers enhanced their willingness and ability to innovate with regard to corporate strategy and industrial relations. Unlike SAIL, MUL has responded to industrial disputes and labor problems not with a short-term policy of appeasement, but with the aim of creating a productive work culture.[1] At the same time, the ability and willingness of MUL management to respond has effectively undermined firm-level trade union-political party ties, improving the company's performance. This, of course, has been possible only because IAS bureaucrats are relatively autonomous from the trade unions.

Thus, state-management relations proved essential for MUL's success for two reasons: (1) They ensured that the bureaucrats in the Ministry of Industry were responsive to MUL's needs; and (2) they enabled management to deal effectively with national trade union federations. The pattern of relations in turn depended on the organizational features of the IAS, its autonomous character, cohesive structure and the strong esprit de corps among its members, and on having a CEO who was a member of the IAS.

As the earlier discussion noted, bureaucrats in the Ministry of Steel, while not predatory, were clearly not developmental. Bureaucrats in the Ministry of Industry acted in a developmental manner only with MUL. The behavior of these bureaucrats is in contrast to the performance of those in the Department of Electronics, who acted in a developmental manner with regard to the industry as a whole. Unlike steel policy, computer software policy was frequently modified and fine-tuned. Why did the state adopt a developmental approach with regard to computer software and not for steel and automobiles?

Consider one possible factor underlying this difference: the greater relative autonomy of the officials in the Department of Electronics from interministerial constraints. Relative to their counterparts in the Ministries of Steel and Industry, Department of Electronics officials were less constrained by decisions and agendas of the Ministries of Finance and Commerce. The greater political restrictions placed on Ministries of Steel and Industry bureaucrats by their political superiors may have limited their policy options and undermined their willingness to innovate.

While this explanation does appear persuasive, it does not explain why the Ministry of Steel was unable and unwilling to respond even when there was political pressure to introduce innovative steel policy. As discussed earlier, ministerial attempts to energize the steel sector in the 1970s, and later under Rajiv Gandhi as Prime Minister in the 1980s, came to naught. When Rajiv Gandhi encouraged the Department of Electronics to change computer policy, the results were clearly different.

The Department of Electronics was better able to respond to industry demands when it was placed directly under the Prime Minister. But the Ministry of Steel had been granted a privileged position in the ministerial hierarchy all along. Steel policy, after all, constituted the core of the various five-year plans. In other words, both state agencies (and sectors) were assigned important positions within the state apparatus, steel as a result of the initially strong Fabian-Socialist ideology and software because of Rajiv Gandhi's interest in technological innovation. And of the two, the Department of Electronics was better able to capitalize on this. The Ministry of Industry, like the Department of Electronics, was able to build on Indira Gandhi's personal interest in MUL and overcome interministerial constraints and thus promote the firm.

It might be argued that Department of Electronics was able to introduce policy innovations because clientelistic politics was present to a greater extent in industries such as steel than in software.[2] However, the relative absence of clientelistic politics alone does not explain why innovations in software policy were introduced at certain times and not others. Moreover, as discussed in chapter 4, entrenched patronage politics was present in the automobile industry, yet Ministry of Industry bureaucrats were able to introduce innovative automobile policy that, by the end of the 1980s, had transformed the industry. The experience of the Indian software and automobile industries suggests that the absence of clientelistic politics alone does not enable or induce a state agency to introduce policy innovations.

What does differentiate the officials in the Department of Electronics and Ministry of Industry from those in the Ministry of Steel is their organizational structure and the pattern of relations between them and the industrial entrepreneurs (the software manufacturers and the management at MUL respectively). First, consider the organizational structure of the Department of Electronics. The department is staffed by mostly technocrats/scientists, with a sprinkling of IAS officials. The technocrats, specialists in their areas, have long tenures within the department. The generalist IAS officials in the department, meanwhile, had noncontractual ties with other IAS members in various ministries. This organizational structure ensured that the technocrats/bureaucrats in the department had the expertise and the time to develop policies with long gestation periods. With some encouragement, they were in a position to introduce innovative policies. Also they had noncontractual ties with bureaucrats in other relevant ministries (Finance, Commerce, and Industry), which were likely to help them get their policy changes adopted.

Second, consider the pattern of relations between the agencies and the industrial actors. Both the Department of Electronics and the Ministry of Industry had informal and noncontractual channels of communication with industrial actors (software entrepreneurs and MUL managers). Such ties were not present between the Ministry of Steel and either the integrated steel plants or the mini-steel plants.

The emergence or the presence of such informal channels of communication is not simply a matter of historical accident (as has been argued in the case of both Japan and South Korea). This becomes clear when we look at the underlying social structural factors. In the case of MUL, such ties emerged due to the presence of a few IAS officials in the upper-levels of management.

In the case of the software sector, the emergence of noncontractual ties has been the consequence of the long tenures of the officials in the Department of Electronics; of the similarity in the training, professional background, and the consciousness of a common interest in technological development; and the structure of the industry. These officials are in place for more than just three to five years (the average tenure of the IAS bureaucrat), a fact that permitted the officials to meet with the entrepreneurs periodically and form noncontractual ties and informal channels of communication. In addition, the technocrats and entrepreneurs had similar backgrounds and professional qualifications.

But such links also create conditions conducive for rent-seeking. Moving bureaucrats around ensures against corruption and patronage, or so goes the classic argument in defense of the IAS policy of transfers. What ensured that the Department of Electronics officials would not be captured by entrepreneurs was the small scale of the overwhelming majority of firms. Infosys (one of India's most successful software firms), for example, was started with an initial capital of Rs. 10,000, a sum inadequate to bribe not just an IAS bureaucrat but even the *peon* in the Department!

The small scale of the enterprises also led them to develop a strong and relatively cohesive industry association, NASSCOM. On its own, each firm is unlikely to have convinced Department of Electronics' officials to introduce policy innovations. Together they were infinitely more successful. The industry association, which is strong and cohesive in comparison to other industry organizations, and has been growing in strength, reinforced the channels of communication between the department and industry.

As discussed in chapter 5, the ability of software entrepreneurs to overcome the free-rider problem and act collectively is a consequence of their export orientation and their dependence on collective goods provided by the Department of Electronics, factors that brought entrepreneurs together and strengthened the industry association. The dominance of an export focus among the software manufacturers has meant that they are not in direct competition with each other. India's small contribution to the international software market has helped eliminate any direct competition. The firms are unlikely to cut into each other's market, at least for now. Unlike the mini-steel industry, the software market is at least not perceived by the firms as a zero-sum game. By not being in direct competition with each other, the software entrepreneurs have come together collectively. This, for precisely the opposite reason, did not happen with either the mini-steel plants or with the automobile manufacturers. This is also true for the computer hardware segment. Primarily focused on the domestic market, the hardware manufacturers pushed for the maintenance of the license-permit-quota raj with limited modifications at the margins. The hardware manufacturers' association, Manufacturers Association for Information Technology (MAIT), unlike NASSCOM, and like SFAI and AIAM was relatively splintered.

The almost 200 mini-steel plants, most with less-than-minimum economic scales of production, were in direct competition with each other. In addition, the collective goods they required (water supply and electricity) could be provided on an individual basis, thus, not necessitating collective action. The automobile manufacturers association was also torn by internal conflicts. As the executive director of the association noted, the association's stated agenda and what each manufacturer sought via political means were entirely different and often contradictory.[3] If the association requested the Ministry of Industry to liberalize regulations, various manufacturers sought the maintenance of protected markets and particularistic benefits. It was only after MUL's entry and its successful performance that the manufacturers collectively and individually called for liberalization. The automobile manufacturers had all along been able to circumvent the restrictive regulations via political patronage.

Apart from long tenures and a strong industry association, the presence of a few IAS bureaucrats within the Department of Electronics also made it willing and able to introduce innovative policy. Having a secretary who was a member of the IAS with noncontractual ties between him and other senior IAS bureaucrats in the Ministries of Finance and Commerce was also advantageous. It ensured that policy changes requiring Finance or Commerce approvals or agreements were relatively easier.

These ties are also what enabled the Ministry of Industry to respond to MUL's needs. The noncontractual intra-IAS ties also made IAS bureaucrats in the Ministries of Finance and Commerce willing and able to support MUL. Thus, initial political encouragement together with the IAS network helped MUL succeed. The importance of the IAS network in MUL's success is also indicated when one compares MUL and the Electronics Corporation of India Limited (ECIL) (and also SAIL). ECIL was not the beneficiary of IAS support; consequently it did not receive as nurturing a policy treatment as MUL did. While the technocrats managing ECIL did have informal ties with those in the Department of Electronics (and in the Electronics Committee), turf battles between the various scientific agencies (Atomic Energy Department, Department of Defense Supplies) undermined their role in promoting ECIL.

One could argue that the absence of entrenched labor interests granted the Department of Electronics more room to maneuver. Unlike the Ministry of

Steel bureaucrats, the technocrats were not constrained by trade union rivalry, union-party ties, and opportunistic politicians dabbling in industrial relations. This conclusion, however, needs to be tempered.

Consider MUL's performance especially in comparison to SAIL's performance. Interunion rivalry and the accompanying tensions were dealt with effectively by MUL management. The MUL union has banned outside leaders, and with only one recognized trade union, the workers are in a stronger position in their negotiations with management. What enabled MUL management to maintain peaceful industrial relations was its intra-IAS ties; but more important, it was the relative autonomy of the bureaucrats in the Ministry of Industry from labor interests. Interaction with the bureaucracy serves two purposes. First, it encourages bureaucrats to be willing and able to respond to the needs of the industry. Second, having the relatively autonomous bureaucracy as an ally enables management to deal more effectively with intransigent unions.

In India, labor leaders and politicians have historically established strong ties. Further, the presence of ties of patronage and rent-seeking between them tends to preempt the development of ties between the trade unions and the senior bureaucrats. The absence of these ties is also a result of the internal structure of the IAS, particularly its generalist character and the frequent transfers of its officials. This pattern of relations restricts the autonomy of the political leadership and of the labor leaders but does not restrict that of the senior bureaucrats.

At the same time, top management of specific companies (e.g., MUL) have noncontractual ties (which do not lead to capture) with the senior members of the bureaucracy. These channels of communication, as discussed earlier, help in the transfer of information between the industrialists and the bureaucrats. In the absence of restrictions on their autonomy by trade unions, and in the presence of noncontractual ties with industrial actors, the bureaucrats are able and willing to formulate and promote policies that foster entrepreneurial perspectives among the industrialists. In other words, they successfully perform the role of policy entrepreneurs.

Thus, when bureaucratic-management ties are present, firms are able to grow, innovate, and succeed despite the constraints imposed by splintered and internally competitive trade union structures. Clearly firms that lack unionized workers (e.g., computer firms, software and high-tech companies) and have noncontractual ties with bureaucrats are the most likely to succeed. Finally, firms that are faced with politicized trade unions and also lack channels of communication with the bureaucracy are in the worst situation, and their performance is likely to suffer. While the trade union structure restricts management's ability to strategize and maneuver, having the bureaucracy as an ally appears to increase this ability to maneuver.

Strengthening industry-bureaucracy ties is crucial for postliberalization growth and investment. These ties have enabled MUL to succeed in ways that SAIL or Premier Automobiles Limited (PAL) could not. In addition, the existing trade union policies grant bureaucrats considerable discretionary power, much as the pre-1991 licensing regime did. The bureaucrats' willingness and ability to use this power to support industry/management (like their willingness and ability to maneuver around industrial regulations) is enhanced by the presence of formal and informal noncontractual ties with industrialists. Therefore, strengthening these ties where they exist, and enabling them where they do not, would help counter the constraints created by the political leadership-trade union nexus. This conclusion would obviously be nullified if the existing labor laws were altered and policies allowing the exit of firms and preventing the splintering of trade unions were adopted. No administration, however, has been unable to amend the labor laws. Until the labor laws are modified, the focus ought to be on working around the existing labor policy regime, and one way of doing this would be to strengthen bureaucratic-industrialist ties.

This discussion also has implications for the debate about labor regime and economic growth. It suggests two conclusions. On one hand, analyses focusing on Mexico have argued that corporatist arrangements among politicians, labor, and capital have been key in enabling the Mexican government to introduce and sustain economic liberalization.[4] Crucial agreements between trade unions and politicians have granted the state greater maneuverability with regard to liberalization. On the other hand, studies focusing on South Korea have identified repressive labor policies as being important for its rapid economic growth from the mid-1960s to the mid-1980s.[5] Close ties between the political leadership and industrialists accompanied by a repressive labor regime have apparently worked in South Korea.

India has neither a repressive labor policy (excluding the period of emergency) nor, despite the close relationship between political parties and trade unions can India be said to have a corporatist arrangement. Yet specific firms have been able to transform the nature of industrial relations. What makes this possible is the presence of noncontractual bureaucrat-industrialist ties. MUL, for instance, was able to counter the splintering and politicization of its unions given its relations with the Ministry of Industry bureaucrats. The ability of MUL managers to negotiate with their unions was enhanced to the extent that the Ministry of Industry supported them. Managers of state-owned enterprises without the backing of Ministry bureaucrats are both ineffective at, and are unwilling of, going out on a limb while negotiating with unions. At the same time, the unions, aware of the managers' potential ineffectiveness, find it more useful to turn to politicians to fulfill their demands. While in South Korea bureaucracy - industry ties promoted industrialization with repression, in India such ties appear to have had a similar result without repressive labor policies. I suggest that the result in India was possible because the trade union structure, while it has eroded the power of labor, did not undermine bureaucratic autonomy.

These answers also help us address three theoretical issues: Why do states not act developmentally? Why are some policies successful in some instances and not others? And what is the institutional basis of developmental state action? Taken together, the answers lead us to an explanation to our theoretical puzzle: Under what circumstances is the state likely to foster long-term entrepreneurial perspectives among the industrial elite?

RETHINKING THE DEVELOPMENTAL STATE

While the comparative institutional perspective is useful for identifying contexts and conditions conducive for developmental state action, the methodological individualist perspective of rational choice theory helps to explain how bureaucrats act within these conditions and contexts. Together the two theoretical perspectives offer a perspective that identifies more comprehensively and clearly than either rational choice or comparative institutional arguments do alone the mechanisms by which some states are willing and able to act in a developmental manner.

Recent institutional and structural arguments about the role of the state in industrial transformation have identified a number of factors as being essential for developmental state action. For Johnson, the critical feature of the developmental state is its internal structure.[6] For Wade, while institutional structures are important, particular policies need to be adopted if the desired economic transformation is to result.[7] Yet others—Amsden for instance—identify the economic/industrial process by which the state can spur industrial growth.[8] According to Evans, successful action depends on state autonomy and embeddedness.[9]

Amsden suggests that a number of countries have institutions that are essential for late industrializing countries, including India, Brazil, Japan, and South Korea. These institutions consist of "an interventionist state that deliberately distorts relative prices to stimulate growth, business groups that diversify widely to compete initially at the lower end of many markets, a strategic focus on shop-floor management, where engineers strive to achieve incremental productivity and quality improvements, and a politically and economically weak labor movement."[10] How effective the institutions are, she argues, is determined by culture and history. In other words, the institutional "paradigm operates especially well in Japan and Korea because the state in both countries is willing and able to exact performance standards from big business."[11] What precisely made the Japanese and South Korean states willing and able to exact such standards?

In a recent contribution to this debate, Evans has examined "how and whether states might facilitate the local emergence of new sectors."[12] He argues that industrial transformation depends on both the structure of the state apparatus and the roles that the state adopts. And further, the transformation "changes the nature of the state's private counterparts, making effective future state involvement dependent on the reconstruction of state-society ties."[13] What leads the state to adopt one role over another depends, according to Evans, on the structure of the state understood in terms of embedded autonomy. The structure of the state "defines the range of roles that the state is capable of playing."[14]

This book has attempted to extend Evans's argument about developmental states in three ways. First, by studying variations in industrial performance within one country, this book has controlled for historical contingency: Evans focuses on one industry in three countries; this book deals with three industries in one country. Second, it examines the micro-foundations of policymaking and in doing so identifies the incentives and constraints influencing state action. This permits an understanding of the institutional mechanisms that promote developmental state action and explains not only why bureaucrats can act entrepreneurially but also what makes them willing to do so. Evans primarily deals with what enabled the state to act developmentally; this book also considers why states and bureaucrats would be willing to act thus. Enabling conditions do not necessarily offer incentives for action. Third, Evans tends to ignore the role of politicians in the process of industrial transformation. This book argues that to understand state action, one must distinguish between bureaucrats and politicians. Statist perspectives often conflate these two sets of actors.

This conflation is especially problematic in democratic countries. As the discussion of the Indian steel, automobile, and software industries demonstrates, politicians and bureaucrats frequently have differing interests. A politician's actions are influenced by the nature of the political system, while a bureaucrat's actions are shaped by the incentives and constraints generated by the structure of state apparatus. The interests of both politicians and bureaucrats influence their specific relations with industrial actors. More important, the interests of politicians indirectly influence the relationship that bureaucrats have with entrepreneurs or labor and vice versa. To understand why some industry actors have close informal relations with bureaucrats, we must conceptually distinguish between politicians and bureaucrats.

For example, if the politician enjoys a close relationship with an industry actor, bureaucrats are likely to steer clear of such an industrialist for fear of treading on the politician's toes. At the same time, industrialists would have little incentive to develop close relations with bureaucrats. The presence of politician-industrialist ties not only does not create incentives for the development of such ties between bureaucrats and industrialists, it might also create disincentives.

Maxfield and Schneider note that to understand the factors underlying state action (especially in democratic countries) we must not only consider the bureaucrats' relations with industrial actors, but also the bureaucrats' relations with politicians.[15] What we also need to consider is the manner in which relations between politicians and industry actors influence relations between bureaucrats and industry actors. As the analysis of the Indian automobile industry indicates, the presence of relations between politicians and industrialists dissuaded bureaucrats and industrialists from developing close relations. As a result, even though bureaucrats had formal autonomy to modify automobile policy during the 1950s and the 1960s, the absence of channels of communication between bureaucrats and industrialists undermined their willingness and also their ability to generate innovate policy modifications.

This book proposes that for industrial transformation to occur, the presence of the developmental ensemble is essential. Such an institutional arrangement makes bureaucrats willing and able to innovate and foster developmental state action. The developmental ensemble has four dimensions: a cohesive organizational state structure, encouragement from political superiors, bureaucratic autonomy from societal interests, and informal channels of communication with industrial actors.

A cohesive bureaucratic structure is likely to generate an esprit de corps among the members and help in intrabureaucratic interaction. Bureaucrats who share common values and norms are in a better position to facilitate interagency interaction than are bureaucrats not so united. Interaction between the Department of Electronics and other ministries, especially powerful ones such as the Ministries of Finance or Commerce, was facilitated by the presence of IAS bureaucrats in the Department of Electronics and these ministries.

Bureaucratic autonomy ensures that policy formulation does not serve the interests of only a few industrialists but rather promotes the growth of the sector as a whole. The maintenance of protected niche markets is likely if bureaucrats are captured by societal (i.e., industrial) interests. A coherent bureaucratic structure and a strong esprit de corps allow bureaucrats to with-stand pressures from societal actors. The likelihood of bureaucratic auton-omy also increases if industrialists are small-scale entrepreneurs who lack the financial resources necessary to capture bureaucrats. But bureaucratic au-tonomy is not simply inversely related to the size of the enterprise. Industri-alists with an export focus (whether large or small) are more likely to cooperate with one another, have strong industry associations, and have less of an incentive to capture bureaucrats individually.

Bureaucratic autonomy and state coherence together influence the ability of bureaucrats to act in an entrepreneurial manner. But bureaucrats still need to be willing to act, ability alone does not guarantee action. Bureaucratic willingness is a function of two factors: political encouragement and infor-mal channels of communication between bureaucrats and industrialists.

Political encouragement is crucial for motivating innovative bureaucratic action, especially in countries such as India, where organizational incentives are lacking. The absence of merit-based promotion for senior bureaucrats and their short tenures generate incentives for non-innovative bureaucratic action. Without a system of rewards for innovation, why should bureaucrats take policy risks? Not rocking the boat is the safer and rational option. Polit-ical encouragement alone, however, is no guarantee of policy entrepreneur-ship. As the case of Indian steel policy indicates, bureaucratic inertia and the lack of embeddedness through informal ties combined to undermine the ef-fect of the political encouragement. In the Department of Electronics, politi-cal encouragement and long tenures came together to generate incentives for innovative software policymaking.

As with political encouragement, informal channels of communication between industrialists (or industry associations) and bureaucrats tend to act as a way of motivating bureaucrats to introduce policy changes. Informal channels of communication enable bureaucrats to understand the needs of in-dustry, adjust policy, and act as policy entrepreneurs more generally. This is especially important in countries where civil service members (as a result of their training, lifestyle and career paths) are insulated from industry.

The development of such relations between the state and industry is more likely when bureaucrats are not transferred often. While longer bureaucratic tenures allow such informal channels of communication to develop, long tenures do not automatically lead to the development of such ties. Industrial-ists also need incentives to form such ties. Individual industrialists who lack the financial capital and political clout necessary to capture politicians have incentives to develop such ties with bureaucrats. Industry associations also can be effective at developing such informal channels of communication. Associations whose members require collective goods from the state and have an export focus (and hence are not in direct competition with each other until export markets are saturated) have an edge here. The stronger and more united the association, the better able it is to develop informal channels of communication with bureaucrats. The behavior of NASSCOM and the Confederation of Indian Industry (CII) as compared to that of the Association of Indian Automobile Manufacturers (AIAM), and Steel Furnace Association of India (SFAI) is evidence of this.

The challenge, therefore, is to construct developmental ensembles. As the discussion above suggests, the presence of a developmental ensemble is not simply a historical accident. By understanding the structure of the developmental ensemble, we are in a better position to say something about its construction. First, having a flexible policy environment is essential. Bureaucrats are able to fine-tune policies only when the policy framework is not rigid. Second, a strong esprit de corps needs to be fostered in the bureaucracy. This unifies the bureaucracy, makes it less susceptible to societal and political pressures, and improves inter-bureaucratic interaction. The construction of such an esprit de corps requires an appropriate training program aimed at generating a common knowledge base and socializing members into a particular lifestyle. It also requires incentives and constraints that distinguish members of the civil service from the rest of the state apparatus.

Third, this study has underlined the importance of industry associations. Industry associations need to work at being more effective. CII's story is instructive here. Until 1990, CII was not much more effective than the Federation of Indian Chamber of Commerce and Industry (FICCI) and the Associated Chambers of Commerce and Industry (ASSOCHAM). During the early 1990s, CII became substantially more powerful. This transformation was a consequence of two key decisions taken by CII's leadership: to focus on exports and to develop informal relations with senior bureaucrats in key ministries. Divisions within CII between Bombay Club members and the rest have in recent years undermined it's performance. CII's abilities have diminished as its membership has broadened. NASSCOM's approach has been identical to CII's more successful initial approach. Fourth, having a liberal trade environment and one that emphasizes exports is helpful not only for disciplining industrialists but also for unifying them. It strengthens industry associations, and they in turn can act as a channel of communication. Bureaucrats hesitate to develop informal or informal ties with divided associations for fear of charges of bias and corruption. Fifth, allowing senior civil servants to have long tenures gives them the opportunity to be able to develop such ties. Bureaucrats with a specialized career focus are likely to be even more effective at establishing informal channels of communication with industrialists, which generates shared interests and understandings among the two sets of actors.

The Developmental Ensemble
in Comparative Perspective

This book offers additional evidence for the critique of neoclassical economics by comparative institutional arguments. It identifies the conditions under which state intervention has positive consequences for growth.

Robert Wade's analysis of Taiwanese development identifies specific policies that can help promote growth and in the adoption of entrepreneurial business strategies. These policy prescriptions include: (a) "Use national policies to promote industrial investment within the national boundaries, and to channel more of this investment into industries whose growth is important for the economy's future growth," (b) "Use protection to help create an internationally competitive set of industries," (c) "If the wider structure calls for heavy reliance on trade, give high priority to export promotion policies," (d) "Welcome multinational companies, but direct them toward exports," (e) "Promote a bank-based financial system under close government control," (f) "Carry out trade and financial liberalization gradually, in line with a certain sequence of steps."[16] However, Wade argues that these policies are a necessary but not sufficient condition for rapid industrialization. These policies are effective when conducive organizational conditions exist.

This comparative analysis of the Indian steel, automobile, and computer sector has helped specify organizational conditions conducive for industrial transformation. Moreover, it suggests that there are different paths to get industrial firms to innovate and adopt entrepreneurial business strategies. What ensured that either path worked in the case of the automobile and computer software industries is the presence of the developmental ensemble. Such institutional arrangements are likely to lead to the emergence of growth-promoting policies. In other words, rather than emphasizing specific industrial policy options and then examining the institutional structures that support their effective implementation, this book suggests that with the developmental ensemble and an overall flexible policy framework effective policies are likely to emerge. Autonomous bureaucrats who have noncontractual relations with industrial actors are able to develop policy responses that enable industrial growth and encourage entrepreneurialism. The policy implication that emerges form this study, therefore, is to have flexible policy frameworks

that grant bureaucrats concerned with different industrial sectors room to maneuver and introduce periodic changes.

If indeed the concept of the developmental ensemble explains industrial
performance more effectively than policies alone, then it should help explain
the variations in the performance of countries that have undergone structural
adjustment and economic liberalization. The economic policy in structurally-
adjusted economies is if not exactly neoclassical, by definition in line with
the prescriptions of neoclassical economic theory. Theoretically, variations in
economic and industrial performance ought not to exist except insofar as
markets, even when allowed a greater play than before, are mixed with government policy in different ways and to different degrees.

It is clear from the experience of a number of sub-Saharan countries that
neoclassical policies alone do not ensure industrial transformation. Institutions matter. However, while the paths of their economies supports my point
that state and societal institutions shape industrial development, they do not
help us understand what kinds of institutional structures are essential. The
theoretical argument developed here cannot be tested with evidence from
sub-Saharan African countries. Structurally adjusted economies with stable
state institutions, however, offer us a valuable testing ground. Are there any
such examples? Consider Venezuela.[17]

The failure of structural adjustment policies introduced in 1989 by the
Pérez government to lead to rapid industrial growth in Venezuela during the
1990s is, plausibly, a consequence of the absence of a coherent, autonomous
state with noncontractual relations with the industrial elite. Senior members
of the bureaucracy were all inexperienced. Moreover, a high turnover ensured that few had the opportunity to stay long enough in a particular position to gain this experience. As Naim notes "the first and second
organizational levels at the ministry [following the 1989 reforms] were
staffed by newcomers with little or no government experience. They, in turn,
lasted less than two years on average."[18]

The state was also not autonomous from the dominant economic interests.
The shift away from an import substitution regime had left the agreements,
pacts, and arrangements among the dominant economic actors in disarray.
These actors were pushed "into a competitive frenzy in which they used every
weapon at their disposal, including government officials [and] . . . politicians
to gain a dominant position in a given industry."[19] This jostling among conglomerates reduced the capacity of the state to act autonomously. The "state
became ever more focused on responding to the pressures, needs, and requests
of influential groups and individuals. This decreased its capacity to implement
policies and make decisions aimed at serving the population as a whole. The

state . . . came to depend for their survival on the political support of specific groups."[20]

Strong and unified industry associations, or the presence of noncontractual relations between the state and the conglomerates and other industry actors, might have prevented this. They were, however, missing. Like FICCI in India, Venezuela's industry associations were concerned primarily with bargaining with the state for benefits and privileges. And the "formal network of business councils, chambers of commerce, and the assorted associations representing business were hard pressed to devise timely and adequate responses to the new situation."[21] The inability of these associations to mediate between the state and industry was especially problematic at a time when frequent policy changes were being introduced. Noncontractual relations between the state and industry might have helped here. But they were nonexistent.

As Thorp and Durand observe, the shift in state-industry relations accompanying the adoption of structural adjustment policies was "akin to going from incest to an abrupt divorce instigated by one partner with no attempt at counseling or intermediation," and they quote Venezuelan businessmen as saying "We have *no* relations with government."[22] Silva observes that policymakers in Venezuela had close links with specific conglomerates but lacked contact with overall business interests. As a result, he argues, "although investment rates rose somewhat during the Pérez administration (1989-94) compared to previous recessionary periods, that rise was on the basis of volatile international financial capital or shot-in-the-arm investment blips in newly privatized companies. Domestic capitalists remained wary. In short, a steady stream of stable investment in production by the national bourgeoisie was not forthcoming, meaning that hard-won macroeconomic stability rests on very uncertain ground."[23]

This brief review of Venezuela's state and industry structure suggests that the absence of the developmental ensemble explains to a substantial extent that nation's recent performance. The absence of these institutions, moreover, undermined the ability of the state to adopt appropriate policies in subsequent years. Under these circumstances a neoliberal policy framework was not able to deliver rapid industrial growth.[24]

If Venezuela's economy has not thrived despite having a neoliberal policy framework because of the absence of the developmental ensemble, China's economy has surged despite its lack of a neoliberal policy framework. Evidence suggests that this anomaly can be explained by the presence of the developmental ensemble at the local level in China.

The most significant contributors to China's rapid industrial growth have been town and village enterprises (TVEs), which are jointly owned and run by town and village governments and private entrepreneurs. In an environment lacking what economists from Adam Smith onward regard as the foundation of a thriving market—clear laws regarding contract and a transparent legal system that applies these laws—private enterprise is flourishing. In an economy seemingly no less entangled in red tape than India's, entrepreneurs are succeeding. Can our argument about the developmental ensemble help explain this? Whatever empirical evidence is emerging from China seems to suggest that it can.

The introduction of market reforms were accompanied by decentralization. The discretionary power and authority of the local government grew substantially from the 1980s onward.[25] These autonomous local governments adopted a proactive approach to industrial development. Moreover, as part of their development strategy, they sought to establish arenas in which entrepreneurs and local government officials could interact. The use of local government resources for investment in these firms gave the former an incentive to actively promote both private firms and town and village enterprises.

Consider the experience of the Chinese automobile industry. While the industry has not performed as well as the South Korea's, it has "made much faster progress than India."[26] However, while some Chinese automobile firms have performed well, others have not. To understand their performance, three sets of actors need to be considered: the political elite in the central government in Beijing, the political elite at the local level in towns and cities, and foreign industrial actors who have established joint ventures. The pattern of relations among these three actors has influenced the performance of the automobile industry.

Automobile production began in China after World War II. Under Mao's leadership, First Automotive Works began production of trucks, utility vehicles, and passenger cars in the 1950s in Changchun. The Great Leap Forward led to a spurt in the number of truck manufacturing enterprises. By the end of the 1970s, there were around 150 automobile manufacturing firms, with each factory producing an average of 1,000 a year. According to Byrd, China's automobile industry was marked by excessively small scales of production and consequently high costs and inefficiency, poor quality and backward technology, a highly dispersed location pattern, an excessive integration of production within plants, and tight controls over product distribution by the central government.[27]

By the 1980s, however, China's automobile industry had begun to change following the decentralization of authority and the establishment of joint ventures (between foreign firms and local governments). Firms such as Shanghai Volkswagen, Guangzhou Peugeot, and the Beijing Jeep Corporation have injected fresh technology and dynamism into the industry. And thanks to the adoption of policies allowing state-owned enterprises (SOEs) to retain a portion of their profits, even the state-owned automobile firms have improved their performance. The Second Automotive Works is a clear success story.[28] However, not all automobile firms (joint ventures or state-owned enterprises) performed well. And the successful firms had close relations with local governments and minimal relations with the central government.[29]

Consider the experience of an automobile firm, a joint venture—Shanghai Volkswagen. The company, which began production in 1982, has grown steadily since. Local support for the firm appears to have been central for its success. The Mayor of Shanghai, Zhu Rongi, made the success of Shanghai's industries his personal mission.[30] Moreover, the mayor had been posted in Beijing previously and also had been involved in the development of another automobile firm there, Beijing Jeep. And he is reported to have used in contacts with the central government to help Shanghai Volkswagen. The Municipal Automotive Small Group, whose members included the mayor, the vice mayor, and representatives from the local economic planning agency, international trade bureaus, and senior management from the automobile company, played a critical role. Their essential task was to improve coordination among the various local government departments. This group provided an arena in which to exchange information.[31]

Comparison of the experiences of Beijing Jeep Corporation, Shanghai Volkswagen, Guangzhou Peugeot, and Panda Motors is illustrative. Encouragement from central political leaders was helpful for growth; lack of encouragement, however, did not undermine successful performance. Second, autonomy from bureaucrats in the quasi-ministerial levels in Beijing helps. Policy differences and political conflicts within central ministries in charge of automobile policy slowed performance. Third, local government politicians tended to play a very positive role. Local government politicians were, however, unable to play a positive role with regard to Beijing Jeep. This is explained by the critical role that Beijing played in national politics, which seriously reduced the autonomy of Beijing's local government from central government politicians.[32]

What explains the ability and willingness of local government politicians to aid joint ventures? The answer has two parts. First, competition between cities offered these politicians incentives to help joint ventures (and also town and village enterprises more generally). Panda Motors, located at Huizhon in Guangdong Province, is a good example. As Harwitt notes: "Panda represented a kind of challenge to the growing Peugeot venture in Guangdong."[33] And this rivalry or competition gave the provincial bureaucrats an incentive to help Panda Motors. Second, close relations between these politicians and the joint venture partners and managers appears to have played a critical role in informing the former of the firm's needs. Local politicians were members of the board of the joint ventures, and in some instances it was hard to tell managers, owners, and politicians apart. As a result, local politicians were both willing and able to promote the automobile joint ventures.

Economists and positive political economists argue that clear property rights are essential for the successful performance of firms. However, what appears to be enabling joint ventures, and even more so the thousands of TVEs, to succeed is the absence of clear property rights and the emergence in their stead of pockets of informal relations and trust. In a recent article, *The Wall Street Journal* noted how one TVE "owner" viewed clear property rights: "[dividing] ownership among managers and employers raises jealousies better left unexplored."[34] The "owner" went on to offer an ancient Chinese proverb to emphasize his point: "if the water's too clear, the fish can't live."

At the local level, then, China's bureaucrats are autonomous from both the central government as well as societal interests and electoral pressures, and they also have established channels of communication with leading industry actors. What has made these bureaucrats *willing* to promote local firms, to the extent that they did is their interest in high returns on the local government investment in these firms and competition among local governments. The reforms of the late 1970s and early 1980s were accompanied by the reinstitution of financial incentives for enterprises and individuals. The TVEs, for example, were owned and run by local government bureaucrats. The financial reforms allowed these officials as individuals and on behalf of their agency to retain a percentage of the profits. Second, competition among local governments also created an incentive for these government officials to promote entrepreneurs.

Chinese local bureaucrats, in other words, are autonomous, have close channels of communication with entrepreneurs, and also have an incentive to be willing to promote industrial transformation. Despite the absence of a market/legal structure regarded as essential by neoclassical economists, the presence of the developmental ensemble appears to have been critical for China's rapid growth since the 1980s.

Developmental ensembles are effective for two reasons: They help counter factors promoting market failures, and they help foster the very entrepreneurial perspectives that neoclassical economists believe the market alone provides. The concept of the developmental ensemble offers a way of understanding not only why neoclassical economic theory remains a theory but, more important, how institutions and social structures foster growth and development. In so doing, it links rational choice and social-structural perspectives. Together these perspectives explain how institutional structures influence economic processes via incentives and constraints, without making simplistic assumptions about human behavior.

SHARED UNDERSTANDINGS

An underlying theme throughout this book has been the importance of "shared understandings" for the better functioning of the economic processes. Whether interpreted as esprit de corps, common values and norms, or a unified focus, shared understandings appear to be essential. Noncontractual relations and informal interactions help strengthen shared understandings. Similarities of educational background and common caste and class identifications are likely to facilitate the emergence of shared understandings insofar as they promote noncontractual and informal interactions.

Shared understandings help overcome bureaucratically and institutionally created divisions. Between bureaucrats, such understandings allow the state not to fall prey to societal and political interests and to function smoothly. Shared understandings among industrialists increase their ability to get the infrastructure and collective goods necessary for further growth. And shared understandings between industrialists and the bureaucracy facilitate the transfer of information between them and the formulation of appropriate policy and thus industrial development. Shared understandings between industrialists and bureaucrats also helps motivate bureaucrats to act.

It is generally believed that relations of trust between bureaucrats and industrial actors help in the transfer of information between them, and this transfer of information is critical for developmental action.[35] However, the evidence presented in this book suggests that relations of trust also play a critical role in motivating bureaucrats to act. The structure of the Indian Administrative Service generates incentives for bureaucrats not to act, making them risk averse in the extreme. Informal interaction with industrialists helps counter these incentives.

Shared understandings help to continually recalibrate the goals and agendas of the concerned actors. Both industrialists and bureaucrats are in a better position to understand the goals of the other and consequently are more likely to act reflexively. While shared understandings do not independently lead bureaucrats to adopt major policy modifications, they do appear to lead to the fine-tuning of policy within the overall policy framework, as evidenced by the development of Indian software policy and automobile policy vis-à-vis Maruti Udhyog Limited. And it this fine-tuning or continuous recalibrating of policy that helped both the Indian software industry and MUL to perform dynamically.

Shared understandings facilitate the formation of communities of trust. As economists have noted, trust in the market acts as a lubricant in interactions with private economic agents, lowering transaction costs. It also helps counter collective action problems. The Prisoner's Dilemma would not be a dilemma if the prisoners trusted one another, and had a set of shared understandings that the police were not privy to. Such trust, according to game theorists, emerges out of repeated interactions.[36]

I propose that shared understandings facilitate interactions that are likely to promote cooperative behavior. I do not assume that shared understandings or trust determines action; I only suggest that communities united by shared understandings are more likely to lead to cooperative decision making and action. More specifically, I propose that under certain circumstances, shared understandings successfully promote cooperation between the state and private actors that facilitates industrial development.

I should also emphasize that shared understandings do not emerge from historical accidents alone. Communities of shared understandings can be constructed. Recent efforts by CII to develop informal relations with senior bureaucrats have been successful in developing shared understandings between them. Bureaucrats interacting with CII not only have a clearer understanding of the formal needs of industry, but they also seem to have a much more intuitive grasp of industry dynamics. CII members, for their part, have a better sense of how the state apparatus operates. This argument is also supported by the experience of NASSCOM, which actively sought to develop a community of shared understanding and has been successful.

Weber's ideal typical bureaucrat is structurally enabled to help the state maintain order in society, to control society, and to retain its monopoly over violence. Routinization and bureaucratization enables the bureaucrat, and more generally the state, to do this. Together they provide the bureaucrat with the skills and incentives to do the necessary tasks. Routinization and bureaucratization help facilitate the emergence of a predictable institutional environment. A predictable institutional structure enables economic calculability. And as neoclassical economists observe, this is essential for market transactions.

To promote development, however, this bureaucrat needs to be willing to take risks, to act innovatively, to counter the restrictions and disincentives imposed by routinization and bureaucratization. And for this the developmental ensemble is necessary. Gerschenkron, Hirschman, and Evans all observe that to promote development, state activity in the economic arena must go well beyond the one identified by Weber.[37] For Evans, embedded autonomy enables the state to increase its range of activity so as to include developmental action. A state that is both autonomous and has close ties with the industrial elite, he argues, is in the best position to undertake developmental action.

Charles Sable has proposed the concept of developmental associations—groups of firms—to help explain how states can both monitor private firms and encourage learning among them. He argues that states can be successful at both regulatory tasks and at developmental action "by creating institutions that make discussion of what to do inextricable from discussion of what is being done and the discussion of standards for apportioning gains and losses inextricable from apportionment."[38] Drawing on evidence from the Japanese experience, Sable argues that developmental associations encourage member actors to "interpret the general rules and expectations to bring them to bear on their actual situation. These reinterpretations proceed through argumentative encounters in which the individual attempts to establish an equilibrium between his or her views and social standards by recasting both."[39]

The experience of the Indian software industry suggests that the presence of developmental associations (i.e., NASSCOM) were important for the industry's dynamic performance. However, NASSCOM was a successful developmental association because the Department of Electronics remained autonomous, its members were closely linked to one another and to the other ministries, and politicians encouraged the growth of the industry. NASSCOM has been successful as a result of the presence of these factors; FICCI and AIAM have been relatively unsuccessful because of the absence of these factors.

Thus, this book offers the concept of the developmental ensemble as one way of extending this discussion further. The concept enables us to understand how relations between concerned actors, situated within specific institutional arrangements, facilitate the formulation of policy best suited for promoting entrepreneurship. As the Indian experience indicates, the presence of communities of trust are critical, and so is the presence of autonomous state institutions. Such an arrangement is effective at continually recalibrating the policy agenda and promoting entrepreneurial goals.

Weber's theoretical understanding of the state drew our attention to the positive role of intra-state cohesion. Properly constructed, such cohesion allows the state to overcome internal collective action problems and act as a corporate actor. What the argument presented here suggests is that for effective state intervention, not only do bureaucrats have to be unified by bonds of trust, but so do industrialists. Moreover, such an institutional arrangement is important insofar as it promotes the emergence of noncontractual relations between the state and industry.[40]

Developmental ensembles promote a rapid industrial take-off of developing economies. The success of the industrial sector hinges not on rational self-interest alone but on the presence of pockets, communities, and groups unified by bonds of shared understandings and trust. The argument about developmental ensembles offers a way of conceptualizing the role of trust in economic processes. Rational self-interested behavior is, of course, essential for the functioning of the market. However, industries and economies are more successful when this behavior is embedded in institutions and social structures. Policies work better when they are supported by developmental ensembles. The state is more successful at fostering long-term entrepreneurial perspectives among the industrial elite in the presence of such institutions. Whether such developmental ensembles can work even after a certain industrial threshold has been achieved and the economy has become modernized and complex is open to question.[41] However, the importance of the developmental ensembles in the take-off period is, to my mind, beyond doubt.

Appendix

TABLE A.1

Steel Production at HSL/SAIL and TISCO
(in million tonnes)

Year	HSL/SAIL Ingot Steel	TISCO Ingot Steel	HSL/SAIL Saleable Steel	TISCO Saleable Steel
1959-60	0.16	1.55	0.06	1.24
1960-61	0.78	1.62	0.48	1.26
1961-62	1.60	1.64	1.10	1.32
1962-63	2.46	1.80	1.71	1.41
1963-64	2.90	1.89	2.17	1.51
1964-65	3.10	1.96	2.33	1.57
1965-66	3.42	1.98	2.50	1.57
1966-67	3.53	2.00	2.58	1.57
1967-68	3.43	1.93	2.43	1.53
1968-69	3.70	1.82	2.65	1.46
1969-70	3.78	1.71	2.60	1.44
1970-71	3.61	1.72	3.34	1.37
1971-72	3.48	1.71	3.15	1.39
1972-73	4.44	1.69	3.44	1.46
1973-74	4.21	1.51	4.32	1.20
1974-75	4.54	1.72	2.27	NA
1975-76	5.46	1.79	5.43	1.46
1976-77	6.52	1.91	5.29	1.49
1977-78	6.46	1.97	5.08	1.55
1978-79	6.29	1.86	4.32	NA
1979-80	6.25	1.78	4.64	1.50
1980-81	5.48	1.87	4.77	1.50
1981-82	6.64	1.96	5.65	1.50
1982-83	6.68	1.95	5.67	1.50
1983-84	5.96	1.97	4.77	1.50
1984-85	6.25	2.05	5.28	1.50
1985-86	6.97	2.10	6.00	1.50
1986-87	6.84	2.25	6.31	1.91
1987-88	7.49	2.28	6.67	1.91
1988-89	8.48	2.31	7.26	1.94

1989-90	8.27	2.32	7.06	1.97
1990-91	8.76	2.29	7.36	1.94
1991-92	9.55	2.41	8.03	2.38
1992-93	9.75	2.48	8.34	2.12
1993-94	9.75	2.49	8.65	2.15
1994-95	10.17	2.79	8.96	2.45
1995-96	10.31	3.02	9.22	2.70
1996-97	10.76	3.15	*9.18	*2.81

SOURCE: Steel Authority of India Limited (SAIL). *Statistics for Iron and Steel Industry in India*, New Delhi: SAIL, 1994, p. 27; N. R. Srinivasan, *The Corporate Story of SAIL,* New Delhi: SAIL, 1990; and Confederation of India Industry (CII), *Handbook of Statistics*, New Delhi: CII (various years).
*Provisional.
NA = not available.

TABLE A.2

Production of Saleable Steel—Mini-Steel Plants
(in million tonnes)

Year	Production	Year	Production
1970-71	0.09	1984-85	2.33
1971-72	0.48	1985-86	2.55
1972-73	0.70	1986-87	2.54
1973-74	0.71	1987-88	2.76
1974-75	0.76	1988-89	2.71
1975-76	0.78	1989-90	2.77
1976-77	1.07	1990-91	3.06
1977-78	1.19	1991-92	3.40
1978-79	1.71	1992-93	3.38
1979-80	1.66	1993-94	2.70
1980-81	1.95	1994-95	3.35
1981-82	2.03	1995-96	4.35
1982-83	2.04	1996-97	*4.39
1983-84	1.98		

SOURCE: SAIL, *Statistics for Iron and Steel Industry in India*, New Delhi: SAIL, 1994, p. 27; N. R. Srinivasan, *The Corporate Story of SAIL,* New Delhi: SAIL, 1990; and CII, *Handbook of Statistics*, New Delhi: CII (various years).
*Provisional.

TABLE A.3

Production of Passenger Cars

Year	HML	PAL	MUL	SMPIL	SAL	DCM	TELCO	Total
1950	1,469	478	—	274	—	—	—	2,221
1951	2,161	703	—	614	—	—	—	3,478
1952	1,185	522	—	386	—	—	—	2,093
1953	1,847	344	—	301	—	—	—	2,492
1954	2,607	1,413	—	975	—	—	—	4,995
1955	4,874	3,581	—	1,546	—	—	—	10,001
1956	5,781	5,722	—	1,836	—	—	—	13,339
1957	5,086	4,866	—	2,251	—	—	—	12,203
1958	4,809	1,843	—	1,462	—	—	—	8,114
1959	5,745	4,459	—	1,789	—	—	—	11,993
1960	9,217	6,516	—	3,364	—	—	—	19,097
1961	11,056	7,197	—	3,409	—	—	—	21,662
1962	13,438	6,247	—	3,641	—	—	—	23,326
1963	8,621	3,750	—	3,340	—	—	—	15,711
1964	15,351	3,868	—	4,008	—	—	—	23,227
1965	15,558	5,673	—	3,559	—	—	—	24,790
1966	19,469	7,030	—	1,098	—	—	—	27,597
1967	20,515	10,055	—	2,774	—	—	—	33,344
1968	22,687	12,266	—	2,345	—	—	—	37,298
1969	21,560	12,218	—	1,405	—	—	—	35,183
1970	22,703	12,054	—	448	—	—	—	35,205
1971	24,656	12,821	—	827	—	—	—	38,304
1972	24,634	13,611	—	583	—	—	—	38,828
1973	25,440	13,883	—	614	—	—	—	39,937
1974	20,129	14,213	—	1,666	—	—	—	36,008
1975	9,322	13,630	—	123	—	—	—	23,075
1976	16,422	14,973	—	161	54	—	—	31,610
1977	20,256	17,481	—	111	171	—	—	38,019
1978	20,987	12,931	—	117	331	—	—	34,366
1979	17,523	11,550	—	56	106	—	—	29,235
1980	21,752	8,729	—	6	51	—	—	30,538
1981	23,197	18,874	—	4	31	—	—	42,106
1982	21,836	20,711	—	1	126	—	—	42,674
1983	23,683	20,929	175	1	302	—	—	45,090
1984	24,376	26,620	12,087	—	930	—	—	64,013

1985	24,064	29,223	48,635	—	523	—	—	102,456
1986	22,387	28,501	63,504	1,557	55	—	—	116,004
1987	25,561	31,191	90,909	484	350	—	—	148,495
1988	27,557	36,567	95,390	217	210	—	—	159,941
1989	29,326	42,033	105,826	5	—	—	—	177,190
1990	26,204	42,737	106,956	—	712	—	—	176,609
1991	18,521	42,154	117,720	—	—	—	265	178,660
1992	19,759	13,407	116,656	—	—	—	4,045	153,867
1993	25,536	20,998	147,389	—	—	—	5,648	199,571
1994	25,164	25,994	174,235	—	—	—	11,887	237,280
1995	28,283	24,289	254,094	—	—	4,443	10,548	321,657
1996	26,263	7,208	313,812	—	—	20,259	8,721	376,263

Source: Association of Indian Automobile Manufacturers (AIAM), *Automan,* Bombay: AIAM (various years).

TABLE A.4A

Production of Commercial Vehicles

Year	TELCO	ALL	PAL	HML	BTL	M&M	SMPIL	Total
1950	—	—	847	1,044	—	—	—	1,891
1951	—	—	1,812	369	—	—	—	2,181
1952	—	—	1,512	1,169	—	—	—	2,681
1953	—	199	1,523	1,032	—	—	—	2,754
1954	120	531	3,531	1,118	—	—	—	5,300
1955	2,338	670	3,887	2,360	—	7	—	9,262
1956	5,153	847	5,285	2,712	—	304	—	14,301
1957	7,401	982	5,944	1,137	—	569	—	16,033
1958	7,694	1,117	4,219	1,431	20,0	569	—	15,230
1959	7,880	1,426	5,409	4,382	533	721	—	20,351
1960	9,665	2,071	6,347	7,079	927	1,429	—	27,518
1961	12,000	2,371	5,528	4,096	793	952	—	25,740
1962	12,196	2,835	5,387	4,947	850	679	—	26,894
1963	12,424	2,732	6,316	5,815	888	307	—	28,482
1964	14,367	3,728	8,749	4,940	1,688	45	—	33,517
1965	17,328	4,285	9,152	4,891	1,681	—	71	37,408
1966	18,900	3,857	4,775	4,101	1,562	953	979	35,127
1967	19,140	4,618	4,076	1,535	1,665	1,057	373	32,464
1968	21,669	4,393	3,355	1,981	1,641	1,453	458	34,940

1969	20,497	4,865	3,563	1,836	2,578	1,483	421	35,243
1970	24,463	5,264	4,893	1,733	3,497	966	156	40,972
1971	24,654	5,472	4,578	2,559	3,322	922	347	41,854
1972	22,441	4,244	3,582	2,670	3,416	912	1,438	38,703
1973	23,107	5,639	5,635	3,161	5,005	1,299	963	44,909
1974	22,277	7,691	4,900	2,078	3,779	954	195	41,874
1975	25,269	7,711	2,917	1,220	4,456	696	765	43,034
1976	26,444	9,179	2,319	1,110	4,654	1,338	1,717	46,761
1977	23,419	8,083	181	969	4,770	953	1,627	41,702
1978	29,108	10,947	1,264	2,383	6,507	1,354	1,907	53,470
1979	31,685	12,315	1,079	2,599	6,509	3,984	2,425	59,696
1980	31,768	12,928	1,235	4,880	9,801	3,617	3,491	68,311
1981	45,034	15,031	3,282	5,303	8,589	7,234	4,459	89,752
1982	43,097	16,363	2,797	2,496	11,708	9,034	4,751	90,246
1983	46,074	13,411	1,293	1,908	9,626	9,658	5,395	87,365
1984	46,740	14,430	952	2,307	12,906	11,515	5,810	94,660
1985	50,768	15,938	475	2,411	13,987	6,368	4,583	101,228
1986	44,122	15,265	46	2,232	13,344	10,928	2,807	95,088
1987	55,666	16,347	1	2,086	16,045	6,776	1,530	108,089
1988	60,924	18,791	—	1,720	15,028	5,569	1,687	117,253
1989	60,991	21,008	2	1,818	16,080	4,630	32	117,598
1990	81,829	107,,97	—	1,536	17,041	4,899	—	145,628
1991	89,304	25,165	—	879	14,547	2,405	—	145,689
1992	89,561	24,425	—	798	13,997	2,941	—	128,095
1993	70,636	22,194	—	1,881	20,442	3,543	—	118,696
1994	115,446	28,039	—	2,100	26,182	5,002	—	176,769
1995	159,340	36,471	—	3,270	25,778	3,846	—	228,705
1996	201,085	43,619	—	2,777	26,750	6,723	—	280,954

SOURCE: AIAM, *Automan,* Bombay: AIAM (various years).
Note: Total production figures for 1980 and 1981 in Table A.4b include 591 and 830 commercial vehicles manufactured by SCL (Simpson & Co. Limited). The total production figures since 1985 also include the production figures of companies listed in Table A.4b.

TABLE A.4B

Production of Commercial Vehicles

Year	MNAL	SML	DCM	EML
1985	—	600	1,323	—
1986	1,654	1,530	2,385	754
1987	1,139	3,146	3,073	2,375
1988	2,338	3,113	3,452	4,631
1989	2,192	3,417	3,288	4,328
1990	3,212	3,465	4,483	4,863
1991	2,594	2,956	3,121	4,742
1992	1,758	2,347	2,028	2,860
1993	—	2,245	2,148	3,029
1994	—	3,404	2,894	4,323
1995	—	4,252	2,071	5,616
1996	—	4,686	1,045	6,452

SOURCE: AIAM, *Automan,* Bombay: AIAM (various years).

TABLE A.5

Production of Two-Wheelers (Scooters, Motorcycles, and Mopeds)

Year	Production	Year	Production
1955	952	1971	121,084
1956	5,757	1972	137,063
1957	8,355	1973	150,256
1958	7,044	1974	169,342
1959	7,179	1975	207,697
1960	16,878	1976	262,561
1961	24,087	1977	266,398
1962	23,657	1978	299,850
1963	24,980	1979	306,883
1964	35,347	1980	417,602
1965	49,122	1981	499,103
1966	50,882	1982	593,288
1967	62,824	1983	759,183
1968	74,916	1984	849,580
1969	94,790	1985	1107,251
1970	113,047	1986	1352,508

1987	1401,926	1992	1477,217
1988	1574,646	1993	1664,427
1989	1750,406	1994	2080,518
1990	1875,522	1995	2551,166
1991	1603,108	1996	2978,332

Source: AIAM, *Automan,* Bombay: AIAM (various years).

Table A.6

Software Production
(in Rupees million)

Year	Production	Year	Production
1987-88	1,700	1993-94	17,150
1988-89	2,410	1994-95	26,000
1989-90	3,450	1995-96	42,000
1990-91	4,750	1996-97	64,000
1991-92	7,500	1997-98	*75,000
1992-93	11,650		

Source: National Association of Software and Service Companies (NASS-COM), *The Software Industry in India-1992,* New Delhi: NASSCOM, 1992; NASSCOM, *Indian Software Scenario,* New Delhi: NASSCOM, 1998; *Dataquest,* various issues and years.
*Provisional.

Table A.7

Software Export Growth

Year	Growth (%)	Year	Growth (%)
1981	70	1990	24
1982	99	1991	33
1983	35	1992	26
1984	39	1993	43
1985	NA	1994	53
1986	40	1995	51
1987	39	1996	64
1988	29	1997	*66
1989	51		

SOURCE: NASSCOM, *The Software Industry in India-1992;* New Delhi: NASSCOM, 1992; NASSCOM. *Indian Software Scenario*, New Delhi: NASSCOM, 1998; *Dataquest* various issues and years.
*Provisional.
NA = not available.

TABLE A.8

Software Export
(in U.S. million)

Year	Export	Year	Export
1990-91	128	**1994-95**	485
1991-92	164	**1995-96**	735
1992-93	225	**1996-97**	1,085
1993-94	330	**1997-98**	*1,800

SOURCE: NASSCOM, *The Software Industry in India-1992*, New Delhi: NASSCOM, 1992; NASSCOM, *Indian Software Scenario*, New Delhi: NASSCOM 1998; *Dataquest*, various issues and years.
*Provisional.

Notes

Chapter 1

1. One computer entrepreneur, for example, sought advise not just about his firm but also about the computer science programs in the United States his son was applying to.
2. This analysis is supported by the experience of other developing economies as well. A recent analysis of Brazil suggests that part of what is preventing the rapid transformation of its economy is the absence of such institutional relations between the state and industry. Analyses of the process of industrial transformation in China and Venezuela also appear to uphold this argument. Jörg Meyer-Stamer, "New Patterns of Governance for Industrial Change: Perspectives for Brazil," *Journal of Development Studies*, 33, no. 3 (February 1997). See also V. Pinglé, "Managing State-owned Enterprises: Lessons from India," *International Journal of Sociology and Social Policy*, 17, no. 7/8 (1997).
3. The term "body-shopping" refers to the practice of sending Indian programmers abroad to work in foreign companies. The foreign companies paid these Indian Programmers considerably less than they would have had pay local programmers. Dewang Mehta, "India: Software Paradise," *Dataquest*, December 15, 1996. Data from NASSCOM, *The Software Industry in India: A Strategic Review 1997-98*, New Delhi: NASSCOM, 1998; and Ministry of Finance, *Economic Survey 1996-1997*, New Delhi: Ministry of Finance, 1997.
4. A number of Indian component manufacturers have become internationally competitive. Sundaram Fasteners is a prominent example. *Business Today*, July 7-21, 1997.
5. Data calculated from Association of Indian Automobile Manufaturers (hereafter AIAM), *Automan 1997*, Bombay: AIAM, 1997; AIAM, *Automan 1991*, Bombay: AIAM, 1991; Centre for Monitoring Indian Economy (hereafter CMIE), *Monthly Review of the Indian Economy*, Bombay: CMIE, various years; and Ministry of Finance, *Economic Survey of India 1996-1997*, New Delhi: Ministry of Finance, 1997.
6. Growth did pick up somewhat during the period 1985-86 to 1988-89, although product quality and production efficiencies still remained poor.
7. Steel data calculated from CMIE, *Monthly Review of the Indian Economy*, various years; Confederation of Indian Industry (hereafter CII), *Handbook of Statistics,* New Delhi: CII, various years; Ministry of Steel, *Annual Report,* New Delhi: Ministry of Steel, 1992; and Ministry of Finance, *Economic Survey of India 1996-1997*.

8. A developmental state has been defined as one that promotes long-term entrepreneurial perspectives among the industrial elite. Peter B. Evans, *Embedded Autonomy: States and Industrial Transformation*, Princeton: Princeton University Press, 1995.

9. Leading exponents of this perspective include: Evans, *Embedded Autonomy*; Peter Katzenstein, *Corporatism and Change: Austria, Switzerland, and the Politics of Industry*, Ithaca: Cornell University Press, 1984; Alice Amsden, *Asia's Next Giant: South Korea and Late Industrialization*, New York: Oxford University Press, 1989; Jeffrey Hart, *Rival Capitalists: International Competitiveness in the United States, Japan, and Western Europe*, Ithaca: Cornell University Press, 1992; Chalmers Johnson, *MITI and the Japanese Miracle: The Growth of Industrial Policy, 1925-1975*, Palo Alto: Stanford University Press, 1982; Robert Wade, *Governing the Market: Economic Theory and the Role of Government in East Asian Industrialization*, Princeton: Princeton University Press, 1990.

10. Dietrich Rueschemeyer and Peter B. Evans, "The State and Economic Transformation," in Peter B. Evans, Dietrich Rueschemeyer & Theda Skocpol (eds.), *Bringing the State Back In*, Cambridge: Cambridge University Press, 1985, pp. 46-47.

11. For a discussion of Weber's understanding of the state, see Evans, *Embedded Autonomy*.

12. Rueschemeyer and Evans, "The State and Economic Transformation," p. 60.

13. Theda Skocpol, "Bringing the State Back In: Current Research," in Evans, Rueschemeyer & Skocpol (eds.), *Bringing the State Back In*, p. 9.

14. Rueschemeyer and Evans, "The State and Economic Transformation," p. 64.

15. For empirical arguments about the role of state autonomy in promoting development, see: Amsden, *Asia's Next Giant*; Thomas Gold, *State and Society in the Taiwan Miracle*, Armonk: M. E. Sharpe, 1986; Moises Naim, *Paper Tigers and Minotaurs: The Politics of Venezuela's Economic Reform*, Washington, D.C.: Carnegie Endowment, 1993.

16. Johnson, *MITI and the Japanese Miracle*, p. 316.

17. World Bank, *World Development Report 1997: The State in a Changing World*, Washington, D.C.: The World Bank, 1997, p. 33.

18. The World Bank refers to this weakness of institutions in Africa as "a crisis of statehood". *World Development Report 1997*, p. 162. See also Robert Klitgaard, *Tropical Gangsters*, New York: Basic Books, 1990.

19. Naim, *Paper Tigers and Minotaurs*; J. Martinez and A. Diaz, *Chile: The Great Transformation*, Washington, D.C.: Brookings/UNRISD, 1996. Evidence from Venezuela suggests that not only did the absence entrepreneurial-institutions undermine industrial growth, it also generated po-

litical instability. Poor industrial performance following the reforms weakened the popular support for them and thus threatened the maintenance of reform policies. The Venezuelan and Chinese experiences are discussed further in chapter 6. See also Rosemary Thorp and Francisco Durand, "A Historical View of Business-State Relations: Colombia, Peru, and Venezuela Compared" and Eduardo Silva, "Business Elites, the State, and Economic Change in Chile," in Sylvia Maxfield and Ben Ross Schneider (eds.), *Business and the State in Developing Countries*, Ithaca: Cornell University Press, 1997.

20. See Eric Harwitt, *China's Automobile Industry: Policies, Problems, and Prospects*, London: M. E. Sharpe, 1996; William Byrd, (ed.), *Chinese Industrial Firms Under Reform*, New York: Oxford University Press, 1992.

21. Peter B. Evans, *Embedded Autonomy.*

22. Anne O. Krueger, "The Political Economy of the Rent-Seeking Society," *American Economic Review*, 64 (1974), pp. 291-303.

23. David Colander (ed.), *Neoclassical Political Economy: The Analysis of Rent-Seeking and DUP Activities*, Cambridge: Ballinger, 1984, p. 5.

24. The larger conceptual implication of the 1997 meltdown in East and South-East Asia is still not clear. Is it a temporary blip, or a major indictment of the strategy followed? Only time will tell.

25. See Amsden, *Asia's Next Giant,* and Wade, *Governing the Market.*

26. Paul Milgrom and John Roberts, "Bargaining Costs, Influence Costs, and the Organization of Economic Activity," in James E. Alt and K. A. Shepsle (eds.), *Perspectives on Positive Political Economy*, Cambridge: Cambridge University Press, 1990, pp. 60-61. R. Coase developed this concept in "Nature of the Firm," *Economica* 4 (1960), pp. 386-405. Oliver Williamson operationalized it within the specific context of business relations. See *Economic Institutions of Capitalism*, New York: Free Press, 1985.

27. David M. Kreps, "Corporate Culture and Economic Theory," in Alt and Shepsle (eds.), *Perspectives on Positive Political Economy*, Cambridge: Cambridge University Press, 1990, p. 96.

28. See also Pinglé, "Managing State-owned Enterprises. "

29. Barry Ames's 'structural coalition theory' is a variation of this argument. See his book: *Political Survival: Politicians and Public Policy in Latin America*, Berkeley: University of California Press, 1990, p. 211.

30. For a theoretical discussion of bureaucracies, see Max Weber, *Economy and Society*, New York: Bedminster Press, 1968.

31. These interests are discussed in detail in chapter 3.

32. Douglass North, *Institutions, Institutional Change and Economic Performance*, Cambridge: Cambridge University Press, 1990, pp. 86, 107. North defines institutions as the rules of the game. He argues that institutions affect the performance of the economy by their effect on the costs of exchange and production. Thus, institutions, together with the standard constraints of economic theory, determine the opportunities in a society. Organizations, on the other hand, are considered to be agents of institutional change.

33. Douglass North, *Structure and Change in Economic History*, New York: Norton, 1981.

34. Ezra Vogel, *The Four Little Dragons: The Spread of Industrialization in East Asia*, Cambridge: Harvard University Press, 1991, p. 92. According to Vogel, historical and structural factors alone do not explain the performance of the four "little dragons." Thus while five "situational" factors—"U. S. aid, the destruction of the old order, a sense of political and economic urgency, an eager and plentiful labor force, and familiarity with the Japanese model of success,"—have been critical for East Asia's growth, they "alone do not account for all that happened. " See also Ronald Dore, *Taking Japan Seriously: A Confucian Perspective on Leading Economic Issues*, Palo Alto: Stanford University Press, 1987.

35. Vogel, *The Four Little Dragons,* p. 92.

36. Peter L. Berger, "An East Asian Development Model?" in Peter L. Berger and Hsin-Huang Michael Hsio (eds.), *In Search of an East Asian Development Model*, New Brunswick: Transaction Publishers, 1990, p. 5.

37. D. Michael Shafer, *Winners and Losers: How Sectors Shape the Developmental Prospects of States*, Ithaca: Cornell University Press, 1994, pp. 226-227. See also Philippe Schmitter, "Sectors in Modern Capitalism: Modes of Governance and Variations in Performance," in R. Brunetta and C. Dell'Aringa (eds.), *Labor Relations and Economic Performance*," New York: Macmillan, 1990.

38. By change, I refer to the development of new patterns, approaches, tools and techniques, or the reformulation of existing ones.

39. Charles Ragin, *Comparative Method: Moving Beyond Qualitative and Quantitative Strategy*, Berkeley: University of California Press, 1987, p. 13.

Chapter 2

1. See, example, the arguments offered by economists such as W. A. Lewis, *The Theory of Economic Growth,* London: Allen and Unwin, 1955; R. Nurkse, *Problems of Capital Formation in Underdeveloped Countries*, New York: Oxford University Press, 1953; and P. N. Rosenstein-Rodan

(ed.), *Capital Formation and Economic Development*, Cambridge: MIT Press, 1964. The approach was also based on the Bombay Plan drafted jointly by Indian industrialists and nationalist leaders in 1943, which is discussed later in this chapter. The development approach was ideologically supported by the Fabian–Socialist views of the ruling Congress party.

2. This goal was stated by the All-India Congress Committee in 1947. According to the committee, it would help create a social structure that would be "an alternative to the acquisitive economy of private capitalism and regimentation of a totalitarian state." All-India Congress Committee, *The Resolutions on Economic Policy and Programme, 1924-1954,* New Delhi: All-India Congress Committee, p. 20.

3. The industries included: automobiles and tractors, machine tools, salt, prime movers, electric engineering, heavy machinery, heavy chemicals, fertilizers, pharmaceuticals and drugs, electrochemical industries, non-ferrous metals, rubber, power, industrial alcohol, cotton and woolen textiles, cement, sugar, paper and newsprint, air and sea transport, and minerals.

4. See Ashutosh Varshney, *Democracy, Development and the Countryside: Urban-Rural Struggles in India*, New York: Cambridge University Press, 1995.

5. Government of India, *Industrial Policy Resolution-1956,* New Delhi: Government of India, 1956, paragraph 7.

6. Planning Commission, *Second Five Year Plan*, New Delhi: Government of India, 1955, p. 25.

7. Ibid., p. 136.

8. Isher J. Ahluwalia, *Productivity and Growth in Indian Manufacturing*, Delhi: Oxford University Press, 1991, p. 3.

9. Planning Commission, *Fifth Five Year Plan*, New Delhi: Government of India, 1974, p. 2.

10. Examining the political-economy of the 1980s, Atul Kohli notes that "although the rhetoric of both socialism and nationalism was maintained, anti-poverty programs were put on the back burner." Kohli, *Democracy and Discontent: India's Growing Crisis of Governability*, New York: Cambridge University Press, 1990, p. 310.

11. United Nations, *Yearbook of International Trade Statistics*, various years.

12. Martin Wolf, *India's Exports*, New York: published for the World Bank by Oxford University Press, 1982.

13. Associated Chambers of Commerce and Industry, *New Industrial Policy*, New Delhi: ASSOCHAM, 1991, paragraph 24.

14. Ibid., paragraph 33.
15. See the section on India's labor structure in this chapter for a discussion of labor laws, and the implications of not having an exit policy.
16. *The Economist,* April 24, 1999.
17. Ibid.
18. For a discussion of India's achievements and failures in food production and in the agricultural sector see Francine Frankel, *India's Political Economy 1957-1977: The Gradual Revolution*, Delhi: Oxford University Press, 1978. See also Amartya Sen, *Poverty and Famines: An Essay on Entitlements and Deprivation,* Oxford: Clarendon Press, 1981; and Varshney, *Democracy, Development and the Countryside.*
19. Ministry of Finance, *Economic Survey 1998-99*, New Delhi: Ministry of Finance, 1999.
20. Data from the World Bank, *World Development Report 1995*, Washington, D.C. : the World Bank, 1995.
21. Data from the World Bank, *Trends in Developing Economies 1990*, Washington, D.C. : the World Bank, 1990, and The Economist, *World in Figures*, London: The Economist, 1994.
22. Ahluwalia, *Industrial Growth in India*, Delhi: Oxford University Press, 1985. For a discussion of India's economic changes of 1991 see Jagdish Bhagwati, *India in Transition: Freeing the Economy,* New York: Oxford University Press, 1993.
23. Ibid., p. 366.
24. The Institute was renamed the Lal Bahadur Shastri Academy of Administration in 1972.
25. D.C. Potter, *India's Political Administrators 1919—1983,* Oxford: Clarendon Press, 1986, p. 185.
26. Ibid., p. 186.
27. Ibid., p. 188.
28. Unless, of course, the IAS official studied economics or related subjects at the undergraduate or masters level prior to joining the IAS.
29. Potter, *India's Political Administrators*, p. 218.
30. Interviews with IAS officials, various dates between September 1991 and July 1997.
31. The transfers of IAS officials follows clearly specified guidelines. Only rarely is an IAS official retained in any post for more than five years. Transfers are usually accompanied by guaranteed promotions. This is in contrast to the transfer system applicable to non-IAS and lower-level bureaucrats, their promotions and transfers are not automatic and are determined by political considerations. In an article Robert Wade argues, that

the system of transfers applicable to non-IAS bureaucrats creates conditions conducive for corruption and undermines bureaucratic initiatives. Wade, "The Market for Public Office: Why the Indian State Is Not Better at Development," *World Development*, 13, no. 4, APR, 1985.

32. Richard P. Taub, *Bureaucrats Under Stress: Administrators and Administration in an Indian State*, Berkeley: University of California Press, 1969, p. 191.

33. For an analysis of corruption at the lower levels of the bureaucracy, see Wade, "The Market for Public Office."

34. Figure 2.1 summarizes the organizational structure of the IAS, and its implications for IAS bureaucrats' ability to act in a developmental manner.

35. Both Nehru and Gandhi were fervent critics of the ICS and argued for its modification and even its elimination.

36. Other important labor laws include: the Minimum Wages Act, Industrial Employment (Standing Orders) Act (which regulates the terms of recruitment), Workmen's Compensation Act, Employees' Provident Fund Act, and Factories Act (regulating work hours and conditions).

37. *Trade Unions Act—1926*, Government of India, Lucknow: Eastern Book Company, 1993, p. 5.

38. C. A. Myers and S. Kannappan, *Industrial Relations in India*, London: Asia Publishing House, 1970, p. 173.

39. New Delhi: Interviews with trade union leaders, Sept. 20, 23, and 28, 1993. See also V. B. Karnik, "National Labour Policy and Union Action," *Proceedings of the Third National Seminar on Industrial Relations in a Developing Country*, New Delhi: Sri Ram Centre for Industrial Relations, 1967.

40. B. Tulpule, "Government Power and Union Recognition," in *Trade Unions and Politics in India*, proceedings of the *Third National Seminar on Industrial Relations in a Developing Economy*, Delhi: SRCIR, vol. 2, 1967, p. 349.

41. Karnik, "National Labour Policy and Union Action," p. 203.

42. Confederation of Indian Industry, *Industrial Relations Policies and Practices*, Case Study, New Delhi: CII, October 1991.

43. Lloyd Rudolph and Susanne H. Rudolph, *In Pursuit of Lakshmi*, Chicago: University of Chicago Press, 1987, p. 261.

44. Ibid., p. 267. New Delhi: Interviews with trade union leader/politicians, September 20, 23, and 28, 1993.

45. Major Indian political parties are: the right-wing Hindu party—Bharatiya Janata Party, two main communist factions—the Communist party of India and the Communist party of India (Marxist), the Congress party, the Janata Dal, and an array of regional parties, such as Dravida Munetra Kazhagam and Telegu Desam.

46. Rudolph and Rudolph, *In Pursuit of Lakshmi*, p. 273. They argue that the political marginality of organized labor is a result of the fact that "workers in the organized economy, the pool for organized labor, constitute only 10 percent of the total workforce; the state, which employs two-thirds of the workers in the organized economy, constitutes an ambiguous adversary because of its claims to be a model employer and the vehicle for socialist objectives; and the multiplication and rivalry of national federations and of industry and enterprise unions lead to the progressive involution of the trade union movement." Ibid., pp. 259-260.

47. Karnik, "National Labour Policy and Union Action," p. 345.

48. Minister P. A. Sanghma quoted in "Exit Policy Ready for Approval," *The Statesman*, March 17, 1993.

49. Ibid.

50. The privatization of the state-owned steel plant in Orissa offers an interesting counterexample. The loss-making plant was sold by the Orissa state government to TISCO in the early 1990s. Labor acquiescence was ensured by promising all unions that no workers would be fired, and given TISCO's higher wages, all workers would also receive higher wages. What made such a negotiation possible was, however, the role of the IAS bureaucrat in charge. This personal interaction with the chairman of TISCO helped ensure that such an offer was possible. Encouragement from political superiors also contributed. No trade union at the plant was willing to prevent the privatization from going through, given the greater benefits workers were likely to receive from it. Thus, fragmentation and inter-union rivalry was countered by ties between the bureaucracy and the industrial actor. Boston: Interview with the Principal Secretary, January 28, 1995.

51. See also Karnik, "National Labour Policy and Union Action," and *Indian Labour: Problems and Prospects*, Calcutta: Minerva Associates, 1974; Myers and Kannappan, *Industrial Relations in India*; Rudolph and Rudolph, *In Pursuit of Lakshmi*; E. A. Ramaswamy (ed.), *Industrial Relations in India: A Sociological Perspective*, Delhi: MacMillan Company of India Ltd., 1978, and E. A. Ramasway, *A Question of Balance: Labour, Management and Society*, Delhi: Oxford University Press, 1997.

52. Bombay: Interviews with trade union leaders, April 30, 1991 and September 1, 3, and 8, 1993.

53. The structure of the IAS also has mitigated against the establishment of noncontractual ties and informal channels of communication with industrialists. Delhi: Interviews with IAS officials in the Ministries of Personnel, Steel, Labor, and Industry, March 1 and 3, and April 28, 1991.

54. Stanley A. Kochanek, "The Transformation of Interest Politics in India," *Pacific Affairs*, 68, no. 4, (Winter 1995-96), p. 532.

55. Stanley A. Kochanek, *Business and Politics in India*, Berkeley: University of California Press, 1974, p. 323.

56. Reproduced in Aurobindo Ghose, "Growth Strategy: Past, Present and Future" in A. Ghose et al. (eds.), *The Indian Economy and Its Performance since Independence*, Delhi: Oxford University Press, 1990, p. 71.

57. Kochanek, *Business and Politics in India*, p. 267.

58. New Delhi: Interviews with senior management of industry association, February 3, 1992.

59. Kochanek, *Business and Politics in India*.

60. Kochanek notes that such "criticism is particularly characteristic of those who depend heavily on personal contacts in government and do not need established patterns of access." *Business and Politics in India*, p. 277.

61. Kochanek, "The Transformation of Interest Politics in India," p. 547.

62. Interviews with bureaucrats and CII members, New Delhi: September 13, 1993; New York: September 4, September 24, October 3, 1997; and Boston: February 6, 1996.

63. Kochanek, "The Transformation of Interest Politics in India," p. 546. He continues that this process of building relationships "involves frequent informal personal contacts, providing up-to-date information, avoidance of public criticism [of the state], and working to help bureaucrats achieve their policy objectives without asking for quid pro quo. Having established a close working relationship, demands are submitted in the form of carefully prepared briefs based on reliable data and well-reasoned arguments. Discussions are held in private and are based on a non-confrontational, constructive, cooperative, problem-solving and bargaining style of negotiations." Ibid., pp. 546-547.

Chapter 3

1. G. Etienne, *Asian Crucible: The Steel Industry in China and India,* New Delhi: Sage, 1992, p. 53.

2. See the appendix, tables A. 1 and A. 2 for India's steel production figures.

3. W. A. Johnson, *The Steel Industry of India,* Cambridge, Harvard University Press, 1966, p. 13.

4. New Delhi: Interviews with World Bank Officials, economic journalists, senior managers at the state-owned steel plants, senior officials in the Department of Steel, Ministry of Steel and Mines, and with former Steel secretaries and chair of SAIL. New Delhi, September 1991-May 1992 and September 9 and 16, 1993.

5. Johnson, *The Steel Industry of India,* p. 79.
6. N. R. Srinivasan, *The Corporate Story of SAIL,* New Delhi: SAIL, 1990.
7. Rakesh Mohan and Vandana Aggarwal, "Command and Controls: Planning for Indian Industrial Development 1951-1990," New Delhi: Ministry of Economic Affairs, 1991, p. 2.
8. Ibid., p. 4.
9. The price paid to the producer is referred to as the retention price.
10. Government of India, *Government Policy and Procedures,* New Delhi: Government of India, Sec. II-2.
11. Besides focusing on the industrial sectors reserved exclusively for state enterprises, the Resolution also specified the relationship between the state and the private units in other industrial sectors. With regard to the industrial sectors not reserved for state enterprises, the resolution stated that the government will assist private or cooperative units "by removing transport difficulties and by facilitating the import of essential raw-materials to the maximum possible extent. The tariff policy of [the] Government will be designed to prevent unfair foreign competition and to promote the utilization of India's resources without imposing unjustifiable burdens on the consumer." Ibid., p. Sec. II-5.
12. Ibid.
13. Johnson, *The Steel Industry of India,* p. 34.
14. Padma Desai, *The Bokaro Steel Plant: A Study of Soviet Economic Assistance,* London: North-Holland, 1972.
15. Srinivasan, *The Corporate Story of SAIL,* p. 67.
16. Johnson, *The Steel Industry of India,* p. 81.
17. Srinivasan, *The Iron and Steel Industry in India: A Monograph,* New Delhi: SAIL, 1982, p. 116.
18. The following list of Steel Secretaries gives as indication of their rapid turnover. Only three Secretaries (marked *) had tenures of four or more years.

*S. Boothalingam	1955-62	Saran Singh	1976-77
R. Venkatanarayanan	1988-91	*N. N. Wanchoo	1962-66
Mantosh Sondhi	1977-80	R. Vasudevan	1991-92
T. Swaminathan	1966-67	S. Samaddar	1980-81
Musa Raja	1992-92	H. Lal	1967-69
A. S. Gill	1981-83	V. Krishnan	1992-93
R. C. Dutta	1969-70	Lovraj Kumar	1983-84
Musa Raja	1993-95	H. C. Sarin	1970-72
P. K. Basu	1984-85	J. K. Bagchi	1995-97
*M. A. Wadud Khan	1972-76	R. P. Khosla	1985-85
A. Banerjee	1997-		

19. Srinivasan, *The Iron and Steel Industry in India,* p. 292.
20. Francine Frankel, *India's Political Economy 1947-1977: The Gradual Revolution,* Delhi: Oxford University Press, 1978, p. 154.
21. New Delhi: Interview with IAS bureaucrats, November 16, 1991, March 13, 1992, and April 20, 1993.
22. Views expressed in a speech entitled "New Model for Governmental Administration of Industry," at Madras, on December 9, 1972. This speech is discussed by Srinivasan in *The Corporate Story of SAIL,* p. 88.
23. Related state-owned enterprises—Hindustan Steelworks Construction Limited (HSCL), Bharat Coking Coal Limited, and National Mining Development Corporation (NMDC)—were also brought under SAIL.
24. Srinivasan, *The Corporate Story of SAIL,* p. 89.
25. According to Srinivasan, the then Minister of Steel and Mines, M. Kumaramangalam, believed that "the culture of the civil services was not conducive to the needs of efficient industrial management, because [the] civil service was procedure oriented whereas, industry was result oriented." Ibid., p. 88. Thus the Minister suggested "the concept of a Holding Company for the twin reasons that a technocrat should be the adviser to the Minister and that decision making should be on the pattern adopted in industry." Ibid.
26. Wadud Khan has been one of only two non-IAS members to be appointed Secretary of the Ministry of Steel.
27. World Bank, *India: Steel Sector Strategy Report,* Washington, D.C. : The World Bank, 1987, p. 44.
28. This was also the primary interest of the IAS bureaucrats in the Ministry of Steel. Frequent transfers, and promotions not linked to accomplishments tend to give IAS officials a relatively short-term perspective. New Delhi and Boston: Interviews with IAS officials, September 20, 1991, February 1, 1992, January 28-31, 1995.
29. New Delhi and Bombay: Interviews with SAIL managers and trade unionists, February 11, March 10 and 31, 1992, and September 12 and 25, 1993. See also B. Tulpule, *Problems of Management and Workers in Public Sector Industries,* Bombay: Lala Lajpatrai Institute, 1974.
30. New Delhi: Interviews with senior managers at SAIL, February 11, 1992, and March 10, and September 12, 1993.
31. Reviewing the mini-steel plants in India, G. Etienne notes that despite the initial plan to license only 15 such plants, the state permitted and even encouraged the establishment of a much larger number of plants. Etienne, *Asian Crucible,* p. 76.

32. Ministry of Steel, *A Strategy for Steel,* New Delhi: Ministry of Steel, 1987, p. 45.
33. World Bank, *India: Steel Sector Strategy Report,* p. 61.
34. The integrated steel plants had their own power generation facilities (i.e., captive power plants).
35. Ministry of Steel, *A Strategy for Steel,* 1987, pp. 45-46.
36. World Bank, *India Steel Sector Strategy Report,* p. 61.
37. Ibid., p. 62.
38. Ibid., p. 15.
39. B. R. Nayar, *The Political Economy of India's Public Sector: Policy and Performance,* Bombay: Popular Prakashan, 1990, p. 141.
40. Ibid., p. 133.
41. This was the second expansion and modernization program undertaken by TISCO. The first such program was in the 1950s.
42. Credit Rating Information Services of India Limited (hereafter CRISIL), *Special Corporate Report on TISCO,* Bombay: CRISIL, 1989, p. 25.
43. Ibid.
44. Etienne, *Asian Crucible,* p. 185. In interviews, senior management at SAIL and TISCO and bureaucrats in the Ministry of Steel all frequently referred to TISCO's management practices in glowing terms. New Delhi: Interviews with senior management at SAIL and TISCO, and Ministry of Steel Bureaucrats, February 11, and March 10, 1992, and September 12, 1993.
45. New Delhi: Interviews with senior officials in the Department of Personnel, and Ministry of Steel, Government of India, March 13, 1992, and April 20, 1993.
46. However, when compared to steel companies in other countries, such as South Korea and Brazil, its performance fell short. Ministry of Steel, *A Strategy for Steel,* 1987.
47. New Delhi: Interviews with Ministry of Steel officials, February 11, and March 10, 1992, and September 12, 1993. Boston: Interview with mini-steel plant manufacturer, June 9, 1994.
48. In issues other than distribution, however, the Ministry of Steel continues to interfere in SAIL's management more or less as before.
49. Confederation of Indian Industry (hereafter CII), *Handbook of Statistics 1996,* New Delhi: CII, 1996; and CII, *Handbook of Statistics 1997,* New Delhi: CII, 1998.
50. N. N. S., "TISCO: Full Benefit of New Facilities," *Survey of Indian Industry 1997,* Madras: The Hindu, 1997, p. 255.

51. Bombay and New Delhi: Interview with journalists, September 1993 and February 1995.
52. "Secondary Steel: Changing Input, Product Profiles," *Survey of Indian Industry 1997,* Madras: The Hindu, 1997, p. 254.
53. New Delhi: Interview with senior bureaucrat, Ministry of Steel, March 12, 1992, and September 12, 1993.
54. Arvind Pande, "Steel: Brightening Near Term Outlook," *Survey of Indian Industry 1997,* Madras: The Hindu, 1997.
55. D. Michael Shafer, *Winners and Losers: How Sectors Shape the Developmental Prospects of States,* Ithaca: Cornell University Press, 1994.
56. Thomas R. Howell et al., *Steel and the State: Government Intervention and Steel's Structural Crisis,* Boulder: Westview Press, 1988, p. 5. See also Chalmers Johnson, *MITI and the Japanese Miracle: The Growth of Industrial Policy, 1925 to 1975,* Palo Alto: Stanford; and Harukiyo Hasegawa, *The Steel Industry in Japan: A Comparison with Britain.* London: University Press, 1982, Routledge, 1996.
57. Howell et al., *Steel and the State,* p. 204.
58. Jeffrey A. Hart, *Rival Capitalists: International Competitive in the United States, Japan, and Western Europe,* Ithaca: Cornell University Press, 1982. p. 85.
59. Ibid.
60. Johnson, *MITI and the Japanese Miracle,* p. 316.
61. Ibid.
62. Richard J. Samuels, *The Business of the Japanese State: Energy Markets in Comparative and Historical Perspective,* Ithaca: Cornell University Press, 1987, p. 286.
63. Alice Amsden, *Asia's Next Giant: South Korea and late Industrialization,* New York: Oxford University Press, 1989. See also Alice Amsden and Yoon-Dae Euh, "Behind Korea's Plunge," *New York Times,* November 27, 1997.
64. Mark L. Clifford, *Troubled Tiger: Businessmen, Bureaucrats, and Generals in South Korea,* Armonk: M. E. Sharpe, 1994, p. 68.
65. Amsden, *Asia's Next Giant.*
66. Leroy P. Jones and Il Sakong, *Government, Business and Entrepreneurship in Economic Development: The Korean Case.* Cambridge: Harvard University, 1980, p. 67.
67. Yoon Je Cho, "Government Intervention, Rent Distribution, and Economic Development in Korea," in Masahiko Aoki et al, (eds.), *The Role of Government in East Asian Economic Development: Comparative Institutional Analysis,* Oxford: Clarendon Press, 1996, p. 229.

68. Peter B. Evans, *Embedded Autonomy: States and Industrial Transformation,* Princeton: Princeton University Press, 1995, p. 52.
69. Ibid., p. 53.
70. While POSCO is not in trouble, Hanbo Steel did experience serious problems beginning in the spring of 1997.

Chapter 4

1. For a breakdown of the production figures by firm and by type of vehicle, see the appendix; tables A. 3, A.4A, A.4B, and A.5.
2. According to Francine Frankel, Gandhi "was always appreciative of his cordial reception by prominent industrialists. He reported, with evident satisfaction, that at his request the rich 'gladly' gave donations to the nationalist cause. . . . It was . . . Tata who first came forward with substantial financial assistance for Gandhi's efforts." Frankel, *India's Political Economy 1947-1977: The Gradual Revolution,* Delhi: Oxford University Press, 1978, p. 34. Sir James Grigg, a senior civil servant at the Treasury, viewed this relationship in ominous terms. He argued that "Birla and Co. can control Congress policy by withholding money." See D. Tripathi (ed.), *State and Business in India,* New Delhi: Manohar Publications, 1987, p. 201.
3. The list of automobile import dealers included Addison, Dewar's, Peninsular, and the French Motor Company.
4. Government of India, *Industrial Policy Resolution 1948,* New Delhi: Government of India, Sec. II-2.
5. The Indian bureaucratic system is discussed in chapter 2.
6. Premier Automobiles Limited, *The Dream Fulfilled,* Bombay: PAL, 1982, p. 5.
7. New Delhi: Interview with a former member of the Planning Commission, February 26, 1992.
8. Premier Automobiles Limited, *The Dream Fulfilled.*
9. Gurcharan Das recounted this incident, Cambridge, Massachusetts, March 1993. Aside from identifying the tension between industrialists and India's political leadership, the incident also emphasizes the sincere belief in the contribution of state-owned enterprises and in the value of controlling the market.
10. This was clearly apparent in the developments in the automobile industry during the 1970s and the 1980s. I will discuss these developments in detail later in this chapter.

11. In 1960 these components included spark plugs, brake parts, mufflers, car and truck bodies, as well as nonmechanical components such as paints, upholstery, and rubber components.
12. This category of automobile ancillaries included mechanical items such as shock absorbers, brake linings, piston and clutch parts, fuel injection equipment, and various filters.
13. These components included electrical equipment and key mechanical parts such as wheels, steering machinery.
14. Krueger, *The Benefits and Costs of Import Substitution in India,* p. 57.
15. Ibid. "O. E." stands for original equipment.
16. World Bank, *India: Review of the Automotive Products Industry,* Washington, D.C.: The World Bank, 1987, p. 31.
17. Frankel, *India's Political Economy 1947-1977,* p. 299.
18. Tata also critiqued the planning process and the extent of economic and industrial regulations. According to Frankel, "Tata's advice to the government was to drastically reduce the role of the planners in the formulation of economic policy." Ibid.
19. Ibid., p. 420. Frankel further notes that the "notion that Mrs. Gandhi was the personal embodiment of a new direction in economic policy aimed at benefiting the poor was meanwhile promoted through large rallies and demonstrations in New Delhi."
20. While this added firmness followed from the recommendations of the 1968 Tariff Commission report, it also reflected the populist interests of Mrs. Gandhi.
21. The final decision was reached by the courts only in 1975.
22. Association of Indian Automobile Manufacturers, *Automobile Production Statistics,* Bombay: AIAM, 1985, p. 18.
23. Frankel, *India's Political Economy 1947-1977,* p. 334.
24. Ibid.
25. Ibid.
26. During the period 1951 to 1979, the largest firms (Indian and multinational) were: Andrew Yule, Bird-Heilgers, Birla, Dalmia, Sahu Jain, Indra Singh, J. K. Singhania, Kasturbhai, Khatau, Mafatlal, Mahindra and Mahindra, Martin Burn, Seshasayee, Shapoorji, Shri Ram (DCM), Tata, Thapar, V. Ramkrishna, and Walchand. The list includes nearly all the automobile companies in India at that time.
27. Aside from the MRTP Act and FERA, the list of populist initiatives included the promotion of small-scale and craft (or cottage) industries, the nationalization of banks, and the restriction of the growth of large private business houses.

28. Passenger cars were classified as luxury products, while two-wheelers and commercial vehicles were not.
29. World Bank, *India: Review of the Automotive Products Industry.*
30. The Fifth Five Year Plan noted that "a large step up in scooter production is envisaged." Government of India, *Fifth Five Year Plan,* 1974, p. 63.
31. World Bank, *India: Review of the Automotive Products Industry,* pp. 2-3.
32. Premier Automobiles Limited, *The Dream Fulfilled,* p. 18.
33. World Bank, *India: Review of the Automotive Products Industry,* p. 11.
34. While TELCO and Ashok Leyland had dominated the commercial vehicle segment from the mid-1960s onward, Premier Automobiles and Hindustan Motors, had been the leaders during the 1950s. Once they began manufacturing passenger cars, however, both companies reduced their contribution to the commercial vehicle segment. By 1980 Premier Automobiles and Hindustan Motors together produced only about 6,000 commercial vehicles.
35. Bajaj Auto's export markets have included South-East Asia, West Asia, and Africa.
36. Interviews with senior officials in the Ministry of Industry as well as other ministries, New Delhi: September 1991-May 1992, September 1993; and New York: October 1997.
37. See chapter 2 for a discussion of the structure of the Indian bureaucracy.
38. New Delhi: Interview with official in the Planning Commission, February 26, and March 1, 1992. This official indicated that political debts incurred by Indira Gandhi during her years in the opposition were primarily responsible for the decision to grant four non-automobile manufacturers licenses to produce light commercial vehicles.
39. R. Venkataramani, *Japan Enters Indian Industry,* New Delhi: Radiant Press, 1990, p. 16.
40. Ibid., p. 136.
41. Indira Gandhi and Rajiv Gandhi's political opponents frequently used this aspect of MUL's performance as political ammunition. One member of Parliament, Madhu Dandavate, joked that "the only indigenous component in [a] Maruti-Suzuki car is the air inside [its] tires." Quoted in *Automobile Engineer and Trader,* (April) 1989, pp. 59-60.
42. *Hindustan Times,* May 30, 1983.
43. Apart from MUL, Sipani Automobiles also produced cars with a capacity of less than 1000cc. Sipani's total production in 1983 was only 302.
44. In addition to the cuts in the various duties, the state directed oil companies to produce 87 octane gasoline rather than the 83 octane currently being produced and used by Premier Automobile and Hindustan Motor vehicles.

45. See Confederation of Indian Industry, *Handbook of Statistics,* New Delhi: CII, 1994; and Venkataramani, *Japan Enters Indian Industry.*

46. See Venkataramani, *Japan Enters Indian Industry.*

47. Planning Commissions, New Delhi: Government of India, *Seventh Five Year Plan,* 1985, p. 41.

48. In both companies, the production figures for buses and trucks are combined since in India the truck and bus chassis are the same. With regard to the ranking, Ford, General Motors, and Daimler-Benz manufactured between 36,00 and 41,000 units each in 1988. Isuzu produced only 5,000 to 6000 units in the same year.

49. Atul Kohli, *Democracy and Discontent: India's Growing Crisis of Governability,* New York: Cambridge University Press, 1990.

50. D. Narayana, *The Motor Vehicle Industry in India,* New Delhi: Oxford and IBM Publishing Co. Pvt. Ltd., and Trivandrum: Centre for Development Studies, 1989, p. 89.

51. "Passenger Cars: Too Many Options for Buyers," *Survey of Indian Industry 1997,* Madras: The Hindu, 1997. Centre for Monitoring Indian Economy (hereafter CMIE), *Monthly Review of the Indian Economy,* Bombay: CMIE, 1997 (various issues).

52. S. Vaitheeswaran, "Commercial Vehicles: Poised for Continued Growth," *Survey of Indian Industry 1997,* Madras: The Hindu, 1997. CMIE, *Monthly Review of the Indian Economy,* various issues.

53. K. Mahesh, "Auto Components: Time to Update Technology," *Survey of Indian Industry 1997,* Madras: The Hindu, 1997.

54. Discussed in chapter 5.

55. See Anthony P. D'Costa, "The Restructuring of the Indian Automobile Industry: Indian State and Japanese Capital," *World Development,* 23, no. 3, (1995), pp. 485-502. D'Costa concludes that the entry of multinational car companies into the Indian market has strengthened rather than undermined domestic automobile production.

56. World Bank, *India: Five Years of Stabilization and Reform and the Challenges Ahead,* Washington D.C., The World Bank, 1996, p. 41.

57. See Oliver Williamson, *Markets and Hierarchies: Analysis and Antitrust Implications,* New York: Free Press, 1975; Williamson *The Economic Institutions of Capitalism,* New York: Free Press, 1985. See also J. Tollison, Buchanan and G. Tullock, *Toward a Theory of the Rent Seeking Society,* College Station: Texas A & M University Press 1980.

58. According to the principal-agent theory, an agency relationship exists when one party (agent) acts on behalf of another (the principal). The theory assumes that the two parties have unequal interests but that they may

be induced to or have an incentive to cooperate. The challenge is to construct contractual relations such that they provide incentives to the agent to act as if he/she were maximizing the principal's welfare. An example of a principal-agent relationship is found between owners and managers in private firms.

59. By high/high industry, Michael Shafer refers to industries marked by high capital intensity, high economies of scale, high production inflexibility, and high asset/factor inflexibility. Michael D. Shafer, *Winners and Losers: How Sectors Shape the Developmental Prospects of States,* Ithaca: Cornell University Press, 1994.

Chapter 5

1. Peter B. Evans, "Predatory, Developmental and Other Apparatuses," Working Paper #11, Center for the Comparative Study of Development, Brown University, 1990, p. 2.

2. See appendix, tables A.6, A.7, and A.8.

3. The Tata Institute of Fundamental Research (TIFR) is one of India's premier scientific research institutes.

4. C. R. Subramanian, *India and the Computer: A Study of Planned Development,* Delhi: Oxford University Press, 1992, p. 3.

5. Government of India, *Report of the Electronics Committee,* February 1966, Table 18, p. 112.

6. New Delhi: Interviews with Department of Electronics officials, both current and former, February 17, 20, and 23, 1992, and September 18, 20 and 29, 1993.

7. Public Accounts Committee, "Computerization in Government Departments: Department of Electronics," 221st Report (1975-76), Fifth Lok Sabha, New Delhi, April 1976.

8. Ibid., p. 177.

9. C. R. Subramanian, *India and the Computer,* p. 5. See also Joseph M. Grieco, *Between Dependency and Autonomy: India's Experience with the International Computer Industry,* Berkeley: University of California Press, 1984.

10. This emphasis on indigenous development and an autarchic approach was reinforced by the policies pursued by Prime Minister Indira Gandhi. In 1973 the Indian government under Mrs. Gandhi's leadership required all multinational corporations in India to reduce their equity to under 40 percent. As I discuss later in the chapter, while ICL agreed to comply, IBM refused eventually and chose to leave India. Interviews with De-

partment of Electronics officials, both current and former, New Delhi, February 17, 20, and 23, 1992, and September 18, 20 and 29, 1993.

11. Department of Electronics, *Software Policy 1974,* 1974.
12. Ibid.
13. Public Accounts Committee, "Computerization in Government Departments," pp. 195-255.
14. O. P. Mehra, "June 1, 1978, IBM Quits India," *Dataquest* (January 1985), pp. 58-59.
15. New Delhi: Interviews with IAS officials, February 10 and 17, 1992, and with Department of Electronics officials, both current and former, February 17, 20, and 23, 1992, and September 18, 20, and 29, 1993. See also Grieco, *Between Dependency and Autonomy,* p. 107.
16. New Delhi: Interviews with IAS officials, February 10 and 17, 1992, and with Department of Electronics officials, both current and former, February 17, 20, and 23, 1992, and September 18, 20 and 29, 1993.
17. New Delhi: Interviews with Department of Electronics officials, both current and former, February 17, 20, and 23, 1992, and September 18, 20 and 29, 1993. See also Subramanian, *India and the Computer.*
18. Problems (i. e., turf battles) regarding ECIL's management, however, remained.
19. New Delhi: Interviews with officials at NASSCOM and the Department of Electronics, both current and former, February 17, 20, and 23, 1992, and September 18, 20 and 29, 1993.
20. Department of Electronics, *Minicomputer Policy 1978,* 1978.
21. Grieco, *Between Dependency and Autonomy,* p. 127.
22. Ibid.
23. Ibid., pp. 127-128.
24. New Delhi: Interviews with officials at NASSCOM and the Department of Electronics, both current and former, February 17, 20, and 23, 1992, and September 18, 20 and 29, 1993.
25. S. S. Oberoi and G. V. Ranganathan, "Indian Software Scenario," *Electronics—Information and Planning* (August 1991), p. 603.
26. Note that software import continued to be regulated by the Department of Electronics.
27. National Association Software and Service Companies (hereafter NASSCOM), *The Software Industry in India—1992,* New Delhi: NASSCOM, 1992.
28. New Delhi: Interviews with Department of Electronics officials, both current and former, February 17, 20, and 23, 1992, and September 18, 20 and 29, 1993. New Delhi, Bangalore, and Bombay: Interviews with

software entrepreneurs, November 15, 26, and December 18, 1991, April 16-28, 1992, and September 4, 5, and 8, 1993.

29. N. Seshagiri, interview in *Dataquest* (December 1984), p. 59.
30. Bangalore: Interview with senior managers at Texas Instruments, March 1992.
31. Brian O'Reilly, "Your New Global Work Force," *Fortune,* December 14, 1992, p. 64.
32. *Dataquest,* (July 1993), p. 177.
33. "Sindbad Story," *India Today* (online edition), March 15, 1999.
34. Oberoi and Ranganathan, "Indian Software Scenario," p. 605.
35. New Delhi: Interview with Secretary, Department of Electronics, September 19, 1993.
36. New Delhi, Bangalore: Interviews with the president and executive director of NASSCOM, February 17, 20, 23, and March 19, 1992.
37. N. Vittal, *The Economic Times,* October 28, 1992.
38. Address by N. Vittal, "The Rama Route to Success," NASSCOM meetings, Bangalore, December 5, 1991.
39. N. Vittal, address to NASSCOM, January 17, 1992.
40. Rahul Sharma, "More Space to Breathe," *The Economic Times,* April 15, 1992.
41. Talk delivered by N. Vittal, "Software and Engineering Industry—Need for Developing a Domestic Market," UNDP, Delhi, August 6, 1991.
42. Department of Electronics, "Note for Supplementaries for Starred Question No. 432 for 14. 8. 91 Regarding Impact on New Industrial and Trade Policies on Electronic Industry," internal memo, p. 6.
43. New Delhi: Interviews with Department of Electronics officials, both current and former, February 17, 20, and 23, 1992, and September 18, 20 and 29, 1993.
44. The only times Department of Electronics officials have faced pressure from the trade union federations have been occasions when the Department has attempted to help state-owned enterprises computerize. For example, when the nationalized banks attempted to introduce computers into their banks, the trade union federations in collaboration with the banks' unions actively resisted any such move (since they perceived computerization as an attempt to reduce employment opportunities). However, even in these instances, while the attempt to computerize might have failed, there was limited, if any, among between the trade unions and the Department of Electronics. The primary interactions were among the political leadership, the concerned administrative ministry (i. e., Finance, Industry, etc.), and the trade unions.

45. Infosys, for example, was established with a mere Rs. 10,000, and was thus hardly in a position, in its early years, to capture bureaucrats. Even a street-level bureaucrat (i. e., a policeman) is likely to demand Rs. 5,000 for doing a "favor."

46. Data from Ministry of Finance, *Economic Survey of India 1996-1997,* New Delhi: Ministry of Finance, 1997; The Hindu, *Survey of Indian Industry 1997,* Madras: The Hindu, 1997; and Centre for Monitoring Indian Economy (hereafter CMIE), *Monthly Review of the Indian Economy,* Bombay: CMIE, (various issues).

47. NASSCOM, *The Software Industry in India—1992,* p. 18.

48. Ibid.

49. "Bangalore Takes on Tasks a World Away," *The Wall Street Journal,* January 6, 1993.

50. *Dataquest,* (1993), p. 66.

51. "Infosys ADR listed on Nasdaq," *Financial Express,* March 12, 1999. See also: "Software Major Infosys to Launch $275 Million American Depository Receipts Issue," *Business Standard,* December 3, 1997.

52. New York: Interview with senior Pakistani bureaucrat, September 30, 1997.

53. N. N. Sachitanand, "Tough Times for Hardware Makers," *The Hindu,* February 24, 1993.

54. Anand Parthasarathy, "Computer Hardware: Last Gasp or Fresh Breath?" in *Survey of Indian Industry 1997,* Madras: The Hindu, 1997, p. 105.

55. Ibid.

56. Dewang Mehta, "Promising a Rich Strike," *The Economic Times,* January 8, 1992.

57. Pronab Sen, "Indian Software Exports: An Assessment," *Economic and Political Weekly,* February 18-25, 1995, pp. M-19 - M-24.

58. New Delhi: Interviews with officials at NASSCOM, MAIT, and the Department of Electronics, both current and former, February 17, 20, and 23, 1992, and September 18, 20 and 29, 1993.

59. New Delhi: Interviews with MUL managers and Ministry of Industry officials, January 31, February 7 and 14, and March 13, 1992.

60. The Japanese and Indian software industries occupy very different market niches: Japan specializes in entertainment software, while India is a leader in custom-designed software. However, they dominate their respective market niches. Remember, this is an industry whose future direction is fuzzy to even its own experts; they can predict that the industry will grow rapidly but can say little about its path. After all, even Bill

Gates put little faith in the role of the Internet in shaping the industry in the early 1990s. The good entrepreneur that he is, he modified his views quickly and emphatically by launching the Microsoft Network. The challenge for any software industry is to develop software products and dominate a market niche and acquire entrepreneurial skills so as to continue to compete in the ever changing high-tech market. It is indeed likely to be futile for either India or Japan to attempt to develop a software company to rival Microsoft. There is no clear path of development for the software industry to follow.

61. See Chalmers Johnson, *MITI and the Japanese Miracle: The Growth of Industrial Policy, 1925-1975,* Palo Alto: Stanford University Press, 1982; Richard J. Samuels, *The Business of the Japanese State: Energy Markets in Comparative and Historical Perspective,* Ithaca: Cornell University Press, 1987; Jeffrey A. Hart, *Rival Capitalists: International Competitiveness in the United States, Japan, and Western Europe,* Ithaca: Cornell University Press, 1982; Daniel I. Okimoto, *Between MITI and the Market: Japanese Industrial Policy for High Technology,* Palo Alto: Stanford University Press, 1989; Peter B. Evans, *Embedded Autonomy: States and Industrial Transformation,* Princeton University Press 1995; Marie Anchordoguy, "Mastering the Market: Japanese Government Targeting of the Computer Industry," *Industrial Organization* 42 (Summer 1988), pp. 509-544.

62. U. S. International Trade Commission, *Advice Concerning the Proposed Modification of Duties on Certain Information Technology Products and Distilled Spirits,* Report to the President on Investigation No. 332-380 Publication 3031, Washington, D. C. : USTIC, April 1997, pp. 3-8.

63. Ibid., pp. 3-8, 3-9.

64. Hart, *Rival Capitalists,* p. 85. See also Evans, *Embedded Autonomy;* Anchordoguy, "Mastering the Market."

65. Hart, *Rival Capitalists,* p. 76.

66. Johnson, *MITI and the Japanese Miracle,* p. 316.

67. Samuels, *The Business of the Japanese State,* p. 286.

Chapter 6

1. See Confederation of Indian Industry, *Case Studies: Industrial Relations Policies and Practices,* New Delhi: CII, October 1991, and R. Venkataramani, *Japan Enters Indian Industry,* New Delhi: Radiant Press, 1990.

2. Peter B. Evans, *Embedded Autonomy: States and Industrial Transformation,* Princeton: Princeton University Press, 1995, p. 115.

3. Bombay: Interview with AIAM staff, April 29, 1991.

4. See K. J. Middlebrook, "The Political Economy of Mexican Organized Labor, 1940-1978," Ph.D. diss., Government, Harvard University, 1981; E. C. Epstein (ed.), *Labor Autonomy and the State in Latin America,* Boston: Unwin Hyman, 1989, and Ruth. B. Collier and David Collier, *Shaping the Political Arena,* Princeton: Princeton University Press, 1991.

5. See F. Deyo, *Beneath the Miracle: Labor Subordination in the New Asian Industrialization,* Berkeley: University of California Press, 1989, and G. E. Ogle, *South Korea: Dissent within the Economic Miracle,* London: Zed Books Ltd., 1990.

6. Chalmers Johnson, *MITI and the Japanese Miracle: The Growth of Industrial Policy, 1925-1975,* Palo Alto: Stanford University Press, 1982.

7. Robert Wade, *Governing the Market: Economic Theory and the Role of Government in East Asian Industrialization,* Princeton: Princeton University Press, 1990.

8. Alice Amsden, *Asia's Next Giant: South Korea and Late Industrialization,* New York: Oxford University Press, 1989.

9. Evans, *Embedded Autonomy.*

10. Amsden, *Asia's Next Giant,* p. 320.

11. Ibid., p. 321.

12. Evans, *Embedded Autonomy,* p. 10.

13. Ibid., p. 17.

14. Ibid., p. 11.

15. Sylvia Maxfield and Ben Ross Schneider, "Business, the State, and Economic Performance in Developing Countries," in Sylvia Maxfield and Ben Ross Schneider (eds.), *Business and the State in Developing Countries,* Ithaca: Cornell University Press, 1997.

16. Wade, *Governing the Market,* pp. 350-368.

17. My attempt here is not to offer a comprehensive argument about Venezuela but rather to draw on the Venezuelan experience to develop some hypotheses.

18. Moreover, the average tenure of ministers of industry was only nine months. Moises Naim, *Paper Tigers and Minotaurs: The Politics of Venezuela Economic Reforms,* Washington, D.C.: Carnegie Endowment, 1993, p. 150.

19. Ibid., p. 129.

20. Ibid., p. 131.

21. Ibid., p. 91.

22. Rosemary Thorp and Francisco Durand, "A Historical View of Business-State Relations: Colombia, Peru, and Venezuela Compared," in Maxfield and Schneider (eds.), *Business and the State in Developing Countries.*

23. Eduardo Silva, "Business Elites, the State, and Economic Change in Chile," in ibid. pp. 179-180.
24. Naim, *Paper Tigers and Minotaurs*; *The Economist*, various issues; United Nations Development Program, *Human Development Report 1997*, New York, Oxford University Press, 1997.
25. See Kenneth Lieberthal and Michel Oksenberg, *Policy Making in China: Leaders, Structures, and Processes*, Princeton: Princeton University Press, 1988.
26. Eric Harwitt, *China's Automobile Industry: Policies, Problems, and Prospects*, Armonk: M. E. Sharper, 1995, p. 159.
27. William A. Byrd, "The Second Motor Vehicle Manufacturing Plant," in William A. Byrd (ed.), *Chinese Industrial Firms Under Reform*, New York: Oxford University Press, 1992, p. 373-374.
28. Ibid.
29. Harwitt, *China's Automobile Industry*.
30. Ibid., p. 102.
31. Ibid. See also World Bank, *World Development Report 1997: The State in a Changing World*, Washington, D.C.: The World Bank.
32. Harwit, *China's Automobile Industry*.
33. Ibid., p. 150.
34. Craig S. Smith, "Municipal-Run Firms Helped Build China; Now, They're Faltering," *The Wall Street Journal*, October 8, 1997. While fuzzy property rights may have aided the performance especially of township and village enterprises in the short run, their long term performance remains somewhat in doubt. Leong Liew and *The World Development Report 1997* suggest that decentralization of authority is at an excessive level in China. The relatively unfettered ability of local governments to borrow from local banks resulted in high levels of inflation. Leong Liew, *The Chinese Economy in Transition: From Plan to Market*, Cheltenham: Edward Elgar, 1997.
35. See Maxfield and Schneider (eds.), *Business and the State in Developing Countries*.
36. Robert Axelrod, *The Evolution of Cooperation*, New York: Basic Books, 1984.
37. A. Gerschenkron, *Economic Backwardness in Historical Perspective*, Cambridge: Harvard University Press, 1962; Albert O. Hirschman, *The Strategy of Economic Development*, New Haven: Yale University Press, 1958; and Evans, *Embedded Autonomy*.
38. Charles F. Sable, "Learning by Monitoring: The Institutions of Economic Development," in Neil Smelser and Richard Swedberg (eds.), *The*

Handbook of Economic Sociology, Princeton: Princeton University Press, 1994, p. 138.
39. Ibid., p. 156.
40. It is important to note that trust alone does not obviate malfeasance. The evidence presented in this book suggests that rational incentives and constraints against corruption generated by organizational forms, together with the esprit de corps within the bureaucracy and strong industry associations, helps restrict the extent of rent-seeking.
41. The current turbulence in East and South-East Asia should lead us to answer this question before long. For a discussion of the institutional factors contributing to the recent crisis in South Korea, see Alice H. Amsden and Yoon-Dae Euh, "Behind Korea's Plunge," *The New York Times*, November 27, 1997.

References

Ahluwalia, Isher J. 1985. *Industrial Growth in India*, Delhi: Oxford University Press.

———. 1991. *Productivity and Growth in Indian Manufacturing*, Delhi: Oxford University Press, 1991.

All-India Congress Committee. *The Resolutions on Economic Policy and Programme, 1924-1954*, New Delhi: All-India Congress Committee.

Ames, Barry. 1990. *Political Survival: Politicians and Public Policy in Latin America*, Berkeley: University of California Press.

Amsden, Alice and Yoon-Dae Euh. 1997. "Behind Korea's Plunge," *The New York Times*, November 27.

Amsden, Alice. 1989. *Asia's Next Giant: South Korea and Late Industrialization*, New York: Oxford University Press.

Anchordoguy, Marie. 1988. "Mastering the Market: Japanese Government Targeting of the Computer Industry," *Industrial Organization* 42 (Summer) pp. 509-544.

Aoki, Masahiko. et al. (eds.). 1997. *The Role of Government in East Asian Economic Development: Comparative Institutional Analysis*. Oxford: Clarendon Press, 1997.

Associated Chambers of Commerce and Industry. 1991. *New Industrial Policy*, New Delhi: ASSOCHAM.

Association of Indian Automobile Manufacturers. 1985. *Automobile Production Statistics*, Bombay: AIAM.

———. 1991. *Automan,* Bombay: AIAM.

———. 1994. *The Automobile Industry: Statistical Profile*, Bombay: AIAM.

———. 1997. *Automan,* Bombay: AIAM.

Axelrod, Robert. 1984. *The Evolution of Cooperation*, New York: Basic Books.

"Bangalore Takes on Tasks a World Away," *The Wall Street Journal,* January 6, 1993.

Bardhan, Pranab. 1984. *The Political Economy of Development in India,* Delhi: Oxford University Press.

Bates, Robert H. 1981. *Markets and States in Tropical Africa: The Political Basis of Agricultural Policies,* Berkeley: University of California Press.

Belassa, Bela. 1985. *Change and Challenge in the World Economy,* London: Macmillan.

Berger, Peter L. 1990. "An East Asian Development Model?" in Peter L. Berger and Hsin-Huang Michael Hsio (eds.), *In Search of an East Asian Development Model*, New Brunswick: Transaction Publishers.

Bhagwati, Jagdish and Desai, Padma. 1970. *India: Planning for Industrialization,* New York : Oxford University Press.

Bhagwati, Jagdish. 1982. "Directly Unproductive Profit-Seeking (DUP) Activities," *Journal of Political Economy* 90 (October), pp. 988-1002.

———. 1993. *India in Transition: Freeing the Economy,* New York: Oxford University Press.

Buchanan, J. Tollison and G. Tullock. 1980. *Toward a Theory of the Rent-Seeking Society,* College Station: Texas A & M University Press.

Byrd, William A. 1992. "The Second Motor Vehicle Manufacturing Plant," in Byrd (ed.), *Chinese Industrial Firms Under Reform.*

Byrd, William A. (ed.). 1992. *Chinese Industrial Firms Under Reform,* Oxford University Press.

Campos, José Edgardo and Hilton L. Root. 1996. *The Key to the Asian Miracle: Making Shared Growth Credible,* Washington, D.C.: The Brookings Institution.

Centre for Monitoring Indian Economy. Various issues. *Monthly Review of the Indian Economy,* Bombay: CMIE.

Chakravarty, Sukhamoy. 1988. *Development Planning: The Indian Experience,* Delhi: Oxford University Press.

Cho, Yoon Je. 1996. "Government Intervention, Rent Distribution, and Economic Development in Korea," in Masahiko Aoki et al. (eds.), *The Role of Government in East Asian Economic Development: Comparative Institutional Analysis,* Oxford: Clarendon Press.

Chopra, B. S. K. S. 1989. *Cases in Corporate Planning,* Pune: The Times Research Foundation.

Clifford, Mark L. 1994. *Troubled Tiger: Businessmen, Bureaucrats, and Generals in South Korea,* Armonk: M. E. Sharpe.

Coase, R. 1960. "Nature of the Firm," *Economica* 4, pp. 386-405.

Colander, David. (ed.) 1984. *Neoclassical Political Economy: The Analysis of Rent-Seeking and DUP Activities,* Cambridge: Ballinger.

Collier, Ruth B. and David Collier. 1991. *Shaping the Political Arena,* Princeton: Princeton University Press.

Confederation of Indian Industry. 1991. *Industrial Relations Policies and Practices,* New Delhi: CII, October 1991.

———. Various years. *Handbook of Statistics,* New Delhi: CII.

Congress Party. *Resolutions on Economic Policy and Programme, 1924-54,* New Delhi.

The Credit Rating Information Services of India Limited. 1989. *Special Corporate Report on TISCO,* Bombay: CRISIL.

D'Costa, Anthony P. 1995. "The Restructuring of the Indian Automobile Industry: Indian State and Japanese Capital," *World Development,* 23, no. 3, pp. 485-502.

Department of Electronics. 1991. "Note for Supplementaries for Starred Question No. 432 for 14.8.91 Regarding Impact on New Industrial and Trade Policies on Electronic Industry," internal memo p. 6.

——. Various years. *Annual Reports.*

——. 1978. *Minicomputer Policy 1978.*

——. 1974. *Software Policy 1974.*

Desai, Padma. 1972. *The Bokaro Steel Plant: A Study of Soviet Economic Assistance,* Amsterdam: North-Holland.

Deyo, F. 1989. *Beneath the Miracle: Labor Subordination in the New Asian Industrialization,* Berkeley: University of California Press.

Dore, Ronald. 1987. *Taking Japan Seriously: A Confucian Perspective on Leading Economic Issues,* Palo Alto: Stanford University Press.

The Economist. 1994. *World in Figures,* London: The Economist.

Electronics Committee. 1966. *Report of the Electronics Committee,* Bombay: Electronics Committee.

Electronics Information and Planning, Various issues and years, New Delhi: Department of Electronics.

Encarnation, Dennis J. 1989. *Dislodging Multinationals: India's Strategy in Comparative Perspective,* Ithaca: Cornell University Press.

Epstein, E. C. (ed.). 1989. *Labor Autonomy and the State in Latin America,* Boston: Unwin Hyman.

Etienne, G. 1992. *Asian Crucible: The Steel Industry in China and India,* New Delhi: Sage.

Evans, Peter B. 1995. *Embedded Autonomy: States and Industrial Transformation,* Princeton: Princeton University Press.

——. 1990. "Predatory, Developmental and Other Apparatuses," Working Paper #11, Center for the Comparative Study of Development, Brown University.

Evans, Peter B. et al. (eds.). 1985. *Bringing the State Back In,* Cambridge: Cambridge University Press.

"Exit Policy Ready for Approval," *The Statesman,* March 17, 1993.

Frankel, Francine. 1978. *India's Political Economy 1957-1977: The Gradual Revolution,* Delhi: Oxford University Press.

Gerschenkron, A. 1962. *Economic Backwardness in Historical Perspective,* Cambridge: Harvard University Press.

Ghose, Aurobindo. 1990. "Growth Strategy: Past, Present and Future," in A. Ghose et al. (eds.), *The Indian Economy and Its Performance since Independence,* Delhi: Oxford University Press.

Ghose, Aurobindo. et al. (eds.) 1990. *Growth Strategy: Past, Present and Future in the Indian Economy and Its Performance since Independence,* Delhi: Oxford University Press.

Gold, Thomas. 1986. *State and Society in the Taiwan Miracle*, Armonk: M. E. Sharpe.

Gopal, S. 1984. *Jawaharlal Nehru: A Biography,* vol. 3: 1956-1964. Delhi: Oxford University Press.

Government of India. 1993. *Factories Act—1948,* Lucknow: Eastern Book Company.

———. 1993. *Industrial Disputes Act—1947,* Lucknow: Eastern Book Company.

———. 1993. *Trade Unions Act—1926,* Lucknow: Eastern Book Company.

———. 1966. *Report of the Electronics Committee*, New Delhi: Government of India.

———. 1956. *Industrial Policy Resolution—1956*, New Delhi: Government of India.

———. 1949. "Prime Minister's Statement in Parliament on Participation of Foreign Capital in Industries," *Documents on Industrial/Licensing Policy*, New Delhi: Government of India.

———. 1948. *Industrial Policy Resolution–1948*, New Delhi: Government of India.

———. Various editions. *Policy and Procedures,* New Delhi: Government of India.

Granovetter, Mark. 1985. "Economic Action and Social Structure: The Problem of Embeddedness," *American Journal of Sociology,* 91, no. 3 (November), pp. 481-510.

Grieco, Joseph. 1984. *Between Dependency and Autonomy: India's Experience with the International Computer Industry*, Berkeley: University of California Press.

Grossack, Irvin M. 1971. "Public Regulation of the Indian Steel Industry," *Journal of Economic Issues,* vol. 5, no. 1 (March), pp. 86-97.

Haggard, S. and R. R. Kaufman,(eds.). 1991. *The Politics of Economic Adjustment,* Princeton: Princeton University Press.

Hanson, A. H. 1966. *The Process of Planning: A Study of India's Five Year Plans, 1950-1964*, Oxford: Oxford University Press.

Hanumanthaiya, K. 1968. "Personnel Administration—The Need for Change," (Inaugural Address) *Indian Institute of Public Administration*, New Delhi: IIPA.

Hart, Jeffrey. 1982. *Rival Capitalists: International Competitiveness in the United States, Japan, and Western Europe*, Ithaca: Cornell University Press.

Harwitt, Eric. 1995. *China's Automobile Industry: Policies, Problems, and Prospects*, Armonk: M. E. Sharpe.

Hasegawa, Harukiyo. 1996. *The Steel Industry in Japan: a comparison with Britain*, London: Routledge.

Hazari, R. K. 1986. *Essays on Industrial Policy*, New Delhi: Concept Publishing Company.

The Hindu. *Survey of Indian Industry 1997*, Madras: The Hindu.

Hiro, D. 1976. *Inside India Today*, London: Routledge Press.

Hirschman, Albert O. 1958. *The Strategy of Economic Development*, New Haven: Yale University Press.

Howell, Thomas R., et al. 1988. *Steel and the State: Government Intervention and Steel's Structural Crisis,* Boulder: Westview Press.

"Infosys ADR listed on Nasdaq," *Financial Express*, March 12, 1999.

Johnson, Chalmers. 1982. *MITI and the Japanese Miracle: The Growth of Industrial Policy, 1925-1975*, Palo Alto: Stanford University Press.

Johnson, W. A. 1966. *The Steel Industry of India*, Cambridge, Harvard University Press.

Jones, Leroy P., and Il Sakong. 1980. *Government, Business and Entrepreneurship in Economic Development: The Korean Case,* Cambridge: Harvard University.

Kanter, Rosabeth Moss. 1986. "Stimulating and Managing Corporate Entrepreneurship: The Auto Industry Connection," in J. C.Campbell (ed.), *Entrepreneurship in "Mature Industry,"* Ann Arbor: University of Michigan Press.

Karnik, V. B. 1967. "National Labour Policy and Union Action," *Proceedings of the Third National Seminar on Industrial Relations in a Developing Country*, New Delhi: Sri Ram Centre for Industrial Relations.

———. 1974. *Indian Labour: Problems and Prospects*, Calcutta: Minerva Associates.

Katzenstein, Peter. 1984. *Corporatism and Change: Austria, Switzerland, and the Politics of Industry*, Ithaca: Cornell University Press.

Klitgaard, Robert. 1990. *Tropical Gangsters*, New York: Basic Books.

Kochanek, Stanley A. 1995. "The Transformation of Interest Politics in India," *Pacific Affairs,* 68, no. 4 (Winter).

———. 1974. *Business and Politics in India*, Berkeley, University of California Press.

Kohli, Atul. 1990. *Democracy and Discontent: India's Growing Crisis of Governability*, New York: Cambridge University Press.

Kreps, David M. 1990. "Corporate Culture and Economic Theory," in J. E. Alt and K. A. Shepsle (eds.), *Perspectives on Positive Political Economy*, Cambridge: Cambridge University Press.

Krueger, Anne O. 1974. "The Political Economy of the Rent-Seeking Society," *American Economic Review,* 64, pp. 291-303.

———. 1975. *The Benefits and Costs of Import Substitution in India: A Microeconomic Study*, Minneapolis: University of Minnesota Press.

Lal, Deepak. 1985. *The Poverty of "Development Economics,"* Cambridge: Harvard University Press.

Leonard, Karen I. 1978. *Social History of an Indian Caste: The Kayasths of Hyderabad*, Berkeley: University of Califonia Press.

Levi, Margaret. 1981. "The Predatory Theory of Rule," *Politics and Society,* 10, no. 4, pp. 431-465.

Lewis, W. A. 1953. *The Theory of Economic Growth*, London: Allen and Unwin, 1955.

Lieberthal, Kenneth and Michel Oksenberg. 1988. *Policy Making in China: Leaders, Structures, and Processes*, Princeton: Princeton University Press.

Liew, Leong. 1997. *The Chinese Economy in Transition: From Plan to Market*, Cheltenham: Edward Elgar.

Lok Sabha Debates, May 30 1957, 2nd series, vol. 2, pp. 2,935-2,959.

Mahesh, K. 1997. "Auto Components: Time to Update Technology," *Survey of Indian Industry 1997*, Madras: The Hindu.

Martinez, J. and A. Diaz. 1996. *Chile: The Great Transformation*, Washington, D.C.: Brookings/UNRISD.

Maxfield, Sylvia and Ben Ross Schneider. 1997. "Business, the State, and Economic Performance in Developing Countries," in Sylvia Maxfield and Ben Ross Schneider (eds.), *Business and the State in Developing Countries*, Ithaca: Cornell University Press.

Maxfield, Sylvia and Ben Ross Schneider (eds.), *Business and the State in Developing Countries*, Ithaca: Cornell University Press.

Mehra, O. P. 1985. "June 1, 1978, IBM Quits India," *Dataquest,* January.

Mehta, Dewang. 1996. "India: Software Paradise," *Dataquest*, December 15.

———. 1992. "Promising a Rich Strike," *The Economic Times*, January 8.

Mehta, Prayag. 1989. *Bureaucracy, Organizational Behaviour and Development,* New Delhi: Sage Publications Ltd.

Meyer-Stamer, Jörg. 1997. "New Patterns of Governance for Industrial Change: Perspectives for Brazil," *Journal of Development Studies,* 33, no.3 (February).

Middlebrook, K. J. 1981. *"The Political Economy of Mexican Organized Labor, 1940-1978,"* Ph.D. diss., Government, Harvard University.

Milgrom, Paul and John Roberts. 1990. "Bargaining Costs, Influence Costs, and the Organization of Economic Activity," in James E. Alt and K. A. Shepsle (eds.), *Perspectives on Positive Political Economy*, Cambridge: Cambridge University Press.

Ministry of Finance. 1999. *Economic Survey 1998-1999*, New Delhi: Ministry of Finance.

———. 1998. *Economic Survey 1997-1998*, New Delhi: Ministry of Finance.

———. 1996. *Economic Survey 1995-1996*, New Delhi: Ministry of Finance.

———. 1995. *Economic Survey 1994-1995*, New Delhi: Ministry of Finance.

———. 1993. *Economic Survey 1992-1993*, New Delhi: Ministry of Finance.

———. 1992. *Economic Survey 1991-1992*, New Delhi: Ministry of Finance.

———. 1991. *Economic Survey 1990-1991*, New Delhi: Ministry of Finance.

———. 1990. *Economic Survey 1989-1990*, New Delhi: Ministry of Finance.

———. 1985. *Economic Survey 1984-1985,* New Delhi: Ministry of Finance.

Ministry of Steel. 1994. *Annual Report,* New Delhi: Ministry of Steel.

———. 1992. *Annual Report,* New Delhi: Ministry of Steel.

———. 1987. *A Strategy for Steel,* New Delhi: Ministry of Steel.

Misra, B. B. 1986. *Government and Bureaucracy in India, 1947-76*, Delhi: Oxford University Press.

Mohan, Rakesh and Vandana Aggarwal. 1991. "Command and Controls: Planning for Indian Industrial Development 1951-1990," New Delhi: Ministry of Economic Affairs.

Myers, C. A. and S. Kannappan. 1970. *Industrial Relations in India,* London: Asia Publishing House.

N. N. S. 1997. "TISCO: Full Benefit of New Facilities," *Survey of Indian Industry 1997*, Madras: The Hindu.

Naim, Moises. 1993. *Paper Tigers and Minotaurs: The Politics of Venezuela's Economic Reforms,* Washington, D.C.: Carnegie Endowment.

Narayana, D. 1989. *The Motor Vehicle Industry in India*, New Delhi: Oxford and IBM Publishing Co. Pvt. Ltd., and Trivandrum: Centre for Development Studies.

National Association of Software and Service Companies. 1998. *Indian Software Scenario*, New Delhi: NASSCOM.

———. 1998. *The Software Industry in India 1997-98: A Strategic Review*, New Delhi: NASSCOM.

———. 1992. *The Software Industry in India—1992*, New Delhi: NASSCOM.

Nayar, B. R. 1990. *The Political Economy of India's Public Sector: Policy and Performance*, Bombay: Popular Prakashan.

———. 1992. "The Politics of Industrial Restructuring in India: The Paradox of State Strength and Policy Weakness," *Journal of Commonwealth and Comparative Politics*, 30, pp. 145-171.

North, Douglass. 1981. *Structure and Change in Economic History*, New York: Norton.

———. 1990. *Institutions, Institutional Change and Economic Performance*, Cambridge: Cambridge University Press.

Nurkse, R. 1953. *Problems of Capital Formation in Underdeveloped Countries,* New York: Oxford University Press.

Oberoi, S. S. & G. V. Ranganathan. 1991. "Indian Software Scenario," *Electronics—Information and Planning,* August.

Ogle, G. E. 1990. *South Korea: Dissent within the Economic Miracle,* London: Zed Books Ltd.

Okimoto, Daniel I. 1989. *Between MITI and the Market: Japanese Industrial Policy for High Technology*, Palo Alto: Stanford University Press.

O'Reilly, Brian. 1992. "Your Global Work Force," *Fortune*, December 14.

Pande, Arvind. 1997. "Steel: Brightening Near Term Outlook," *Survey of Indian Industry 1997*, Madras: The Hindu.

Parthasarathy, Anand. 1997. "Computer Hardware: Last Gasp or Fresh Breath?" *Survey of Indian Industry 1997*, Madras: The Hindu.

"Passenger Cars: Too Many Options for Buyers," *Survey of Indian Industry 1997*, Madras: The Hindu, 1997.

Pinglé, Vibha. 1997. "Managing State-owned Enterprises: Lessons from India," in *International Journal of Sociology and Social Policy*, no.7/8.

Planning Commission. 1991. *Eight Five Year Plan,* New Delhi: Government of India.

———. 1985. *Seventh Five Year Plan*, New Delhi: Government of India.

———. 1980. *Sixth Five Year Plan*, New Delhi: Government of India.

———. 1974. *Fifth Five Year Plan*, New Delhi: Government of India.

———. 1969. *Fourth Five Year Plan,* New Delhi: Government of India.

———. 1961. *Third Five Year Plan,* New Delhi: Government of India.

———. 1955. *Second Five Year Plan,* New Delhi: Government of India.

———. 1951. *First Five Year Plan*. New Delhi: Government of India.

Potter, David C. 1986. *India's Political Administrators 1919-1983,* Oxford: Clarendon Press.

Premier Automobiles Limited. 1982. *The Dream Fulfilled*, Bombay: PAL.

Public Accounts Committee. 1976. "Computerization in Government Departments: Department of Electronics," *221st Report (1975-76), Fifth Lok Sabha*, New Delhi, April.

Raghavan, T. C. A. S. 1993. "INTUC's Problem," *The Economic Times,* May.

Ragin, Charles. 1987. *Comparative Method: Moving Beyond Qualitative and Quantitative Strategy,* Berkeley: University of California Press.

Ramamurti, Ravi. 1987. *State-Owned Enterprises in High Technology Industries,* New York: Praeger.

Ramaswamy, E. A. 1997. *A Question of Balance: Labour, Management and Society,* Delhi: Oxford University Press.

———. 1995. *India Briefing, 1994,* New York: Asia Society.

Ramaswamy, E. A. (ed.). 1978. *Industrial Relations in India: A Sociological Perspective,* Delhi: MacMillan Company of India Ltd.

Rosenstein-Rodan, P. N. (ed.). 1964. *Capital Formation and Economic Development,* Cambridge; MIT Press.

Rudolph, Lloyd and Susanne H. Rudolph. 1987. *In Pursuit of Lakshmi,* Chicago: University of Chicago Press.

Rueschemeyer, D. and L.Putterman. 1992. *State and Market: Synergy or Rivalry,* Boulder: Lynne Riener.

Rueschemeyer, Dietrich, and Peter B. Evans. 1985. "The State and Economic Transformation," in Peter B. Evans, Dietrich Rueschemeyer, and Theda Skocpol (eds.), *Bringing the State Back In,* Cambridge: Cambridge University Press.

Rueschemeyer, Dietrich. 1990. "Different Methods—Contradictory Results?" Working Paper [#13], Center for the Comparative Study of Development, Brown University.

———. 1990. "Planning Without Markets: Knowledge and State Action in East German Housing Construction," *East European Politics and Societies,* 4, no. 3 (Fall).

Rueschemeyer, D., E. H.Stephens and J. D.Stephens. 1992. *Capitalist Development & Democracy,* Chicago: University of Chicago Press.

Sable, Charles F. 1994. "Learning by Monitoring: The Institutions of Economic Development," in Neil Smelser and Richard Swedberg (eds.), *The Handbook of Economic Sociology.* Princeton: Princeton University Press.

Sachitanand, N. N. 1993. "Tough Times for Hardware Makers," *The Hindu,* February 24.

Samuels, Richard J. 1987. *The Business of the Japanese State: Energy Markets in Comparative and Historical Perspective,* Ithaca: Cornell University Press.

Schmitter, Philippe. 1990. "Sectors in Modern Capitalism: Modes of Governance and Variations in Performance," in R. Brunetta and C. Dell'Aringa (eds.), *Labor Relations and Economic Performance,* New York: Macmillan.

Sen, Amartya. 1981. *Poverty and Famines: An Essay on Entitlements and Deprivation,* Oxford: Clarendon Press.

Sen, Pronab. 1995. "Indian Software Exports: An Assessment," *Economic and Political Weekly,* February 18-25, pp. M-19-M-24.

Shafer, D. Michael. 1994. *Winners and Losers: How Sectors Shape the Developmental Prospects of States,* Ithaca: Cornell University Press.

Sharma, Rahul. 1992. "More Space to Breathe," *Economic Times,* April 15.

Silva, Eduardo. 1997. "Business Elites, the State, and Economic Change in Chile," in Sylvia Maxfield and Ben Ross Schneider (eds.), *Business and the State in Developing Countries,* Ithaca: Cornell University Press.

Skocpol, Theda. 1985. "Bringing the State Back In: Current Research," in Peter B. Evans, Dietrich Rueschemeyer, and Theda Skocpol (eds.), *Bringing the State Back In,* Cambridge: Cambridge University Press.

Smith, Craig S. 1997. "Municipal-Run Firms Helped Build China: Now, They're Faltering," *The Wall Street Journal,* October 8.

"Software Major Infosys to Launch $275 Million American Depository Receipts Issue," *Business Standard,* December 3, 1997.

Srinivasan, N. R. 1982. *The Iron and Steel Industry in India: A Monograph,* New Delhi: SAIL.

———. 1990. *The Corporate Story of SAIL,* New Delhi: SAIL.

Statistical Outline of India. Various years. Bombay: Tata Industries Limited.

Steel Authority of India Limited. 1994. *Statistics for Iron and Steel Industry in India,* New Delhi: SAIL.

Subramanian, C. R. 1992. *India and the Computer: A Study of Planned Development,* Delhi: Oxford University Press.

Taub, Richard P. 1969. *Bureaucrats Under Stress: Administrators and Administration in an Indian State,* Berkeley: University of California Press.

Thorp, Rosemary and Francisco Durand. 1997. "A Historical View of Business-State Relations: Columbia, Peru, and Venezuela Compared," Sylvia Maxfield and Ben Ross Schneider (eds.), *Business and the State in Developing Countries,* Ithaca: Cornell University Press.

Tripathi, D. (ed.). 1987. *State and Business in India,* New Delhi: Manohar Publications.

Tullock, Gordon. 1980. "Rent-Seeking as a Negative Sum Game," in James M. Buchanan, Robert Tollison, and Gordon Tullock, (eds.), *Toward a Theory of the Rent-Seeking Society,* College Station, Texas A&M University Press.

Tulpule. B. 1974. *Problems of Management and Workers in Public Sector Industries*, Bombay: Lala Lajpatrai Institute.

———. 1967. "Government Power and Union Recognition," in *Trade Unions and Politics in India*, proceedings of the *Third National Seminar on Industrial Relations in a Developing Economy*, Delhi: SRCIR, vol. 2.

U.S. International Trade Commission. April 1997 *Advice Concerning the Proposed Modification of Duties on Certain Information Technology Products and Distilled Spirits*, Report to the President on Investigation No. 332-380; Publication 3031, Washington, D.C.: USTIC.

United Nations Development Program. 1997. *Human Development Report 1997*, New York: Oxford University Press.

United Nations. Various years. *Yearbook of International Trade Statistics*, New York: United Nations.

Vaitheeswaran, S. 1997. "Commercial Vehicles: Poised for Continued Growth," *Survey of Indian Industry 1997*, Madras: The Hindu.

Varshney, Ashutosh. 1995. *Democracy, Development and the Countryside: Urban-Rural Struggles in India*, New York: Cambridge University Press, 1995.

Venkataramani, R. 1990. *Japan Enters Indian Industry*, New Delhi: Radiant Press.

Vittal, N. 1991. "Software and Engineering Industry—Need for Developing a Domestic Market," Talk presented at the UNDP, New Delhi, August 6.

———. 1991. "The Rama Route to Success," Talk presented at the NASSCOM meetings, Bangalore, December 5.

———. 1992. Talk presented at the NASSCOM meetings, January 17, 1992.

Vogel, Ezra. 1991. *The Four Little Dragons: the Spread of Industrialization in East Asia*, Cambridge: Harvard University Press.

Wade, Robert. 1990. *Governing the Market: Economic Theory and the Role of Government in East Asian Industrialization*, Princeton: Princeton University Press.

———. 1985. "The Market for Public Office: Why the Indian State Is Not Better at Development," *World Development*, 13, no. 4, APR.

Weber, Max. 1968. *Economy and Society*, New York: Bedminster Press.

Williamson Oliver. 1985. *The Economic Institutions of Capitalism*, New York: Free Press.

———. 1975. *Markets and Hierarchies: Analysis and Antitrust Implications*, New York: Free Press.

Wolf, Martin. 1982. *India's Exports*, New York: Oxford University Press.

World Bank. 1997. *World Development Report 1997: The State in a Changing World*, Washington, D.C.: The World Bank.

———. 1996. *India: Five Years of Stabilization and Reform and the Challenges Ahead*, Washington, D.C., The World Bank.

———. 1995. *Bureaucrats in Business: The Economics and Politics of Government Ownership*, New York: Oxford University Press.

———. 1995. *World Development Report 1995*, Washington, D.C.: The World Bank.

———. 1993. *The East Asian Miracle: Economic Growth and Public Policy*, New York: Oxford University Press.

———. 1990. *Trends in Developing Economies 1990*, Washington, D.C.: The World Bank

———. 1987. *India: Steel Sector Strategy Report*, Washington, D.C.: The World Bank.

———. 1987. *India: Review of the Automotive Products Industry*, Washington, D.C.: The World Bank.

Zysman, John. 1977. *Political Strategies for Industrial Order: State, Market, and Industry in France*, Berkeley: University of California Press.

Newspapers and Periodicals

Automobile Engineer and Trader
Business India
Business Standard
Business Today
Business Week
Dataquest
Economic Times
Economist
Financial Express
Financial Times
Fortune
The Hindu
Hindustan Times
India Today
Indian Express
The New York Times
The Statesman
Times of India
The Wall Street Journal

Index

94, 97, 99-100, 103, 109-110,
112-113, 116-117, 145, 162-
164, 166
Ministry of International Trade and
Industry (MITI), 81, 156
Ministry of Labor, 32, 40
Ministry of Steel, 1, 14, 32, 38, 40,
54, 56, 60, 61, 63-65, 67-68,
71-74, 76, 78, 80, 83, 117,
145, 160-161, 163-164
Ministry of Steel and Mines, 59,
68
Mitsubishi, 105, 115
Modi Group, 42
Mohan, Rakesh, 52
Monday Club, 81
Monopolies and Restrictive Trade
Practices (MRTP) Act, 23, 25,
27, 46, 97-98, 109, 114, 128
Monopolies and Restrictive Trade
Practices (MRTP)
Commission, 27
Mostek Electronics, 137
Motorola, 148
Murthy, N. R. N., 141
Myers, C. A., 37
Mysore Iron and Steel Works, 51

Naim, Moises, 175
Nanda, H. P., 102
Narayana, D., 114
Narsimhan, Professor, 123, 126-
127
National Academy of
Administration, 30
National Association of Software
and Service Companies
(NASSCOM), 48, 141, 144,
146, 151, 152, 155, 157, 165,
166, 173, 181, 182

Nayar, B. R., 69
NEC, 155
Nehru, Jawaharlal, 20-21, 26, 52-
54, 59, 73, 87, 92-93, 95, 97,
110, 117, 123, 155, 162
NELCO, 148
Neoclassical argument, 12-13, 17,
118
Nigeria, 159
Nippon Steel, 81
Nissan, 105
North, Douglass, 15

oil crisis (1973), 23-24, 62, 98,
100

Pakistan, 149
Pakistan, war with (1965), 22, 95
Panda Motors, 178-179
Pande, Arvind, 78, 116
Park Chung Hee, 82
Park Tae Joon, 82
Parliamentary Public Accounts
Committee (PAC), 128
Parthasarathy, Anand, 150
Patni Computer Systems (PCS),
141
Paul, Swaraj, 105
Pentafour Software, 142
Peugeot, 105, 109, 115
plan holiday, 22
Planning Commission, 20, 58, 59
Pohang Iron and Steel Company
(POSCO), 82
political encouragement, 8-9, 172
political parties, 39-40. *See also*
Bharatiya Janata Party;
Congress Party; Janata Dal
politicians, 9, 12, 61, 170-171
populism, 43, 46, 95-96, 98